GURU DEV

Paul Mason learned the practice of transcendental meditation in 1970 when he visited Maharishi's ashram at Rishikesh after having hitchhiked to India. This experience spurred him to dig deeper into the history of the teaching of meditation, which in turn led to his being commissioned by Element Books to write the biography of Maharishi Mahesh Yogi - published in 1994 as *'The Maharishi: the Biography of the Man Who Gave Transcendental Meditation to the World'.*

Maharishi's *guru,* referred to simply as Guru Dev, was Swami Brahmananda Saraswati, Shankaracharya of Jyotirmath (the most prominent religious position in Northern India). Paul Mason hopes that by offering Guru Dev's lifestory and teachings, readers will be able to obtain a clearer perspective on traditional Indian teachings.

Titles by Paul Mason:

Via Rishikesh: A Hitch-Hiker's Tale

The Maharishi: The Biography of the Man Who Gave Transcendental Meditation to the World
Element Books - First English edition 1994
Evolution Books - Revised English edition 2005
Maharishi Mahesh Yogi - Aquamarin - German edition 1995
O Maharishi - Nova Era - Portuguese edition 1997

Mala: A String of Unexpected Meetings

108 Discourses of Guru Dev:
The Life and Teachings of Swami Brahmananda Saraswati,
Shankaracharya of Jyotirmath (1941-53) - Volume I

The Biography of Guru Dev:
The Life and Teachings of Swami Brahmananda Saraswati,
Shankaracharya of Jyotirmath (1941-53) - Volume II

Guru Dev as Presented by Maharishi Mahesh Yogi:
The Life and Teachings of Swami Brahmananda Saraswati,
Shankaracharya of Jyotirmath (1941-53) - Volume III

Kathy's Story

The Knack of Meditation:
The No-Nonsense Guide to Successful Meditation

Dandi Swami: The Story of the Guru's Will, Maharishi Mahesh Yogi, the
Shankaracharyas of Jyotir Math & Meetings with Dandi Swami Narayananand
Saraswati

Roots of TM: The Transcendental Meditation of Guru Dev &
Maharishi Mahesh Yogi

The Beatles, Drugs, Mysticism & India:
Maharishi Mahesh Yogi - Transcendental Meditation- Jai Guru Deva OM

* All titles are published by Premanand, other than *'The Maharishi'* biography

The Biography

of

GURU DEV

The Life and Teachings of
Swami Brahmananda Saraswati,
Shankaracharya of Jyotirmath (1941-53)

Volume II

by
Paul Mason

PREMANAND
www.paulmason.info
premanandpaul@yahoo.co.uk

First published by Premanand, 2009
© Paul Mason 2009, 2016, 2017
ISBN 978-0-9562228-1-7

Cover design by Premanand

Introduction

*

It was a long arduous journey from Delhi to Rishikesh. Having spent several days there I continued on my way further, onward into the Himalayan foothills, into the area known as Devabhoomi, the land of the gods. Information about the area had been difficult to acquire. It was in the late 1978 when I was back in London that I was lucky even to have managed to obtain the pencilled sketch map of the main roads. Whether for national security or out of religious secrecy, or a combination of both, information about the area was a closely guarded secret. But on the basis of the scant information that I obtained, I planned a journey. My hope was to visit two places associated with Maharishi Mahesh Yogi and his master Guru Dev. My first goal was to find the monastery of Jyotirmath, and after that to visit Uttarkashi, where at different times they had both spent time in *sadhana*.

From Rishikesh it took the best part of two days to get to Joshimath, a market town high in the mountains. I found a rest-house there where I left my backpack and then went off to visit the monastery. It was a thrill to become enveloped in the sanctity and talk with the monks there. Later, back at the rest-house I met with the manager who was reclining on a bed, reading. I was astonished to notice the book had a photograph of Guru Dev on the cover! The manager explained that the book was a biography of the former Shankaracharya, and if I wanted we could go and get a copy the next day. I was soo-o-o-o excited!

I had arranged a little trip to a destination a few miles away where I was assured that I would meet some holy men with perfected 'powers' or '*siddhis*' – that was at Tapoban, and in particular a certain *baba* I had heard of. But the place was deserted and I discovered that Gudri Baba had died a little while back. At his shrine I found two young *sadhus* and there I watched with mild interest and detachment as they chopped and sliced a quantity of marijuana. When I got up to leave they insisted that I accept '*prasad*' (blessing) of Gudri Baba and presented me a handful of marijuana. After I returned to Joshimath I passed on the *prasad* to an Indian acquaintance. Later in the day I happened to meet the mananger of the rest-house again. This time he was dressed as a beggar and was being led about by my Indian friend. Both of them were very merry, and it turned out they had swallowed the marijuana washed down with a mouthful of honey. So the manager was pretending to be blind and the other man was guiding him about, they found their prank hilarious. As I observed them I realised that my trip to the monastery would have to wait, as I couldn't possibly go to a holy shrine with this guy completely stoned out of his mind! However, the manager was not to be dissuaded, and was soon urging me to follow along with him to the *peeth*. I dreaded the reaction of the monks there. Surprisingly, the presence of the stoned manager presented no particular problem and an old *swami* found me the biography and other books too.

I held the books close to me at all times – I wouldn't even trust them to be left in my luggage on my flight home to Britain, I just had to keep them with me, all the time. I resolved to learn Hindi and share the contents.

With the passage of time my knowledge of Hindi increased slowly and by the time I was ready to embark on the translation the biography had become lost to me, …. and so I took another trip to Joshimath, but the book was now out of print and no longer available. However, thankfully, I was able to obtain a photocopy of the pages and eventually I finally got around to starting to translate the books on Guru Dev. I would do some translation then post the roughs on my website for all to share. And now, here is that work, completely revised, rewritten and polished up, and presented as a book.

In his introduction to the Hindi biography, published in 1965, Rameshwar Tiwari. wrote; '*In the upadesha of Maharaj Shri he spoke mostly from his own experience, therefore your upadeshas were always fresh. Whosoever was listening, his audience were always eager and this is the cause of getting these colourful descriptions of your solitary life. In this book are quotations of your talks about those occurrences. Those devotees took note of what they heard from your lotus mouth. Therefore this biography is just a collection of occurrences gained by way of your nectar speech..'*

So, this book is essentially Guru Dev's autobiography. But it has also been suggested that Maharishi Mahesh Yogi claimed the work as his own, apparently telling an assistant, Australian TM teacher Edna Linnel, *'We shall see what they have done with it.'* There might be an element of truth to this story as the Hindi copy has a serious timeline error in Chapter Six which hitherto no one seems to have picked up on, but which would have been obvious to the compiler. But I am still puzzled as to who actually compiled the biography!

Before I tackled this project both Prem Pasricha and Raj Varma had also attempted translations, but although both were seemingly using the same Hindi text, curiously, both translators omit material, embellish and generally alter the contents. In the first attempts at translation I pursued quite a different policy, actually attempting to purge the work of all but Guru Dev's recollections, only later deciding to include translations of the narrative too.

Thanks go to Dr Cynthia Hume who helped organise a photocopy of the Hindi text after my copy disappeared. And to Tom Anderson, whose copy of the Hindi book it was which was photocopied, and for his getting all sorts of material across to me, and providing feedback, support and great friendship. My thanks also go to Bjarne Hansen in Sweden for his feedback, support and material.

Initially, as I worked, I uploaded the translations onto my website (www.paulmason.info) where they attracted a lot of attention. I am pleased to now be able to present my translations in book form and make them available through the website.

To render the Hindi into a printed form I had first to type the entire text into ITRANS and then convert that to a Devanagari font, which I achieved by using a program called *Itranslator99*. I am indebted to Omkarananda Ashram for developing and making this software freely available, and to Swami Satchidanand for working through some technical problems with me.

The entire translation process was made so much easier with the help of Richard Mason, who suggested I make a database of Hindi words which he then connected to MS Access with a little program he created called *Handi Hindi Gizmo Innit*. Thanks Richard, I don't know what I would have done without it!

I dedicate these volumes to Dandi Swami Narayanand Saraswati, a close disciple of Guru Dev, who told Rajiv Malik for the August 1995 issue of *'Hinduism Today'*; "I am seventy-two years old. I lead a very disciplined life. My main message to the people is to go through Holy Scriptures and remember God always. If you live in this way, your life will be happy and blissful."

Premanand Paul Mason

Contents

※ जय प्रभो ※

※ श्री ज्योतिष्पीठोद्धारक ※

ब्रह्मलीन जगद्गुरु शंकराचार्य श्री ज्योतिष्पीठाधीश्वर
स्वामी ब्रह्मानन्द सरस्वती जी महाराज
ज्योतिर्मठ - बदरिकाश्रम (हिमालय) की
संक्षिप्त - जीवनी

ॐ – OM

* Jaya Prabho * Victory to the Lord *

* Shri Jyotishpeethoddharak *
* Blessed Restorer of Jyotir Peeth *

Samkshipt Jivani - Abridged Biography

of

Brahmaleen Jagadguru Shankaracharya Shrii Jyotishpeethadhishwar

Swami Brahmananda Saraswati Ji Maharaj

Jyotirmath - Badarikashram (Himalaya)

१

पहला अध्याय

बाल्यावस्था और वैराग्य

सर्वाधिष्ठान स्वप्रकाश परब्रह्म परमात्मा के साकार विग्रह कौशलेन्द्र भगवान् श्रीराम की लीलाभूमि अयोध्या के सन्निकट सरवार प्रान्त अपनी पवित्रता के लिये उत्तर भारत में प्रसिद्ध है। यह पञ्च गौड़ ब्राह्म[ान्तर्गत सरयूपारीण ब्राह्मणों का प्रधान क्षेत्र है। यहाँ गाना ग्राम की विशेष प्रतिष्ठा है। महाराज श्री का इसी गाना नामक ग्राम के एक श्रेष्ठ प्रतिष्ठित सम्मानित सरयूपारीण पंक्तिपावन् गाना मिश्र ब्राह्मण

कुल में मार्गशीर्ष शुक्ल दशमी, विक्रम सम्वत् १९२८, तदनुसार दिसम्बर २१, १८७० ई। दिन वृहस्पतिवार को प्रादुर्भव हुआ। एक सम्पन्न ज़मीन्दार रईस परिवार के बालक होने के नाते जीवन के सभी सुख-वैभव प्राप्त थे। परन्तु कौन जानता था कि मखमली गद्दों में पला हुआ बालक संसार का परम विरक्त सिद्ध योगी होगा और शंकराचार्य की गद्दी को सुशोभित करेगा?

महाराज श्री का प्रारम्भिक जीवन बहुत ही चमत्कारिक और आदर्शमय रहा। बाल्यावस्था से ही आपकेमन में संसार की क्षण-भंगुरता भासने लगी। जन्म से ही तेजस्वी शरीर में वैराग्य का भाव प्रबल था। व्यावहारिक जीवन में आप प्रायः उदासीन ही रहते थे। एकान्तप्रिय थे। सदैव गम्भीर मुद्रा में निवास करते थे। चञ्चलता का

नाम तक न था। आपका अलौकिक तेजपूर्ण मुखमण्डल सभी को प्रभावित कर लेता था। नाना प्रकार के स्वादिष्ट खाद्य पदार्थ और अच्छे-अच्छे सुन्दर वस्त्रों पर, जो बालकों को स्वाभाविक ही प्रिय होते हैं, आपकी दृष्टि ही नहीं गई। जीवन के आमोद-प्रमोद की सामग्री और बच्चों के नाना प्रकार के खेल-खिलौने कभी भी आपको आकर्षित नहीं कर सके। मित भाषण और हस्तपादादि इंद्रियों को भी यथासाध्य निरोध करना आपकी स्वाभाविक विशेषता थी। जहाँ बैठते बैठे ही रह जाते, न जाने किस् विचारधारा में निमग्न रहते। आपकी प्रत्येक क्रिया में गम्भीरता और बोलचाल में अलौकिकता देख कर कुटुम्बीजन विस्मित हो जाते थे और आपकी भावी महानता का आभास पाया करते थे। आपमें बुद्धि प्रखर, विचारशक्ति प्रबल और निर्णय करने की क्षमता अद्वितीय थी।

आप अपने पितामह के बहुत प्यारे थे। उन्हीं के प्रेम पूर्ण अङ्क में आपकी दिनचर्या का अधिकांश समय व्यतीत होता था। जो कुछ आपके हृदय में प्रेमभाव या मान्यता थी, वह मानों सारी पितामह के लिये ही थी। पितामह वृद्ध थे ही लगभग सौ वर्ष की अवस्था में उन्होंने अपने प्रिय पौत्र से सदा के लिये विदा होकर अपनी लौकिक जीवन यात्रा समाप्त कर दी। सात वर्ष तक जिनकी गोद में खेले थे, उस परम प्रिय पितामह का शरीर छूट गया। घरवालों की सतर्कता के कारण बालक अपने पितामह के शव को नहीं देख सका, पर जब वे घर से बाहर निकाल कर ले जाये गये तब कुछ दूर चले जाने के बाद एक नौकर ने दिखाया कि देखो वे सब लोग पितामह को लिये जा रहे हैं। बालक ने भीड़ को बार बार कहते सुना "राम नाम सत्य है"। बालक के नेत्रों ने पितामह को ओढ़े हुये, सोये हुये, जाते हुये देखा और कानों ने सुना "राम नाम सत्य है"। सोचा, पितामह का

यह अंतिम उपदेश है । बालक के मन में दो बातें जाग्रत हुईं –

(१) पितामह अब कभी नहीं मिलेंगे;

(२) 'राम नाम् सत्य है ।'

अवस्था ७ वर्ष की थी । बालक अपने पितामह की स्मृति में जब भावमग्न होता तो अपने आस-पास पिता, माता, काका, ताउ आदि सम्बन्धियों को देख कर यही सोचता कि ये भी किसी न किसी दिन इसी प्रकार छूट जाएँगे । किसको अपना समझें? एक को अपना माना था, वे चले गये, यह कोई रहनेवाला नहीं दिखता । हमारा शरीर भी इसी प्रकार एक दिन छूट जायगा । जब यहाँ कोई रहने वाला नहीं है तो फिर यह सब क्या है, कौन सी चीज है जो यहाँ रहेगी? बालक के मन में यह भाव आते ही, कानों में गूंज उठता "राम नाम सत्य है ।"

जैसे-जैसे समय व्यतीत होता गया "राम" के सम्बन्ध में अधिकाधिक विचार बढ़ता गया । यही "राम नाम सत्य" बालक के हृदय पटल पर अंकित हुआ, उसी का मनन हुआ । वही उसके भावी जीवन-प्रासाद की सुदृढ़ नींव बना । उसी "राम नाम सत्य" के साँचे में उसने अपना जीवन ढाला । बालक के मन में संसार का मिथ्यात्व दृढ़ हो गया । घरवालों ने देखा कि बालक के मन में पितामह की छाप अमिट पड़ी है । सबको चिन्ता होने लगी कि कैसे इस बालक के अन्तःकरण से पितामह की दुःखद स्मृति हटाई जाय । लगभग एक वर्ष व्यतीत हुआ । अवस्था ८ वर्ष की हुई और उपनयन संस्कार का समय आ गया । सब ने विचार किया कि उपनयन कराकर कुछ समय के लिये काशी पढ़ने को भेज दें ।

आठ वर्ष की आयु में यज्ञोपवीत संस्कार के पश्चात् आप वेदाध्यायनार्थ काशी भेज दिये गये। काशी पहुँचते ही वहाँ की सांस्कृतिक विशेषता की छाप आप पर पड़ी। आपने अपना जीवन आध्यात्मिक उन्नति की ओर लगाने का संकल्प किया। इधर तत्कालीन प्रचलित सुकुलीन ब्राह्मण कुलों की प्रथो के अनुसार अयोध्या प्रांत के सरयूपारीण प्रतिष्ठित पंक्तिपावन गाना मिश्र कुल में पुत्र विवाहोत्सव का समय आ गया। कुटुम्बीजन प्रयत्नशील हो उठे। कुछ लोग काशी आये कि बालक को बुला ले चलें। आपको मालूम हुआ कि गृह से विवाह के लिये बुलावा आया है। अभी दूध के दांत पूरे गिरे भी नहीं थे और जिस अवस्था में सहस्रों बालक धूलि-धूसरित, अबुद्धावस्था में आपस में लड़ते-भिड़ते, हँसते-खेलते इतस्ततः बालक्रीड़ा में निमग्न रहते हैं, उस ८-९ वर्ष की सुकोमल अवस्था में आपके कानों में 'विवाह' का शब्द पड़ा। हृदय चौंक उठा। रोमांच हो आया-विवाह? विवाह और उससे सम्बन्धित संसार?

निर्मल नवीन बालन्हृदय के मानस-पलड़े पर तुल गया संसार रत्ती भर। उधर प्रवृत्तिमार्ग ने बालक के मानस पटल पर अपनी निराली छवि दिखलाई। अगणित सामग्रियाँ उपस्थित कीं कि समस्त इन्द्रियों के विषय को यथेच्छा भोग कर आनन्द प्राप्त किया जाय, इधर निवृत्ति मार्ग ने अपना निराला अनिर्वचनीय आकर्षण उपस्थित किया। किन्तु इसमें क्षण-भंगुरता नहीं, स्थिरता थी; कोलाहल नहीं, शान्ति थी, आवागमन नहीं, प्रत्यक्ष मोक्ष था। निस्संदेह इसका पलड़ा भारी था। आपने निश्चय किया कि निवृत्तिमार्ग ही श्रेयस्कर है और यही अपनाने योग्य है। सहसा इस पथ का द्वार खुला।

नन्हा-सा बालक त्याग वैराग्य की मूर्ति बनकर भगवती भागीरथी

के पुनीत तट को पकड़े हुये चल पड़ा। आपने गंगाजी के किनारे-किनारे ही चलते रहने की ठान ली। एकाग्रमन से अपनी अलौकिक विचारधारा सम्भाले हुये आप भागीरथी के तट पर निरन्तर बढ़ने लगे। प्रातःकाल का समय बीत गया। धूप कड़ी हो गई। ऊपर से सूर्य भगवान् की तेज किरणें, निचे गंगाजी की तप्त बालुका। परन्तु क्या बालक इन विषमताओं से किंचित् मात्र विचलित हो सका? उसने तो जीवन की ऐसी विषम परिस्थितियों के साथ हँस-हँस कर खेलने का व्रत ही ले लिया था। उसे ये क्षुद्र बाधाएँ कहाँ तक रोक पातीं?

भगवती भागीरथी का हृदय द्रवीभूत हो उठा। दो चुह्लू जल पिलाकर वृक्ष की शीतल छाया में कुछ समय रोकना चाहा; किन्तु उत्तर मिला "माँ, तेरे सहारे ही जीवन का यह वृहत पथ व्यतीत होना है। अभी से रुकने का स्वभाव मत बनने दे। एक बार हिमालय की किसी एकाकी गुफा तक पहुँच जाने दे, जहाँ बैठकर जीवन की साध पूरी कर सकूँ।" यह कहते हुए तपसी हृदय ने जाह्नवी को प्रणाम कर आगे का पथ सम्भाला।

थकावट नहीं, नींद नहीं, निर्जन और अर्द्धरात्रि में अकेले पन का भय भी नहीं। बढ़ते चले गये। जब भूख लगती तब चुह्लू से गंगाजल पी लेते और जब प्यास लगती तब चुह्लू से गंगाजल पी लेते। पहिला दिन गया, दूसरा बीता और तीसरा भी ढल गया, गंगा का चुह्लू चुह्लू जल पी-पी कर। वह सुकोमल अवस्था और विधि की इतनी उपेक्षा क्यों? क्या यह परीक्षा का समय है? परीक्षा भी हो तो भी विधना, क्या यह अति नहीं है? किन्तु हमें सन्तोष है उस ओर से यदि अति है तो इस ओर से भी तो उसका यथार्थ प्रत्युत्तर हो रहा है। बस आगे बढ़ना ही उसका एक कार्य है। परन्तु तीसरे दिन

भावी चौक उठी; सूर्य भगवान् के विदा होते-होते परीक्षा समाप्त हुई । एक ज़मीन्दार ने गंगा के उस पार से देखा कि कौन यह नन्हा सा बालक गोधूलि में झाड़ी-झंखाड़ बेधता, लाँघता बीहड़ पथ पर बढ़ा चला जा रहा है । उसने अपने नौकर को भेजा कि उसे बुला ले आये । किन्तु क्या यह सम्भव था? किसकी सामर्थ्य थी कि उस परम स्वतंत्र एकनिष्ठ बाल तपस्वी को अपने पास नौकर द्वारा बुलावा सके? ज़मीन्दार को स्वयं समीप जाना पडा ।

पूछा - "आप कौन हैं?"

उत्तर - "हमें जानकर क्या करोगे? अपना अर्थ कहो ।"

उसने फिर प्रार्थना की - "महाराज, मेरा अर्थ यही जानना है कि आप कौन हैं और इस असमय में इस बीहड़ पथ पर कैसे बढ़े चले जा रहे हैं?"

बाल तपस्वी ने कहा - "यह समय है या असमय, और यह कुमार्ग है या सुमार्ग, इसका ज्ञान तुम्हें नहीं हो सकता । इतना ही जान लो कि हम काशी से चलकर हिमालय में तपस्या करने जा रहे हैं । जाओ अपना काम करो, हमें व्यर्थ छेड़ने से कुछ लाभ नहीं ।"

जमीन्दार ने कुछ साहस बटोर कर धीमें स्वर में कहा - "महाराज, क्या मैं जान सकता हूँ कि आपने मार्ग में कहाँ और कब भिक्षा की है?"

उत्तर मिला - "अभी तक गंगोदक ही अन्न-जल का काम कर रहा है ।"

"तो चलिये, ग्राम में कुछ जलपान करके आगे बढ़िये तो हमें भी

संतोष होगा । रात्रि भी हो रहो है ।''

"भिक्षा के लिये तो हम किसी के दरवाजे जायेंगे नहीं । रही बात तुम्हारे संतोष की, तो हमें कुछ खिलाने-पिलाने से तुम्हें संतोष हो जायगा, यह भी नहीं माना जा सकता । संतोष तो तब माना जाय जब उसके बाद फिर कोई इच्छा न उठे । यह हमें भिक्षा कराने से तो होगा नहीं । यह तो तभी हो सकता है जब उस परम तत्व को जान लो जिसके जानने से सब जाना जाता है और जिसकी प्राप्ति होने पर फिर कोई वस्तु अप्राप्य नहीं रह जाती । इसलिये कुछ ऐसा प्रयत्न करो जिससे वास्तव में संतोष हो जाय ।''

नन्हें से दुधमुहें बालक के मुख से परमार्थ का ऐसा उपदेश! आश्चर्य! सोचा, जिस केन्द्र से यह ज्ञानधारा बह रही है क्या उसकी चरम स्थिति और विकास की सीमा का अनुमान लगाया जा सकता है? मानव शरीर तो है किन्तु यह निश्चय नहीं होता कि मानवी लालवाणी है ।

वहीं गंगातट पर ही दूध की व्यवस्था की गई । आपने दो तिहाई दूध से गंगा जी का भोग लगा दिया । दुग्धधारा जल में समाहित हो गई, भगवती भागीरथी से जितना जल तीन दिन में पिया था वह एक ही बार में दूध से चुका दिया । माता का हृदय गद्गद् हो उठा । वरदान मिला – अब जीवन में जल से जठराग्नि शान्त करने की आवश्यकता नहीं पड़ेगी । माता अन्नपूर्णा ने गोद में उठा लिया । फिर क्या था, वर्षों सघन वन-पर्वतों की एकाकी गुफाओं में रहे, वर्षों आकाश के नीचे मैदानी स्वामी के नाम से मैदानों में स्वच्छन्द व्यतीत किये न कभी किसी से याचना की और न किसी से संकेत किया । किन्तु खाद्य सामग्री की कभी कमी नहीं हुई । कितनी ही बार

जंगलों में घनघोर अँधेरी रातों में न जाने कौन सेरों मलाई और टोकनियों में फल लाकर रख जाता ।

दायें-बायें न देखकर सीधे हिमालय के लिये गंगा के किनारे-किनारे ही यात्रा चली । सन्ध्या-वंदन का नित्यकृत्य नहीं छूटा और जब जैसा प्राप्त हुआ भगवद्प्रण बुद्धि-पूर्वक क्षुधा निवृत्ति की । पीने को अंजलि में गंगाजल, विश्राम के लिये वृक्षों की शीतल छाया में पवित्र भूमि-शैय्या सर्वत्र उपलब्ध हुई ।

शरीर पर विशिष्ट ओज तेज होने से जिसने देखा समीप अवश्य आया । विचित्र आकर्षण था । दर्शकों की आँखों में ध्रुव, प्रह्लाद की छवि साकार होकर झूल पड़ती थी । इस प्रकार दिन बीत रहे थे, रातें बीत रही थीं जब तक पैरों ने मन का साथ दिया तब तक चले और जब पैर थके तो किनारे गंगा की बालू में किसी वृक्ष की छाया में विश्राम किया और नींद खुलते ही आगे चल पड़े तीन दिन के बाद मालूम पड़ा कि गंगा बहुत चौड़ी हो गई हैं बालक को यह ज्ञान न था कि यह गंगा यमुना का संगम है । कुछ और आगे बढ़े तो लोगों से मालूम हुआ कि प्रयाग आ गये ।

त्रिवेणी का माहात्म्य तो पितामह से सुना ही था । श्रद्धापूर्वक गोते लगाये । आगे आकर थकान मालूम हुई तो दशाश्वमेध घाट पर किनारे एक चौकी पर बैठ गये । कुछ समय व्यतीत हुआ – ध्यान में बैठे थे कि एक महाशय बगल में आकर बैठ गये और बाल तपस्वी की मुद्रा को चुपचाप देखने लगे । काफी समय व्यतीत हो गया । देखा कि यह बालक तो है परन्तु बालकपन की चेष्टाओं से सर्वथा रहित है । चेहरा थका हुआ सा है पर तेजयुक्त है । उसने अपनी जेब से एक कागज निकाला, पढ़ा और ध्यान पूर्वक एक बार पुनः बालक

की मुखाकृति को देखा । तब बिलकुल पास ही सामने जाकर उसी चौकी पर बैठ गया । बाल तपस्वी अपनी अंतर्निष्ठा से चौंक पड़ा और समीपस्थ पुरुष की ओर निहारा । अपनी ओर देखते जानकर उस पुरुष ने आपके सामने अपनी जेब का कागज निकालकर रख दिया ।

बाल तपस्वी   – "यह क्या है?"

उत्तर   – "आपकी हुलिया ।"

बाल तपस्वी   – "आप कौन हैं?"

उत्तर   – "मैं पुलिस का दारोगा हूँ ।"

बाल तपस्वी   – "क्या चाहते हैं?"

दारोगा   – "आपके नाम की यह हुलिया है । आप घर से भाग आये हैं ।"

बाल तपस्वी   – "अधिक बात की क्या आवश्यकता है, हुलिया ही है न?"

दारोगा   – "हाँ"

बाल तपस्वी   – "तो जिसने हुलिया कटाई है, उसे सूचना दे दो कि हम यहाँ हैं । किसी का पशु खो जाता है तो वह उसकी हुलिया कटा देता है । हम तो किसी के लड़के ही हैं । सूचना दे दो कि हम यहाँ पर आ गये हैं । वह चाहेगा तो आकर ले जायगा ।"

दारोगा   – "हाँ, सूचना तो मैं कर ही दूँगा? पर आप घर से क्यों चले आये कुछ मालूम भी तो हो ।"

बाल तपस्वी   - "यह तो अच्छा प्रश्न है, घर से क्यों चले आये? हम पूछते हैं कि आप घर ही में क्यों रहते हैं?"

दारोगा अपनी पुलिसगीरी भूल गया - छोटे से बच्चे के मुँह से दर्शनशास्त्र का इतना ऊंचा तर्क सुनकर उसकी बुद्धि चकरा गई उसका दारोगापन जाता रहा। आवाज में नरमी आ गई उसने कहा - "घर में तो सभी रहते हैं, क्योंकि घर में आराम रहता है। घर के आराम को छोड़कर आप इस तरह दरिया के किनारे दोपहर में मारे-मारे फिर रहे हैं इसका क्या कारण है?"

बाल तपस्वो - "जाईये दारोगा जी, अपना काम कीजिये और घर का आनन्द लीजिये। गंगातट पर माता की गोद में, रेती में, एकान्त दोपहरी में और निर्जन, नीरव स्थली में हम मारे-मारे फिरते हैं या आनन्द करते है यह आपकी समझ में नहीं आ सकता।"

नन्हें से बालक के मुख से ऐसे मार्मिक शब्द सुनकर दारोगा जी की आँखें खुल गई। पुलिसपन का नशा उतर गया और श्रद्धापूर्वक बोले - "आपकी छोटी उमर है। किसी बड़े घर का जन्म मालूम पड़ता है। क्या इस प्रकार अनाथ से फिरने में आपको संकोच नहीं होता?"

बाल तपस्वी   - "हम छोटे हैं, आप तो अपने को बड़ा ही मानते हैं न? बड़े होकर भी आप यह नहीं समझते हैं कि अनाथ और सनाथ कौन है? थोड़ा विचार तो कीजिये तो स्वयं ही पता लग जायगा कि सर्वत्र सर्व शक्तिमान् परमात्मा ही सब का एक "नाथ" है। उसकी शरण में जिसने अपने को डाल दिया वह अनाथ रहा कि सनाथ हो गया। हम आपसे पूछते हैं कि जिसने उस परम पिता से अपना सम्बन्ध नहीं बनाया क्या उसे आप "सनाथ" कहेंगे?"

एक बालक के मुख से परमार्थ का सारगर्भित उत्तर सुनकर दारोगा जी निरुत्तर हो गये और उनके मन में आया कि यह कोई साधारण बालक नहीं, कोई होनहार महान् आत्मा है ।

दारोगा जी विनम्रतापूर्वक बोले, – "आप एक काम करें कि अब हमारे साथ चलें, क्योंकि आपके नाम की हुलिया है । वैसे तो आपको हम यहाँ छोड़ कर जा नहीं सकते । पर हम आपको पुलिस थाने में नहीं ले चलेंगे । आप हमारे साथ हमारे घर पर चलें । वहाँ रात्रि में रहें फिर सबेरे जो विचार होगा वह कीजिएगा ।"

बाल तपस्वी को समझा बुझा कर दारोगा उन्हें अपने घर पर ले गया । रात्रि में अनेक प्रकार की सत्संग-वार्ता में उसने यह भलीभाँति समझ लिया कि बालक तीव्र वैराग्यवान् है और वास्तव में हिमालय पहुँचकर भगवान् की प्रत्यक्षानुभूति के लिये तपश्चर्या में ही अपना जीवन लगाना चाहता है । दारोगा ने यही निश्चय किया कि उन्हें जल्दी ही हिमालय के निकट भेज दिया जाय । प्रातःकाल दारोगा ने कहा हम आपके इस पवित्र मार्ग में बाधक नहीं होना चाहते । परन्तु आपकी हुलिया देश भर के लिये है । यदि इसी प्रकार गंगा के किनारे-किनारे पैदल चला करेंगे तो कहीं न कहीं अवश्य ही पकड़ जायेंगे इसलिये हम सोचते हैं कि आपको चुपचाप रेल पर बैठा कर हरिद्वार तक भेज दें ।

जो बाल तपस्वी चाहते थे हुआ । इनके मन में था कि जल्दी से जल्दी हरिद्वार पहुँच जाय । उसकी भूमिका स्वतः बन गई । जो बाधक बनकर आया था । वही साधक बन गया । भगवान् के भक्तों की बातें ऐसी ही हुआ करती हैं । भगवान् की शक्ति से ही भक्तों के संकल्प पूरे होते हैं । सर्वशक्तिमान् सर्वज्ञ भगवान् की सर्वशक्तिमयी

The reply:- 'I am a police Sub-Inspector.'

Child ascetic:- 'What do you want?'

Sub-Inspector:- 'This description is in your name. You are running away from home.'

Child ascetic:- 'Why is it necessary to talk excessively? It is only a description. No?'

Inspector:- 'Yes.'

Child ascetic:- 'Then he who lodged the description, give him the information that I am here. Any cattle that is lost, that description is lodged. I then are only a child. Inform him I have come here. If he wants then having come he will take me.'

Sub-Inspector:- 'Yes, to inform. Only then I will investigate. But why did you come walking from home? Apparently there is something else then?'

Child ascetic:- 'This then is a good question. 'Why go from home?'

I am asking. 'Do you really stay in the home?'

From hearing the remark from the mouth of the young child who had such apparent great philosophical reasoning, the Sub-Inspector forgot his own police-speech. The Sub-Inspector's mind was going to be widened. With a soft voice he said:- 'All are staying in the home because it is a pleasure staying in the home. What is the reason you are renouncing the comfort of home and then afterwards staying on the river shore at midday?'

Child ascetic:- Sub-Inspector Sir, you ought to go! You should do your work and take the pleasure of home. On the shore of Ganga in the lap of Mother, in the sandy soil, I am wandering alone in the midday and are secluded. You cannot understand.having this bliss.'

From the mouth of a tiny lad he heard touching words, thus the

प्रकृति का यह कार्य है कि प्रिय भक्त की इच्छा के अनुकूल परिस्थितियाँ बना दे और भक्त के संकल्प की पूर्ति कर दे । दारोगा ने उन्हें टिकट लेकर गाड़ी पर बैठा दिया । बाल तपस्वी दूसरे दिन हरिद्वार पहुंच गये ।

जब आप गंगा-स्नान को जा रहे थे, एक पुलिस इन्सपेक्टर से भेंट हुई । इन्सपेक्टर ने देखा कि यह तो वही बालक है जिसको ढूँढ़ हो रही है । क्यों न इसे उनके घर भेजवा दिया जाय और पारितोषिक लिया जाय? इतना सोचते सोचते वह बालक के साथ हो गया । इन्सपेक्टर ने पूछा – "बच्चा, तुम घर से क्यों चले आये और कहा जा रहे हो?" । उनका उत्तर था "परम पिता का साक्षात्कार करने के लिये सीधे हिमालय की ओर यात्रा हो रही है ।" पुलिस इन्सपेक्टर ने कहा "मैं आपको आपके घर भेजना चाहता हूँ, क्योंकि इससे हमें पारितोषित्क मिलेगा । उत्तर दिया "मैंने निश्चय कर लिया है और उसी पर अटल हूं । यदि आप मुझे भेज भी देंगे तो मैं वहाँ रह नहीं सकता, दूसरे ही दिन मेरी फिर यहीं के लिये यात्रा होगी । इसलिये आप मेरे लिये विघ्न न बनें और मुझे जाने दें । किन्तु यदि पारितोषिक का लोभ विशेष है तो मुझे हमारे घर भेजवा कर अपना पारितोषिक ले लें । जैसा उचित समझें वैसा करें ।" पुलिस इन्सपेक्टर धार्मिक प्रकृति का साधुसेवी सज्जन था उसने बालक की बातें मान ली और चला गया । परन्तु दूसरे ही दिन जब आप ऋषीकेश की ओर यात्रा कर रहे थे दूसरे पुलिस इन्सपेक्टर मिल गये । उन्होंने भी देखा कि यह बालक तो वही बालक हैं जिसकी हुलिया कटी है और पारितोषिक निकला है । उसने नहीं माना और बाल तपस्वी को घर मेज दिया ।

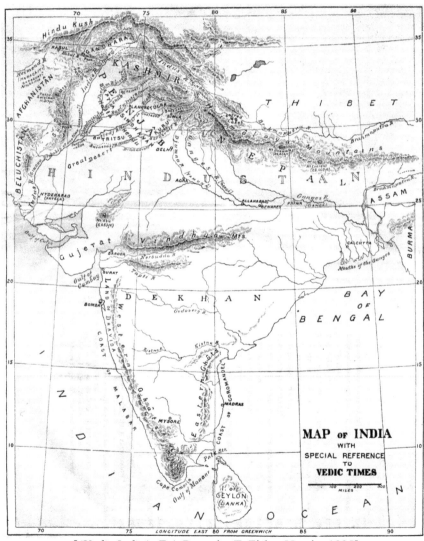

[*'Vedic India'*, Z A Ragozin, T. Fisher Unwin, 1895]

Chapter 1
Childhood & Asceticism

That which is Omnipresent, Self-illuminating, the Supreme Soul, took form from the body of Kaushaleya (as Rama). The area closeby to Ayodhya is renowned in North India as a place of sanctity of Shri Rama's *leela bhoomi* (earthly performance). This is the principal place of the five 'hidden' Brahman subcastes of the Saryupareen Brahmans. [The Saryupareen Brahmans are said to descend from those Brahmans who assisted Lord Rama after the killing of Ravana (the son of a Brahman) in Lanka. Allegedly, out of gratitude for assistance in performing a ritual, Rama gave them land to the edge of the River Sarayu to dwell in, hence "Saryuparin" meaning; 'on the bank of the Saryu (or Sarya)']

Maharaj Shri (Guru Dev) was of the village named Gana [near Ayodhya, which is a city between Lucknow and Gorakhpur, about 175km north of Allahabad]. He was of the respected noble Saraupareen Gana Mishra Brahman caste, and born on the tenth day of the bright half of the month of Margashirsh in the Vikram year 1928 - accordingly, 'December 21st 1870'. [Actually, the month of Margashirsha in the Vikrami year of 1928 corresponds to 1871 in the Gregorian calendar, so Guru Dev was likely born on Thursday December 21st 1871. It is believed he was given the name Rajaram (meaning 'King Rama'), therefore his full name was Rajaram Mishra.] The day he came into existence was a Thursday.

Of a well-off *zamindar* (landlord) family, all comfort and wealth was available for this young child. But who knew that the young child being reared on velvety cushions would become a *siddha yogi,* detached from worldly existence and be gracing the seat of the Shankarcharya?

Maharaj Shri's early life is very portentous and exemplary. Really, right from his childhood, *samsara* (worldliness) appeared transitory. Actually, from birth he had a noble-spirited strong feeling of asceticism, a freedom from bodily desires. In everyday life he was generally retiring being a lover of privacy. He dwelt always giving the impression of seriousness, he was not known for being playful. His unworldly perfectly effulgent face impressed everyone. Although it is natural for children to love varied kinds of tasty foodstuffs and nice clothes, he was not really interested. Neither was he attracted to things to make life merry or the various kinds of children's playthings and toys. His natural specialness was his moderate speech, and according to his capacity he was restrained in the action of hands, feet and senses. Wherever he was sitting he sat engrossed in who-knows-what stream of thought. The family was astonished at the seriousness of his every action but from the rare conversation they obtained a hint of his great future destiny. His sharp mind, powerful reasoning and decisiveness were matchless.

You greatly loved your grandfather. A greater part of your daily routine was spent in the embrace of the full love of only them. Although small, the emotion of love in your heart was considerable, that measure was entirely only for grandfather. Really, grandfather was old, his age was about one hundred years old, he completed his passage of earthly life and departed his beloved grandson forever. Until he was seven years old he had played in his lap, now the body of that highly beloved grandfather's was gone away. Due to the vigilance of those of the household the young lad could not see the dead body of his grandfather, but when they took it out of the house, after they had gone a little way a servant showed him all the people coming for the grandfather. The young child heard the crowd saying again and again;

"राम नाम सत्य है"

"raama naama satya hai"
'Rama's name is truth'.

The young child's eyes saw that grandfather had been covered, saw that he had gone to sleep, and his ears heard *"raama naama satya hai"* - 'Rama's name is truth'. He considered this his grandfather's last instruction. In the mind of the young child he awoke to two ideas:-

(1). Grandfather will not be met with now.

(2). *"Raama naama satya hai"* - 'Rama's name is truth.'

He was seven years old, and when the young lad recalled his grandfather he became drowned in emotion, then having father, mother, paternal uncle, etc, seeing relatives, he considered this, that some day they too will have this kind of leaving. What will we understand? One that was considered one's own, they will go, there is nobody who stays. Our own body too, one day will go this way too. When there is none who stays, then again what is all this? What thing is there that stays here? In the mind of the young lad this feeling came, the echo rising in his ears *"Raama naama satya hai"* - 'Rama's name is truth'.

As time passed more and more he considered the relationship with "Raama". *"Raama naama satya hai"* - 'Ram's name truth' become stamped in the young child's heart. He came to be just that very thought. That same thought he made the strong basis of his life. Really, in truth that phrase *"Raama naama satya hai"* - 'Rama's name truth' shaped his life. In the young lad's mind he became resolved about the falsehood of *samsara* (worldliness). Those of the household saw the indelible impression that grandfather had on the mind of the young lad. All thought; 'How to drive away the trouble-giving memory of grandfather on the inner conscience of this young lad?'

About a year elapsed.

'Hindu Temples, Benares'
[*'Indian Pictures'*, Rev. W. Urwick, Religious Tract Society, c1885.]

Being eight years old it came to be time for the ceremony of investiture with the sacred thread. All decided on performing the initiation and then sending him for some time to Kashi (Benares, Varanasi) to study. *Having become eight years old, and after the performance the ritual of the sacred thread, you were sent to Kashi to study the wealth of the Vedas. On arriving there you made a special impression in the study of Sanskrit. You resolved to devote your own life in advancing spiritually.*

At this age, according to the prevailing custom of the caste of Brahmans on the edge of Ayodhya, the celebrated Saryuparin/Mishra Brahmans of Gana, the time of the marriage feast came. Relatives made an effort. Some folk came to Kashi to summon the young child to go with them. *It became obvious to you that they came from the house to call you for the marriage.* Just now all the milk teeth had not yet fallen out and at that age thousands of young lads are dusty and dirty, in a state of ignorance playing hither and thither, wrestling and fighting with one another, and laughing, remaining wrapped up in childhood. *At that very delicate age of eight to nine years old, into your ears falls the word "vivaaha", 'marriage'. The heart arose with a sudden start. The hairs stood up on end, - "vivaaha"? Marriage, and a relationship with worldliness?*

Pure, youthful of a child-heart, on one side of the balance of his mind was the full weight of *samsara* (mundane existence). On the other side the youth was seeing the proximity of his own particular light. There ready at hand, all the uncounted things to be acquired for the pleasure of the senses, and here, the way of salvation, and his own indescribable attraction for personal solitariness. But this was not a fragile moment for him as he was already resolved. There was no hue and cry for he was peaceful, no uncertainty about *moksha* (freedom) was apparent. Certainly this pan of the balance was weighty. He was convinced that the road to salvation is propitious and that it really suited him. Suddenly the door to this path opened.....

Resembling a small child but taking to the form of non-attachment and asceticism, he left, keeping to the shore of pure Goddess Bhagarathi (Ganga River). He resolved to keep walking on the banks of his own Ganga Ji. With an untroubled mind he kept watch over his transcendental stream of thought. *You proceeded along on the bank of the Bhagarathi (Ganga) [from Varanasi].*

The time of daybreak came and it became bright and unbearably hot. From above, the hot rays of light of Bhagwan Surya (the Sun), and below was the heated sand of [the shore] of Ganga Ji. But would the young child get somewhat unsettled by these extremes? He took a vow to take the very difficult surroundings along with the swans at play (taking the rough with the smooth). Was he going to let these trifling issues stop him from being able get to reach where he was going?

The heart of Bhagavati Bhagirathi (Goddess Ganga) melted:- 'You need to drink a couple of handfuls of water, stay some time in the cool shade of the tree.'

But he answered:- 'Mother, this great way of life has only been taken to with your support. From now on please don't give me the habit of stopping. Once I am given to arrive at some solitary cave of the Himalayas, then I can fulfil the life of a hermit wherever I sit.'

Having said this, the ascetic heart did *pranaam* (salutations) to Jahnavi (Ganga Ji) to help on the way ahead.

Ganga Ji

No fatigue, no sleep, solitary too half the night, he resolved not to be scared to be alone. Further he went. When he became hungry he drank a handful of Gangajal (water from the Ganges) and when he became thirsty he drank Gangajal from the hollowed palm.

The first day passed, another passed, and a third also rolled by drinking handfuls of water from the Ganga. Why so much disregard for this delicate condition and behaviour? What is this time of test? If this is a test, then that is also fate, [but] is it not excessive? But to us there is gratification that if there is a lot [of testing] from one direction, then from that direction is a good answer coming. Really, the one task is proceeding far enough. But the third day he reached Bhavi Chauk ('the courtyard of destiny'); Surya Bhagwan (the Sun) was departed - the test had been completed. In the twilight, a landowner from the other side of the Ganga looked to see whom this little boy was who was walking on the rugged path making his way through the bushy thicket. He sent his own servant to call out to him. But was it possible? What could be the adequacy of sending one's servant to call to this extremely free god-devoted young hermit? The *zamindar* (landowner) reached nearby.

He asked:- 'Who are you?'

The answer:- 'Why do you have to know about us? Tell me your purpose.'

Again the *zamindar* requested:- 'Maharaj, my intention right here is to know who you are and why you are going along this rough path at this improper time?

The young ascetic said; 'Whether this is the time or the improper time, and whether this is an evil path or a good path, you cannot have this knowledge. Understand this much though, that I am walking from Kashi to go to do *tapasya* (austerity) in the Himalayas.' [The distance along the Ganges between Kashi (Varanasi) and the Garhwal Himalayas, where for time immemorial many ascetics have resorted to, is about a thousand kilometres.] 'Go and do your own work. To no purpose you bother us, to know advantage.'

The *zamindar* collected together a little courage and said in thoughtful tone; 'Maharaj, what I want to know is the where and when of the *bhiksha* (food gained by begging, charity or alms) on your way?'

He was met with this response; 'Up until just now the water of the river Ganga has been working as food and water.'

[The *zamindar*;] 'Then you should come to the village, you can have some *jalpan* (refreshment, snack) then you can proceed farther, then I will also be satisfied. Moreover, it is becoming night time.'

[Young ascetic;] 'For *bhiksha* (charity) I will not go to any door. Really, this talk of your satisfaction... then will you become satisified causing us to drink so to be burst in the middle? Then this satisfaction also cannot go to be measured, after it has been measured, then no desire will arise again. And this will not be from this doing *bhiksha* to us. For this to be, only when you take to that *param tatwa* (Supreme Essence), from knowing that knowledge all is known and there is nothing which is going to be unobtainable. Therefore, make some effort after this manner, become satisfied in that which is genuine.'

From the mouth of a small milk-sucking lad, such an *upadesha* (sermon) of *paramarth* (salvation)! Astonishing! Consider; what is the origin that this stream of knowledge is issuing from? How could one guess the limit of his eventual status and development? A human being's body it is then, but this is certainly not the voice of a dear human boy.

At that very place on the shore of the Ganga came a measure of milk. Two-thirds of the milk was given for the pleasure of Ganga Ji. The stream of milk became merged in the water, to repay Bhagavati Bhagarathi (goddess Ganga) with milk the water he had drank in the three days. Mother's heart rose to be very happy. He got granted a boon - now in the life it won't be necessary to pacify the fire of the stomach which helps digest the food with water, because Mother Annapurna got up to embrace him (*"anna"* = food, *"puurnaa"* = sufficient).

What was to be the future? Years living alone in caves in dense forests and mountains, years on the plains beneath the sky with the name of 'Swami'. According to his own will he spent time in open fields. On no occasion did he beg or give any hint [of need]. But there was no shortage of things to eat. How many times, in jungles on terrible dark nights, no one knows who brought and placed seers of cream and baskets of fruit?

Not looking towards the right or towards the left, he walked along the banks of the Ganga on his pilgrimage to the Himalayas. Regular evening prayer was not omitted, and according to God's gift earlier, all thought of hunger disappeared. In hollowed hands he drank Gangajal (the water of the Ganga). He gained rest on the pure cold ground everywhere, in the cooling shadows of the trees.

Those who came near him could see that his body had a special lustre of vitality, was curiously attractive. The eyes of those who saw him beheld in him the brilliant form either of Dhruva or Prahlad (celebrated child saints of India).

In this way days were passing, and nights were passing too. Whilst the feet went then with a mind he walked, and when the legs were tired then he relaxed in the shade of any tree, in the sand of the shore of the Ganga. Awaking, he arose to move on ahead. The winding riverside route from Varanasi to Allahabad is perhaps 200km.

After three days he realised the Ganga was becoming very wide. The young lad did not know this is the *sangam* (meaning confluence) of the Ganga and the Yamuna rivers. After going a little further ahead he then learnt from people that he was coming to Prayag (Allahabad).

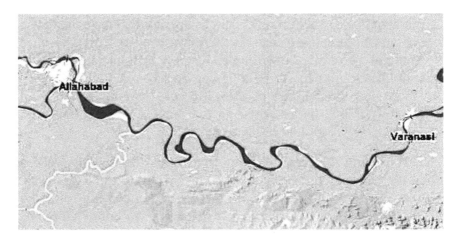

He had heard of the greatness of Triveni (the confluence of the three rivers, viz., Ganga, Yamuna and Saraswati rivers) from his grandfather. Reverently proceeding there he immersed himself. Going further on, it became obvious he was fatigued, so then he sat on a bench on the shore at Dashashvamedha Ghat.

Some time passed – he was sitting in meditation.

A well-intentioned person came and stared at the countenance of the young ascetic. Some time passed. Though he appeared a young child, yet he was completely without the demeanour of infancy. He appeared to be weary, yet lustrous. The man drew out a note from his pocket, read it and considered it again before looking at the intent face of the young child. Then, having come quite close, face-to-face, he sat down on the bench.

The young ascetic emerged from his meditation, he looked in the direction of the man. *Having seen from his side, that man compared you with the paper he took out of his pocket, and that he passed to you.*

Child ascetic:- 'What is this?'

The reply:- 'Your description.'

Child ascetic:- 'Who are you?'

eyes of the Sub-Inspector were opened.

The pride of the policeman was taken down. He spoke with reverence:- 'Your age is little. It is obvious you are born to a great family. Are you not ashamed in wandering in this way like an orphan?

Child ascetic:- 'I am small. Then you assume you are great? No? However, you do not understand who has a lord, and who is without a master? You ought to consider a little, then you will really have knowledge of the self, that the one *"naatha"* – 'lord' is really everpresent All-Powerful Paramatma. He who casts himself on the protection of Him, he who is *"anaatha"*, an 'orphan' he becomes *"sanaatha"*; 'possessed of a master'. I ask you why don't you make a relationship with the *param pitaa;* the 'ideal father'?

'Are you saying you are *"sanaatha"* – 'with master'?'

Hearing the pithy answer of salvation from the mouth of one a young child, the Sub-Inspector became speechless and it came to his mind that this is no ordinary boy, but someone who is a promising great soul.

Humbly, the Sub-Inspector spoke:- 'There is one thing to do. You will come along with me now because of your name and description. So, then I cannot set you free here to go, but I will not take you to the Police Station. You will come with me to my home and there you will stay the night. Tomorrow I will be considering what to do.'

The dejected young ascetic understood and was taken to the Sub-Inspector's home.

In the night there was much *satsang* (spiritual discussion). The policeman well understood that the young lad passionately wanted the recluse life, and genuinely wanted to reach the Himalayas, as he desired to set his life in austerity for the experience of endless bliss of Bhagwan, Paramatma. Thus the Sub-Inspector resolved to send him near to the Himalayas.

At daybreak the Sub-Inspector said; 'I do not want to be an obtruction to your spiritual path. But your description is for all the country. If you go by foot on the shores of the Ganga, somewhere or other you will be captured, therefore I am considering sending you on the railway quietly to Hardwar.'

What the child ascetic desired, occurred. It was in his mind to arrive quickly to Haridwar. His introduction was made spontaneously. He who come to obstruct him, the very same went on to become a facilitator. Such is the speech of Bhagwan's devotees. Only by the strength of Bhagwan is the will of the devotees fulfilled. The nature of the Omnipotent, Omniscient, Almighty Bhagwan is to make favourable surroundings for the wish of the beloved *bhakta* (devotee), and give fulfilment to the resolve of the *bhakta* (devotee). The inspector booked a ticket and got him a seat in a railway carriage.

The child ascetic arrived at Haridwar the next day. *There, when you were going to bathe in the Ganga, a police inspector interviewed you.* The inspector saw that this is the very boy whom is being sought. So for the sake of the reward why not go and cause him to be sent to his home? Considering as much, he came alongside the youth. The inspector asked:- 'Child, why have you walked from home and where are you going?'

Their answer was:- 'For the meeting of the *param pita* (the Best Father) I am on a *yatra* (pilgrimage, journey) in the direction of the Himalayas.'

The police inspector said:- 'I wish to send you to your home as from this I will get a reward.'

He gave an answer:- 'For certain I am decided, and on that I am steadfast. If you have me sent [back] then I cannot stay there, so indeed a second time I will be making a *yatra* (pilgrimage, journey) to this very place. Therefore, don't make yourself into an obstacle for me, let me go. But, if it is greed for the reward, then cause me to be sent home, so that you can take your reward. Do that which is suitable to your understanding.'

The police inspector was of a spiritual nature, gentle, of service to *sadhus* (religious or holy men). He took the measure of the lad's words and went away.

But the next day, when he (the child ascetic) was travelling in the direction of Rishikesh he met with another police inspector who said; 'This is the youngster then, the very same youngster in the description lodged, and he turns out to have a reward.'

The inspector was not to be dissuaded, and the child ascetic was sent home.

२

दूसरा अधयाय

गृह त्याग और सद्गुरु की खोज

हूर पहुंचने पर सभी बड़े-बूढ़ों से ज्ञान-वैराग्य की ही चर्चा करते रहे। एक ९ वर्ष के अबोध बालक की ज्ञान वैराग्य की बातों को कुट्वम्बीजनों ने बाल्यावस्था की सनक समझ कर टाल दिया। जितना ही बालक ने उन लोगों से प्रार्थना की कि उन्हें घर गृहस्थी के जंजाल में न बाँधा जाय उतनी ही तेजी से लोगों ने विवाह का कार्य प्रारम्भ किया। उन्हें भय था कि बहका हुआ बालक कहीं हाथ से निकल न जाय। परन्तु बालक के दृढ़ विश्वास और अटल निष्ठा ने साथ दिया। वह अपने पूर्व संकल्प पर दृढ़ रहा और अपने घर और पारिवारिक जीवन के बंधन में बँधना कदापि स्वीकर नहीं किया। बड़े बूढ़ों को आपके भविष्य की चिन्ता थी। यद्यपि वे जानते थे कि बालक एक श्रेष्ठ मार्ग का अनुसरण करने जा जा रहा है, जिससे केवल अपना ही नहीं वरन् कुल परिवार और संसार का कल्याण है। परन्तु फिर भी आजीवन ब्रह्मचर्य के कठिन तप और वैराग्य के कंटीले जीवन की कल्पना से वे भयभीत हो उठते थे। उन्होंने बहुत कुछ समझा बुझा कर विचार बदलने का प्रयत्न किया। परन्तु वह बालक महात्मा अपने निश्चय पर ही अटल रहा। उन्हें दृढ़ विश्वास था कि भगवान् वे दर्शन और तत्वज्ञान के बिना कुछ भी कर सकना असम्भव है। घर के सभी लोग अपने प्रयत्न में असफल रहे। फिर गाँव के सर्वमान्य कुलगुरुजी को बुलाया गया। पंडित जी ने अपने अनुभव और पाण्डित्य के बल पर बहुत कुछ समझाने की चेष्टा की। उन्हें विश्वास था कि बालक का मन बदल देना बड़ा सरल है। परन्तु

जितनी ही बुद्धिमानी से वे अपनी दलीलों को उपस्स्थित करते गये, उतनी ही बुद्धिमानी के साथ उन्हें उनका उत्तर मिलता गया। जब पाण्डित्य के तर्क वितर्क में पंडितजी जीत न सके, तो उन्होंने भावुकता की शरण ली। बोले, "बेटा, तुम एक मात्र अपने माता-पिता की संता अ हो। उनकी सारी कल्पनाएँ तुम्हारे जीवन के सहारे बनी हैं। उनकी आशाओं के भंडार हो तुम। माता पिता की इस वृद्धावस्था में सेवा करना ही परम धर्म, और कर्तव्य है। उन्हें छोड़ कर अनाथ मत करो। उनका सारा बचा हुआ जीवन अंधकारमय और दुःखपूर्ण हो जाएगा। अभी तुम्हारी बाल्यकाल है। यह जंगलों में तप करने की अवस्था नहीं है। यदि यह निश्चय ही है कि संन्यास लेकर वैराग्य का अभ्यास करना है तो अभी उसका अवसर नहीं आया। पहिले पारिवारिक उत्तरदायित्व को पूर्ण करो, विवाह करके घर गृहस्थी के अनुभव प्राप्त करो; फिर संन्यास का समय आने पर जंगलों में चले जाना। अपूर्ण जीवन से तो साधन न हो सकेगा।"

परन्तु जिस व्यक्ति को भविष्य में धर्म-सम्राट की गद्दी सुशोभित करनी है, उस पर क्या इन लचर दलीलों का प्रभाव पड़ सकता था? ब्डी दृढ़ता के साथ उत्तर दिया "भगवन् आप की आयु ८० वर्ष की हो गई, परन्तु कितने दुःख को बात है कि आपको अब तक तत्वज्ञान प्राप्त करने की इच्छा ही नहीं हुई। लज्जा की बात है कि आप सांसारिकता में इस तरह जकड़े हुए हैं कि अपने कल्याण का मार्ग आपको नहीं सूझता। यदि बालक होने के नाते मुझे घर पर रहना चाहिये तो वृद्ध होने के कारण आपको जंगल के लिये प्रस्थान करना चाहिये। मैं उचित निश्चय पर पहुंच चुका हूँ। मैं अपना कर्तव्य सही ढंग से निभाने जा रहा हूँ और सभी को सही मार्ग का ही अनुसरण करना चाहिये। अपने आगे कहा कि शास्त्रों का कहना

हैं कि यदि परिवार में एक भी मनुष्य को तत्वज्ञान प्राप्त हो जाय तो वह परिवार का परिवार तर जाता है । यदि शास्त्रों का कथन सत्य है तो भगवत्-साक्षात्कार और ब्रह्मज्ञान से मैं सारे परिवार का कल्याण कर्नेवाला बनूंगा ।''

इस पाण्डित्यपूर्ण उत्तर को पाकर वयोवृद्ध पुरोहित महाराज अवाक् रह गये । उन्हें धीरे-धीरे अनुभव होने लगा कि जिसे वह एक अबोध और नासमझ बालक समझ कर सही मार्ग पर लाने की चेष्टा कर रहे थे, वह भविष्य का एक परम तपस्वी और सिद्ध महात्मा है । पंडित जी ने परिवार वालों को संबोधित करते हुए कहा, ''यह आपके कुल में ध्रुव उत्पन्न हुए हैं और आपके कुल को उज्वल बनायेंगे'' इतना कहा कर उठ खड़े हुए और बड़ी श्रद्धा-भावना से उस बाल महात्मा को शीश नवा कर प्रणाम किया और फिर परिवार के सभी छोटे-बड़े सज्जनों ने बारी-बारी से उन्हें प्रणाम किया ।

परन्तु परीक्षा का अंत अभी नहीं हुआ । कुछ लोगों ने फिर भी प्रयत्न किया कि माता के वात्सल्य-प्रेम के प्रभाव से बालक के निश्चय को बदला जाय । उनकी सारी बातें उनकी माता जी पर्दें के भितर बैठी हुई सुन रही थीं । कुछ माताएँ उनकी माता जी के पास गईं और अपना आशय उनसे प्रकट किया । उस समय बालक के हृदय में यह चिन्ता हुई और संकट उत्पन्न हुआ कि कहीं माता की ओर से न रोक लिया जाऊँ । परन्तु जैसा विशाल हृदय-वाला पुत्र था, माता भी वैसी ही विशाल हृदयवाली थीं । वह पुत्र की इस प्रकार की ज्ञान-विकसित भावना को कैसे ठुकरा सकती थीं? वे यह नहीं सहन कर सकीं कि अपने पुत्र के श्रेष्ठतम उन्नतिशील पवित्र और उज्वल भविष्य के सामने रुकावट बन कर खड़ी हों । उन्होंने उत्तर दिया, ''जो इतने ऊँचे मार्ग का अनुसरण करने जा रहे हैं और जिन्हें हमारे कुलगुरु

भी प्रणाम कर रहे हैं, उन्हें हम गज से उतार कर गधे पर बिठाना उचित नहीं समझतीं। कल्याण मार्ग से हटाकर गृहस्थी के जंजाल में प्रवेश करने की आज्ञा नहीं दे सकतीं" उस पर आपने माता जी से प्रस्थान करने की आज्ञा माँगी। उत्तर मिला "जाओ भजन करो। किन्तु भिखमंगा साधु नहीं बनना और जब कभी भी गृहस्थी करने की इच्छा हो तुरन्त घर चले आना।"

दो दिन बाद उन्होंने घर छोड़ दिया। छोड़ दी उसके साथ संसार की माया और ममता। विशाल जन समूह के कोलाहल के बीच से अनन्त ब्रह्मांड के किसी निर्जन कोने में रमने के लिये चल दिया एक बोध दृढ़-प्रतिज्ञ बालक। कौन जानता था उस समय कि यही बालक एक दिन पथ - विहीन, लक्ष्यहीन आध्यात्मिकता के प्रतिकूल विकराल प्रवाह के सामने एक ठोस चट्टान बनकर खड़ा होगा?

आप प्रयाग पहुँचे। यहाँ संगम में स्नान करके बालू पर एकान्त निर्जन स्थान में ध्यानस्थ होकर बैठ गए। दिनचर्या विलक्षण और आकर्षक थी। इसी स्थान में तीन दिन बीत गए। एक पुलिस के दारोगा जी जो तीन दिन से इस अलौकिक तेजपूर्ण बालक की क्रियाशीलता देख रहे थे कुछ विस्मित होकर निकट आये और साधारण सा प्रश्न किया -

"महाराज, किधर से आना हुआ है और किधर जाना है?"

उत्तर असाधारण था -

"मैं वहीं से आया हूँ, जहाँ से सारा जगत् आया है और वहीं जा रहा हूँ जहाँ सारा जगत् ज रहा है।"

दारोगाजी ने फिर प्रश्न किया -

"परन्तु बिना पैसे के जीवन्-निर्वाह तो नहीं हो सकता है?"

अधिक दृढ़ता से उत्तर मिला -

"अनेक जन्मों से मैं शुभ कर्म करता आ रहा हूँ, उनका फल ही मेरा धन है। मेरा शरीर तब तक चलेगा जब तक यह पुण्यरूपी धन है और जिस दिन इसका अन्त हों जायगा, उसी दिन नश्वर शरीर भी शा त हो जायगा। आप मेरी चिन्ता न करें और जाकर अपने कार्य में लगें।"

इस नन्हें से बालक की दृढ़ता, विश्वास और तेजपूर्ण मुख-मण्डल के दर्शन से दारोगा जी पहिले ही प्रभावित हो चुके थे। प्रारब्ध, पुरुषार्थ और इच्छा–शक्ति का इतना सुन्दर विवेचन सुन कर नत-मस्तक हो गये और बड़ी श्रद्धा से उस बालक महात्मा को प्रणाम किया ओर चले गये।

अपने प्रारब्ध और विश्वास के सहारे आप फिर हरिद्वार पहुँचे। यह स्थान धार्मिक जनता का केन्द्र तो है ही। शीघ्र ही लोग इस दिव्य स्वरूप की ओर आकर्षित हो गए। परन्तु बालक महात्मा को अपने ध्यान पूजन के अतिरिक्त किसी ओर देखने का भी अवकाश न था। एकान्त में भजन होता रहा और इस प्रकार कुछ दिन व्यतीत हो गये।

घूमते-घूमते आप ऋषीकेश पहुँचे। यह पुण्यस्थल है और प्राचीन समय से ही एक महान् तीर्थ रहा है। उत्तरी भारत और विशाल हिमालय के क्षेत्र में बसा हुआ यह छोटा सा नगर हिमालय का द्वार है। बड़ा ही रमणीक स्थान है, साधु, महात्मा, मुमुक्षुओं और साधकों को तो विशेष प्रिय है। चारों ओर सुन्दर जंगल है, जहाँ

एकान्त में युग-युग से कितने ही साधक अपने अभीष्ट की सिद्धि प्राप्त कर लोककल्याण में सहायक हुए हैं । यहाँ आपका विचार हुआ कि स्वतन्त्र रूप से जप-तप अभ्यास मर्यादा के विरुद्ध होगा । भगवान् आदि शंकराचार्य ने भी गुरु की शरण ली थी । इसलिए मर्यादा का उल्लङ्घन उचित नहीं और किन्हीं सद्गुरु की खोज करनी चाहिए । सद्गुरु कैसा होना चाहिये

"श्रोत्रियं ब्रह्मनिष्ठम्" इन दो शब्दों में अपने दो शब्द और जोड़े – "क्रोधरहित और बाल ब्रह्मचारी ।"

बहुतों की प्रतिष्ठा सुनी । जा जा कर साक्षात्कार किया । कहीं कोरा पाडित्य था, कहीं शुष्क त्याग वैराग्य, कहीं श्रोत्रियता और ब्रह्मनिष्ठता दोनों प्रतीत हुई, तो बाल ब्रह्मचारी न होने के कारण गुरु जी आपकी कसौटी पर खरे न उतर पाये । एक दण्डी स्वामी महात्मा बाल ब्रह्मचारी सुने गये । उनके योगा-भ्यास की भी ख्याति सुनी । उनके समीप गये । वहाँ आश्रम के सेवकों से विदित हुआ के स्वामी जी अभी समाधि में हैं । अतः प्रतीक्षा में बाहर बैठ गए । स्वामी जी समाधि से उठकर सीधे बाहर आये । आँखों में कुछ गुलाबीपन था । प्रतीत होता था कि प्राणायाम की गरमी अभी शान्त नहीं हुई है । बड़ी नम्रतापूर्वक दोनों हाथ जोड़ कर कहा "ॐ नमो नारायणाय । स्वामिन् कुछ अग्नि की आवश्यकता है, मिल जाय तो बड़ी कृपा होगी" यह सुनना था कि स्वामी जी की अग्नि भड़क उठी । आँखें लाल हो गईं । क्रोधपूर्वक बोले ॥ । ॥ ॥ (कुछ अप शब्द) "जानता नहीं, दण्डी के पास अग्नि कहाँ? मुझसे अग्नि माँगने आया है ॥ ।" स्वामी जी के आवेश के कारण कुछ दो एक कदम पीछे हट कर बोले – "स्वामिन् अग्नि रही नहीं, तो आई कहाँ से?"

बस, सहसा हवा बदल गई। क्रोध जाता रहा। एक नन्हें से बालक से इस तरह परास्त होकर स्वामी जी के हृदय में ठंडापन उतर आया। वे रुक न सके, दौड़ कर गले लगा लिया। बोले, "बेटा, हम अवश्य अपने स्थान से च्युत हो गये। यह तो अनतःकरण का धर्म है। निमित्त पाकर गड़बड़ हो ही जाता है। अपने वास्तविक रूप में आत्मा तो सदा निर्लेप है। तुम धन्य हो जो इस अवस्था में अग्नि प्रज्वलित करने की उत्कट इच्छा रखते हो। आपने कहा "स्वामी जी, आपकी अग्नि की पहली लपट ने ही मुझे भयभीत कर दिया है।"

"धन्य हो, बेटा, धन्य हो," यह कहते हुये बालक की अपूर्व बुद्धि की प्रशंसा करते हुए बड़े प्रेम से दो तीन दिन अपने आश्रम में रखा, कुछ उपदेश दिये। इच्छा थी कि ये समीप में रह जायण् तो इन्हें योगाभ्यास कराया जाय। किन्तु, छुटा हुआ तीर फिर हाथ नहीं आता। पहिले ही स्वामी जी के क्रोधी होने का प्रमाण मिल चुका था। खेद रहा कि स्वामी जी भी आपकी सद्गुरु कसौटी में उन्नसि ही उतरे।

आगे बढ़े। सद्गुरु की खोज थी। कितने ही घाट का पानी पीना पड़ा, कितनी ही कठिनाइयाँ उठानी पड़ीं। किन्तु खोज जारी रही श्रोत्रिय ब्रह्मनिष्ठ संन्यासी की। कई प्रतिष्ठित महात्माओं के समीप रहे, परन्तु कोई कसौटी पर ठिक न उतरा। ढूँढ़ते-ढूँढ़ते हिमालय स्थित उत्तरकाशी पहुँचे। उत्तरकाशी के शृंगेरीपीठ ले शिष्य परम तपस्वी बाल ब्रह्मचारी योगिराज दण्डी संन्यासी श्री स्वामी कृष्णानन्द सरस्वती जी महाराज की शरण में गये और अखण्ड ब्रह्मचर्य की दीक्षा लेकर उन्हीं के समीप रहने लगे। गुरुदेव ने आप का नाम "ब्रह्म चैतन्य ब्रह्मचारी" रखा।

स्वामी जी भारतीय दर्शनशास्त्र के आचार्य और पूर्ण सिद्ध योगिराज थे। जीवन के उच्चतम् सिद्धान्तों को वास्तविक जीवन में घटाने की उनकी कोई समता नहीं कर सकता था। तत्वज्ञान की पराकाष्ठा को पहुँचे हुए स्वयं ब्रह्मस्वरूप साक्षात् ईश्वर स्वरूप भगवान् थे। स्वामी जी के आश्रम में अनेक नवयुवक साधक जीवन के सभी सुख ममता और मोह को त्याग कर परमात्म-दर्शन की उत्कट अभिलाषा से रहा करते थे। सानिध्य होते ही आपने समझ लिया कि जिस गुरु की खोज थी, वह मिल गये और गुरुदेव ने भी जान लिया कि एक उपयुक्त अधिकारी शिष्य तत्वज्ञान की प्राप्ति हेतु उनकी शरण में आया है। ऐसे साधन सम्पन्न अधिकारी की पाकर आप्तकाम, परम निष्काम, सदा एकान्त सेवी अद्वैत निष्ठ महात्मा शास्त्र का कपाट खोल कर कुञ्जियाँ प्रदान करते हैं और दर्शा देते हैं कि तत्व यह है।

गुरु जी विशेष प्रसन्न हैं। उन्हें अपने आश्रम के छोटे ब्रह्मचारी पर स्नेह है, प्रेम है। अलपवयस्क ब्रह्मचारी एवं जन्मजात तपस्वी पर गुरु की असीम अनुकम्पा की बाढ़ सी आ गई है, कुछ विशेष आकर्षण हो गया है। गुरु जी के इतने लगाव का कारण - यह अनुभव का विषय है। शिष्य और गुरु के दो हृदयों के बीच सूक्ष्मातिसूक्ष्म भी कोई ऐसा स्तर नहीं है जो भेद का कारण हो। शिष्य अपने अहंभाव को समस्त वासनाओं सहित भस्म कर अपने अन्तःकरण में सद्गुरु का स्थान बना लेता है। मन को वह अपने सद्गुरु के चरणों में अर्पित कर चुकता है और सद्गुरु के अन्तःकरण की भावनाओं से प्रभावित होकर उसके मन, बुद्धि, चित्त, अहंकार, ज्ञानेन्द्रियों एवं कर्मेन्द्रियों की सूक्ष्म स्थूल हलचलें होती हैं। उसके भाव उसके अपने भाव नहीं, वे तो गुरु की भावनाओं के

आभास हैं। उसके विचार उसके अपने विचार नहीं वरन् सद्गुरु की विचारधारा के प्रतीक हैं। उसका व्यक्तित्व उसका अपना व्यक्तित्व नहीं वह तो गुरु की धरोहर है। शिष्य के आत्म-समर्पण की इस ऊँची सीढ़ी पर गुरु का सर्वस्व शिष्य का है और शिष्य उस सर्वस्व के सहित अपने को सद्गुरु के चरणों में समर्पित आनन्द लेता है। आश्रम के छोटे ब्रह्मचारी की आत्म-समर्पण की भावना इसी प्रकार परमोत्कृष्ट है।

Chapter 2

Forsaking Home
&
the Quest for a Sadguru

On being returned home he discussed asceticism with the old folks. His family members were given to understand his was but a childish whim, just an ignorant nine-year-old young lad talking about ascetic knowledge. However much the youngster requested those people not to tie him down to the difficulties of the duties of a householder, just as much those people quickly began effecting his marriage for their fear was that the youngster would again slip from out of their hands. However, the young child was of resolute trust and he stayed immovable and on his initial vow he remained resolute, so it was unlikely he would accept being tied by the restraints of the family life.

The elders were anxious about your future, although they knew that by his going to follow the One Great Path the youngster was not just doing this for himself but for the happiness and welfare of his family and the world. But then again, by their speculating on the difficult penance of celibacy throughout life and the thorny life of asceticism, they become increasingly afraid for you. So they knew well to make an effort to dampen his desire and to change his thinking. But that young child *mahatma* (great soul) remained steadfast in his determination. His resolute trust was of obtaining Bhagwan's *darshan* (seeing) and the *tatvagyaana* (Essential Knowledge), without which nothing can be possible. Everyone in the family was unsuccessful in their efforts, so the *guru ji* whom all the community respected was then called for.

The *pandit* wanted to explain his own experience and learning as he believed that the boy's mind could be changed straight away. But however intelligent were the arguments he presented, he was met with that much more intelligent responses. When the *pandit* could not win in reasoned debate, then he took recourse to sentiment. Saying:-

"Son, you are the lone offspring of your mother and father. All their plans depend on your life. They have set their store of hopes on you. To serve one's mother and father in the old age is the highest duty, and it is a duty. Don't leave them helpless! You are all of their protection else they will go and live an unreasonable and unhappy life. Right now is your period of childhood and not the age to be doing *tapa* (penance) in the jungles. Certainly, the moment has not come to take to the practice of *sannyas vairagya* (renunciation and asceticism). First, you should fulfil the family responsibilities, of being married and gaining the experience of the duties of the *grihasthi* (householder). Afterwards, when the time of *sannyas* (renunciation) comes, then go walk in the jungles. With an incomplete life then there can be no *sadhana* (spiritual practice leading to realisation)."

But what effect could these arguments have on him he who in the future would be *dharma-samrat* (Emperor of Dharma), and seated on the *gaddi* (seat of Shankaracharya? The answer came with great confidence;

"Bhagwan, you are eighty years old, but how painful it is to say that you really have no desire to acquire knowledge of the divine. Shame to say, you are tied to the worldly, you have not understood the way to happiness. If with regard to my being a young child I should stay at home, then on account of your being old, you should depart for the jungle. I have arrived at a reasonable decision. I am going to take care of my situation correctly, properly, and really all should follow the correct path. You have already said that it is declared in the *Shastras* that if in a family a person gains True Knowledge then the family of that family attains salvation. If the statement of the *Shastras* is true, then meeting by God and having knowledge of Brahman I will make the whole family happy."

Having received this perfectly erudite answer, the aged family priest became speechless. Slowly he got the impression, an understanding that this ignorant and stupid youngster was acually applying his desires to the correct path of action, that in the future he would become extremely ascetic andan accomplished and great soul.

The Pandit called out aloud to the family saying:- "In this your tribe has been born a Dhruva (the boy saint famous throughout India) and he will make your race radiant [with pride]."

Having said as much he stood up, and with great reverence bowed his head and did *pranaam* (reverently placing the palms together in salutation) to that *bal mahatma* (young high soul), and then all the men of the family, from the youngest to the eldest, in turn did their *pranaam*.

However, even now an end to the test had not occurred. Some people then made an effort to shift the determination of the boy by influencing with his mother's fondness. His mother had been seated behind a curtain listening to all their words. Some mothers went near to his mother and made their intent clear. In his heart the young boy had been worried about this time and concern arose because maybe his mother says he cannot go. However great a hearty son he was, as heary too was his mother. So how could she kick out that feeling, for unfolding knowledge, of the son? Surely she could not suffer this, standing as an obstruction to her own son's natural excellent advancement, obstructing his bright and pure future?

She gave this answer; 'He who is going following the upwards path this much and who our own *guru* of the tribe is doing *pranaam*, I do not think it reasonable that we take him off the elephant to cause him to sit on an ass. I cannot command him to withdraw from the *kalyana marg* (the way to happiness, salvation) to enter into the difficulties of the householder.'

He asked the permission to leave of his own Mata Ji. He was met with the answer,

"जा भजन करो"

"jaao bhajana karo"
'Go do *bhajan* (sing praise).'

'But don't become a *bhikhamangaa sadhu* (begging *sadhu*) and when you get the desire sometime, for being a *grishasthi* (householder) then come home at once.'

Two days later he left home and was released from delusion of worldly existence and feeling of attachment towards his family. In the midst of the tumult of the vast multitude of humanity the boy felt a resolve to go and dwell in an uninhabited corner of the infinite universe. At that time, who was to know that this very boy one day will be standing solid as a rock, face-to-face with those without a path, the terrible stream of aimlessness contrary to spirituality?

You reached Prayag. [Prayag is named from the Sanskrit word prayag meaning 'place of sacrifice' – Prayag is also known as Allahabad).] Here he bathed in the Sangam (the confluence of the rivers at Allahabad) and sat alone on the sand solitarily musing. This was the unusual and charming routine of his day and three days passed like this. A policeman noticed him over this period of three days and was astonished at the unusual inclination of the energy of the youth. He came close and made the usual enquiry; 'Maharaj, Where are you from and where you are going?'

The uncommon reply he received was; 'I came from that very place from where the whole world came and I am going where the whole world is going.'

The policeman again questioned him; 'But without *paise* you cannot maintain life?' [*paise* are one hundredth parts of a *rupee*, the currency of India.]

He was met with an answer with more strength; 'From many lifetimes I am coming doing auspicious actions, and the results of that is my wealth. My body will proceed whilst there is this holy form of wealth, and will go on until the day that ends, then that transient body will also become still. Don't think about me any more, apply yourself to your own work.'

From seeing the strong trust in the round face of this small boy before him, so full of glory, the policeman became completely impressed. Having heard such a beautiful investigation concerning wealth created by destiny and of the power of desire, his head became bowed and with great reverence he did *pranaam* to the great-souled boy and went away.

With the support of destiny and trust you arrived again at Haridwar. [Hari-dwar or Hara-dwar means 'Gateway to the Lord'. Hardwar is an ancient town marking the start of the Sivalik foothills of the Himalayas.]

Brahmakund Ghat, Haridwar, 1880's

That place is indeed a centre of spiritual folk. Quickly people became attracted towards his divine form. But the boy *mahatma* devoted himself to his meditation and to worship, and did not have time to look in any other direction. He worshipped alone and in this way some days passed.

Wandering on you arrived at Rishikesh. This is a holy place and from ancient times it has been an important sacred place of pilgrimage. This little town has become a gateway to the area of the immense Himalayas of Northern India. Indeed, it is a pleasing place. It is especially beloved by *sadhus* (religious people), *mahatmas* (great souls), those seeking salvation and *sadhakas* (those engaged in spiritual discipline). How many sadhakas, from age-to-age have been guided and have fulfilled their desire in finding aworld of happiness in the beautiful jungles on all four sides of Rishikesh? *Here you discerned that by practicing japa (repetition of mantra) and practising tapa (austerity) of your own initiative would be against the code of conduct.*

Bhagwan Adi Shankaracharya took refuge of a *guru* too, therefore it is not proper to transgress the code of conduct, but he sensed he should make a search for someone who is really a *sadguru* (good *guru*). Of what sort a person should a *sadguru* be?

"श्रोत्रियं ब्रह्मनिष्ठम्"

"Shrotriyam brahmanishtham"
'One who has studied the *Vedas* thoroughly, - a devotee of a
Brahman (one possessing knowledge of the immortal Self)'
[from *Manduka Upanishad* 1:2:12]

To these two words he added two of his own. *Krodharahita* –
devoid of *krodha* (anger, heat, fury) and *balbrahmachari* –
celibacy since boyhood.

He heard of many who were honoured, and had meetings with
them. Some just had empty book learning, some just dry ascetic
detachment), and some they were who were acquainted with both
shrotriyata and *brahmanishthata* but who were not celibate from
childhood. Notwithstanding, he would not climb down and lower
the criteria for his *guru*.

He heard of a Dandi Swami Mahatma (a staff bearing high-
souled swami) who was lifelong celebate, and he also heard of his
fame as a *yogabhyasa* (living and practicing by the rules of *yoga*).
He went near to him and the servants there at the *ashram* made it
known to him that the *swami* was just now in *samadhi* (engaging
in meditation). Therefore he sat waiting, not making a sound. The
swami came out of meditation, stood up and came outside. There
was a little pinkness in his eyes, and just now wasn't serene
having become acquainted with the heat of *pranayama* (breathing
exercise).

With great courtesy [the boy ascetic] joined his hands together
and said:- ' *"AUM namo naaraayanaaya"*. Swami, it is necessary
for me to get some fire, if I got this I would be very grateful.'

Hearing this, fire arose in the swami. The eyes became red. He
spoke angrily (in a somewhat harsh tone); 'Don't you understand?
Where does a Dandi Swami) have fire? Yet you have come calling
for fire from me!'

Because of Swami Ji's wrath the boy took one or two steps back out of the way, saying; 'Swami, if there is no fire, then from where is it coming?'

Okay, so suddenly the wind changed, and the anger was going. From one tiny boy came this kind of defeat. The heart of swami cooled down, he could not restrain himself and he rushed over and to give him a hug. He said, 'Son, I have certainly become fallen from my own position. This then is the *dharma* of the inner self, that we become uneven. The true form of the self is always pure. You are blessed, who desire to contain this intense burning fire.'

You said, 'Swami Ji, the first glow of your fire gave me a fright.'

[Dandi Swami Ji responded] 'Congratulations son, congratulations.'

Having said this he applauded the boy's unique mind. With increased love he kept him at his ashram for two or three days, giving him some instruction. *It was his desire that you stay there, to go live and practice yoga.* But [as the saying goes] having loosed the arrow it does not return to the hand again. He had discovered the measure of the swami's hot-temperedness and was sorry that swami really did not pass the third criteria of being his *sadguru* (that of being without anger).

So he went further searching a *sadguru*. Really, at how many *ghats* did he drink the water, indeed how much difficulties befell him? But the search was proceeding for a *guru* that was *shrotriya brahmanishtha*. He stayed near many respected *mahatmas* (high-souled people) but none appeared to exactly match the criteria. Searching and searching he arrived at Uttarkashi, situated in the Himalayas.[Uttarkashi is a town situated in a valley approximately midway on the route between Rishikesh and the head of the Ganga river at Gangotri. The Ganga River is known in this area as Bhagairathi. Uttarkashi is the northern Varanasi, *'uttari'* means 'northern', *'kaashi'* is another name for Varanasi.]

At Uttarkashi he sought refuge from Dandi Swami Shri Swami Krishnananda Saraswati Ji Maharaj, a lifelong celibate *yogi* and great disciple of Shringeri Peeth. There he took initiation wholly as a monk. *And Gurudeva gave you the name 'Brahma Chaitanya Brahmachari'.*

Swami Ji was an instructor of Indian *Shastras* (treatises) and a perfectly accomplished ascetic of the highest order. Really he lived by the highest principles, there was nobody who could equal or surpass him in living. He had arrived at the highest degree of knowledge of the divine, he was himself in the self of Brahman, in the presence of god Shiva, the Self of Paramatma.

In Swami Ji's ashram were many young men who were devoting their lives to spiritual accomplishment. *Abandoning all comfort, affection of family and ignorance, having an earnest desire to see Paramatma (the Supersoul, God) you had searched to get near to a guru in order to understand your Self. You had got him and Gurudeva who was a worthy authority, which was a reason to become a disciple under their auspices in order to gain knowledge of the divine.* Thus he acquired a master possessed of realisation, desireless, always alone, worshipping, engaged in *advaita* (undivided, non-dualism), one who is high-souled and with the keys to the door of the *Shastra* which gives sight of the essential nature.

At his ashram the little *brahmachari* is liked, loved. Guru Ji is abundantly pleased. The *guru* becomes especially drawn to the young *brahmachari* giving unbounded compassion to the born *tapasvi,* overcoming any difficulties,. The reason for this much support of Guru Ji – this is the transaction of knowledge. Between the *shishya* (disciple) and *guru* there is only a fine distinction between the two hearts, so this is the reason there is no separation. The disciple's own ego and all his desires are reduced to ashes. One's own self becomes the place of the *sadguru*. He completely fixes the feet of his *sadguru* in his mind and the influence of the *sadguru* on his inner self, his mind, intelligence, reasoning, egotism, the senses of perception, and the subtle and gross agitations of the organs of action. His emotions… he is not having his own emotions, they are but the reflection of the emotions of the *guru*. His thoughts, they are not his own thoughts but a signs, hints of the *sadguru's* thinking. His personality is not his own personality, it is in the trust of the *guru*. The *shishya* (disciple) surrenders himself. On the steep climb of the ladder the *guru* is everything to the *shishya* and the *shishya* happily dedicates everything to the feet of the *sadguru*. The ashram's little *brahmachari* was extremely drawn to dedicate his soul and feeling in this way.

*

[On the approach road to Uttarkashi is an area known as Gyansu – the word *gyaansu* roughly means the wise one. Until recent years there was a small temple here called Gyan Mandir with adjoining several buildings and a modest expanse of land. However, what with severe erosion due to periodic flash flooding of the Bhagarathi River (Ganga) in monsoon time, a landslide in 1980, the quake in 1991, and another landslide in 2003, the area has changed beyond recognition. However, vestiges of the *ashram* remain, including the small temple with its large *shivalinga*. I am of the opinion that this was formerly the site of Dandi Swami Krishnanand's *ashram*, so it is probable that as a youngster Guru Dev stayed in the *antim kutiya* (end hut) here. When I visited Gyan Mandir in 1978 the *ashram* was lived in mainly by elderly *swamis*. For several days I stayed in the single-storey *kutir* at the back and one morning a *brahmachari* pointed to this *kutir* as being the place where Brahmachari Mahesh (aka Maharishi Mahesh Yogi) had lived (during the months he spent doing *sadhana* here in 1953-4). Beneath the bed of the *kutir* was a tiny *gupha* (cave), hollowed out, just large enough for one person to crawl in and sit cross-legged to meditate on the sand.]

३

तिस्रा अधयाय

गुरुनिष्ठा

एक बार उत्तरकाशी में कोई विशिष्ट दार्शनिक व्याख्यानदाता आये। वह भारतीय दर्शन शास्त्र पर व्याख्यान दिया करते थे। सभी साधु-महात्मा आमंत्रित थे। गुरु जी तो कभी कहीं जाते नहीं थे। आश्रम के सभी विद्यार्थी साधकों की इच्छा हुई उनका व्याख्यान सुनने की और गुरुदेव से आज्ञा माँगी। आज्ञा हुई कि सब लोग चले जाना, जाते समय प्रमुख द्वार पर बाहर से ताला बन्द करते जाना और जब आना तो खोल कर चले आना। समय हुआ और सभी आश्रमवासी व्याख्यान सुनने चल दिये, ताला बाहर से बन्द कर दिया गया। इधर छोटे ब्रह्मचारी का हृदय धड़कने लगा। विचार हुआ कि सभी दर्शनशास्त्रों के पंडितों के भी आचार्य परम श्रेष्ठ तपस्वी तत्वज्ञान-प्राप्त श्री गुरुदेव जिनकी कृपा के बल पर अभ्युदय और भगवत्साक्षात्कार करना है, जिनके श्री चरणों में जीवन समर्पित है, उनके श्री चरणों् को छोड़कर कहाँ जाना है? जिनके एक शब्द से ही कल्याण हो सकता है जिनकी कृपा-कटाक्ष से हृदयपटल की पंखुरियाँ विकसित होकर तत्वज्ञान का प्रकाश करा सकती हैं, उनको छोड़कर अनभिज्ञ, केवल पुस्तकों के ज्ञाता और साधनहीन व्याख्यानदाता के व्याख्यान में क्या सार मिलेगा? उसमें ऐसी क्या वस्तु मिल जायगी जो अपने इष्ट के इस घोर अपमान का बदला चुका सकेगी? उन्हें इस प्रकार ताले में बन्द कर सब लोगों का जाना

कितना लज्जास्पद है । पग-पग पर इस प्रकार की भावना पुष्ट होती गई और थोड़ी ही दूर जाने पर यह निश्चय किया कि सब जाते हैं तो जाने दो, अपना लौट पड़ना ही ठिक है ।

किन्तु लौटने के लिये कोई प्रत्यक्ष कारण साथियों को बताना आवश्यक था । यह तो कह नहीं सकते थे कि गुरु जी को ताले में बन्द करके जाना ठिक नहीं, क्योंकि सब कहने लगते कि तुम्हीं एक बड़े भक्त हो गुरु जी के । इतने पुराने-पुराने सब सेवक लोग चल रहे हैं क्या वह गुरु जी का अपमान कर के आये हैं । इसलिए कहा, "व्याख्यान में उत्तरकाशी के विद्वान महात्मा आयेंगे, इसलिये व्याख्याता का भी भाषण क्लिष्ट होगा । हमारी समझ में तो आयेगा नहीं, इसलिये हमारा जाना व्यर्थ ही होगा । हम लौट जाते हैं," तत् पश्चात् फाटक की कुञ्जीलेकर लौट आये ।

पीछे कदम रखा ही था कि दो दण्डी संन्यासी महात्मा आश्रम की ओर जाते हुए दिखाई पड़े । जल्दी बढ़कर ताला खोला । उन्हें अपनी कुटिया में आसन देकर पूछा "महाराज भिक्षा हुई है कि नहीं?" उन्होंने कहा "इसी उद्देश्य से आये हैं कि यहाँ कुछ भिक्षा करके व्याख्यान सुनने जायँगे" । विचार किया कि व्याख्यान का समय तो प्रायः हो ही गया है । जल्दी से हलुवा बना कर उन्हें जलपान कराया । तब वे व्याख्यान सुनने चले गये ।

इधर आप नित्य-कृत्य में संलग्न रहे । सायंकाल सब लोग व्याख्यान सुनकर लौटे । वे दोनों दण्डी संन्यासी भी आये । गुरु जी ने दण्डी महात्माओं को देखकर पूछा "आप लोगों की भिक्षा हुई है?" उन्होंने कहा "हाँ महाराज, यहीं आश्रम में व्याख्यान सुनने जाते समय भिक्षा करके गये थे" गुरु जी ने सोचा कि आज तो आश्रम

बन्द ही रहा। उन्होंने इधर कहाँ भिक्षा की? पूछा, "आश्रम में कहाँ?" संन्यासियों ने बताया "अन्तिम कुटिया में एक छोटे ब्रह्मचारी थे, इन्होंने जल्दी से हलुवा बना कर हम लोगों को भिक्षा करा दी थी जिससे व्याख्यान में भी समय पर पहुँच गये थे।" नित्य की भाँति जब छोटे ब्रह्मचारी प्रणाम करने गये तब गुरु जी ने पूछा "क्या तुम व्याख्यान सुनने नहीं गये थे?"

"नहीं, महाराज! झमने सोचा कि हमारी समझ में तो आयेगा नहीं, जाना व्यर्थ ही होगा। इसलिये नहीं गये।" दण्डी संन्यासियों के अतिथि सत्कार की बात पूछी। जैसा किया था बता दिया। गुरु जी ने सोचा इस अवस्था में तो सभा समारोह बच्चों को स्वाभाविक ही आकृष्ट करते हैं, इनके न जाने का कोई विशेष ही कारण होगा। कुछ सूक्ष्म विचार किया। योगी थे ही, परिस्थिति स्पष्ट चित्रित हो गई। विदित हो गया कि इनकी गुरुनिष्ठा आश्रम के सभी सेवकों से उत्कृष्ट है। फिर क्या था उत्कृष्ट अधिकारी के लिये उत्कृष्ट पथ निर्धारित हो गया। दूसरे दिन रात्रि के समय जब प्रणाम करने गये तब गुरु जी ने रोक लिया। सब प्रणाम करके चले गये तब कहा – "जितना शास्त्र-अध्ययन हो गया, पर्याप्त है। अब हम तुम्हें साधन में लगाना चाहते हैं जिससे जो बात शास्त्र से जानी गई है उसका अनुभव कर लो।" "जो आज्ञा महाराज।" "जो साधन तुम्हारे लिये निश्चय किया गया है, वह हमारे साथ इस आश्रम में रहकर नहीं हो सकेगा, क्योंकि तुम्हारा वह मार्ग होगा॥ ॥ ॥ जो बहुत उत्कृष्ट साधन है। इस आश्रम में कई लोग बीस-बीस, पच्चीस-पच्चीस वर्ष से पड़े हैं। साधन-सम्पत्ति न होने के कारण कोई उस अध्यात्म विद्या के अधिकारी नहीं हैं इसलिये यह मार्ग किसी को नहीं बताया गया। यदि यहीं रह कर तुम उसमें दत्त-चित्त होगे, तो ये लोग ईर्ष्यावश

तुम्हारे मार्ग में बाधक हो जायँगे । यहाँ से समीप ही, तीन मील की दूरी पर एक स्थान है, वहीं जाकर इस प्रकार से अभ्यास करो । सात दिन में एक बार सन्ध्या समय चले आया करो और एक रात्रि यहाँ बिताकर प्रातःकाल चले जाया करो । कल हम तुमको वहाँ जाने की आज्ञा देंगे, पर अभ्यास करने के लिये वहाँ जाओ ऐसा नहीं कहेंगे । सब लोगों के सामने तुमको जोर से डाँटेंगे और आश्रम से हट कर वहाँ जाकर रहने के लिये कह देंगे तुम घबड़ाना नहीं । चुपचाप अपना सामान लेकर वहाँ चले जाना जिससे लोग समझें कि इन्होंने कोई बड़ी भुल की है जिससे गुरु जी ने अप्रसन्न होकर आश्रम से हटा दिया है ।"

गुरु जी दूसरे दिन किसी निमित्त को लेकर आश्रम के सभी लोगों पर बिगड़े । कुछ हल्ला सा हुआ । सभी लोग एकत्र हो गये । गुरु जी अप्रसन्न हैं । सभी अपनी-अपनी गर्दन झुकाये खड़े हैं, डाट खा रहे हैं । छोटे ब्रह्मचारी के आते ही मानो सबको छुटकारा मिल गया – उन्होंने आकर मानो सब की लाज रख ली सब का दोष अपने ऊपर ले लिया । गुरु जी की दृष्टि इन्हीं पर केन्द्रित हो गई । बोले "हटो, यहाँ से निकलो । यह स्थान बच्चो के लिये नहीं है । तुम्हारा यहाँ कोई काम नहीं है । कोठारी! झटाओ इनको, अभी कुटिया खाली कराओ । जाओ, यहाँ तुम्हारा कोई काम नहीं ।"

"कहाँ जायँ महाराज?"

"जाओ, जहाँ ठिक समझो, रहो । कोठारी! तीन मील दूर वह स्थान इन्हें बता दो । रहना चाहें, तो वहीं रहें या चले जायँ जहाँ ठिक समझें ।" "जो आज्ञा" कह कर दण्डवत प्रणाम किया । अपना सामान लिया । सदा की भाँति कोठारी ने एक सप्ताह की खाद्य

सामग्री दे दी। सब कुछ लेकर वहाँ चले गये और रहने लगे।

दिन-रात बीतने लगे। साधन-पथ अग्रसर होने लगा। गुरुवार को गुरु चरणों के दर्शनार्थ जाते और सात दिन किये हुये अभ्यास का अनुभव सुनाकर नवीन आदेशोपदेश ले कर चले आते। गुरु-चरणों के दर्शन से हृदय को नवीन स्फूर्ति मिलती साधन-पथ पर प्रकाश मिलता। निष्ठा दृढ़ होकर क्षमता बलवती होती और सद्गुरु कृपा के सहारे इष्ट उतरता आता। ब्रह्मचारी जी श्री गुरुकृपा से साधन पथ की उच्चतम सीमा की ओर जिस तीव्र गति से बढ़े वह अद्वितीय, प्रशंसनीय और अनुकरणीय रहो।

गुरु जी ने एक बार एक सेवक भेज कर पुछवाया "हम आना चाहते हैं क्या वहाँ पर स्थान खाली है?" उत्तर मिलाट्टृस्थान बिलकुल खाली नहीं है?" सेवक ने समझाया "गुरु जनों से व्यवहार बहुत संभल कर करना चाहिये। जैसा आपने कहा वैसा यदि हम जाकर कहेंगे, तो आप पर तो प्रायः गुरु जी अप्रसन्न हैं ही हमारी भी आफत आ जायगी। ठीक से तो हम यही कह देंगे कि वहाँ गुफाओं में कई कमरे खाली हैं। हम देख आये हैं आप चल सकते हैं।" उत्तर मिला, "देखिय, आपकी आयु, आपकी विद्या, और आपकी गुरुभक्ति को हम सभक्ति नमस्कार करते हैं। आप हम से बड़े हैं आपका हम सम्मान करते हैं। परन्तु इस समय आप दूत की हैसियत से आये हैं। गुरु जी का प्रश्न आपने हमें सुनाया है हमारा उत्तर जैसा हम कहते हैं श्री चरणों में निवेदन कर दीजिये कि यहाँ पर एक भी कमरा खाली नहीं है। इसके बाद अपनी ओर से जो कुछ आपको कहना हो आप अच्छी तरह से कह सकते हैं। परन्तु हमारा उत्तर हमारे ही शब्दों में कहियेगा। गुरु जी अप्रसन्न होंगे तो हम भुगत लेंगे आपको क्या? आप तो सूचनावाहक हैं, इस समय।"

दूत ने आकर उत्तर सुनाया। सुन कर गुरु जी मौन रहे। परन्तु छोटे ब्रह्मचारी की यह धृष्टता की बात आश्रम भर में फैल गई। उन्होंने गुरु जी का बहुत अपमान किया है। अबकी गुरुवार को आयें तो इन्हें ठिक करना चाहिये। इस प्रकार की भावना सारे आश्रम में व्याप्त हो गई। आश्रम के बड़े पुराने सेवक गुरुवार की प्रतीक्षा करने लगे। गुरुवार आया और सन्ध्या होते-होते ब्रह्मचारी भी गुरु जी के समीप आ पहुंचे। देखा प्रायः सभी लोग एक के बाद एक गुरु जी के समीप आ बैठे। आज सभी की आँखों में ब्रह्मचारी की ओर एक विधेष गम्भीर दृष्टि है। आपस में एक दूसरे की आँखें मिल कर कह लेती हैं कि देखो इनकी धृष्टा का फल अब मिलता ही है। अब सभी बुद्धिमान अपनी-अपनी बुद्धि टटोल रहे थे कि किस प्रकार उस प्रसंग को गुरु जी के सम्मुख उपस्थित करें। एक, जो गुरु जी के कुछ विशेष कृपापात्र समझे जाते थे, बोल हो पड़े, – "महाराज, गुरु की इच्छा की अवहेलना करने वाला किस प्रायश्चित्त का भागो होता है। इच्छ की अवहेलना तो एक प्रकार से गुरु की अवज्ञा ही हुई। इससे तो वह गुरुद्रोही ही सिद्ध होता है। फिर ऐसे गुरुद्रोही के साथ क्या बर्ताव होना चाहिये?" गुरु जी आश्रम् के वातावरण से परिचित थे ही, किन्तु उन्होंने कुछ तटस्थ से होकर कहा – "अपना प्रश्न किसी उदाहरण से स्पष्ट करो। अभी तुम्हारा तात्पर्य ठिक स्पष्ट हुआ नहीं।" अब तो प्रश्नकर्ता संकोच में पड़ गये। सामने स्पष्ट कैसे कहें। किन्तु गुरु आज्ञा थी, कहना ही पड़ा। कह गये – "उस दिन की बात है जब महाराज ने उस स्थान पर जाने की इच्छा प्रकट की थी और पुछवाया था छोटे ब्रह्मचारी से स्थान के सम्बन्ध में, तो वहाँ गुफाओं में कई कमरे खाली रहते हुये भी इन्होंने कह दिया कि स्थान बिलकुल खाली नहीं है। श्री चरणों के प्रति इनकी इस धृष्टता से आश्रम के सभी लोगों को महान् क्षोभ है

और महाराज जी से अब हम जानना चाहते है कि इनके साथ हम लोगों का कैसा व्यवहार हो?"

गुरु जी बोले, "क्यों जी, इस सम्बन्ध में तुम क्या कहना चाहते हो?"

छोटे ब्रह्मचारी ने कहा, "मेरे साथ आश्रमवासी कैसा व्यवहार करें यह अनुशासन तो श्री चरण ही देने में समर्थ हैं। हाँ, हम इतना ही कह सकते हैं कि उस दिन जो कहा था वही सत्य था और अब भी वही परिस्थिति है कि वहाँ गुरु जी के लिये कोई स्थान खाली नहीं है।"

उस पक्ष से आवाज आई – "क्यों, ब्रह्मचारी, क्या कोने के वे दो कमरे और सामने के दो कमरे खाली नहीं हैं?"

उत्तर मिला, "आपको तो वहाँ का बोध है नहीं। आप से हम अधिक विश्लेषण क्या करें!"

"समझा दो इन लोगों को। जो बात हो, स्पष्ट कह दो।" गुरु जी ने कहा।

"महाराज, इन लोगों से बताने की बात तो है नहीं हम क्या कहें? हम तो प्रार्थना रूप में ही कह सकते हैं।"

"अच्छा, हमी से कह दो। ये लोग सुनना चाहते हैं तो सुना दो।"

छोटे ब्रह्मचारी ने कहा, "जहाँ तक हम समझ पाये हैं गुरु चरणों का निवास मिट्टी पत्थर के कमरों में तो होता नहीं। उनके निवास के लिये भक्तों के हृदय का कमरा चाहिये। मेरे पंचकोशों के समस्त

कमरों में श्री चरणों का निवास पहिले से ही हो चुका है। जिस दिन हमने श्री चरणों का पवित्रतम चरणोदक ग्रहण किया था, उसी समय अपने हृदय के कमरों को पूरा खाली कर इन्हें वहाँ आसीन करा दिया था। अब हमारे पास कोई खाली कमरा नहीं है। गुरु देव तो रोम-रोम में व्याप्त हो चुके हैं। यदि हमें पहिले दिन विदित होता कि भविष्य में फिर कभी स्थान की माँग होगी तो पंचकोशों में से कोई एक दो रिक्त रख लेते। पर अनभिज्ञतावश अपने सब कमरे पहिले ही भर रखे हैं – और रही बात उन मिट्टी-पत्थर के कमरों की तो महाराज जी जानते ही हैं कि सब खाली पड़े हैं यदि वहीं निवास की इच्छा होती तो पधार ही जाते। हमसे पुछवाने की आवश्यकता ही न थी। इसलिये जिन कमरों के लिये महाराज जी ने पुछवाया था उन्हीं के लिये हमने उत्तर दिया था।"

इतना कह कर ब्रह्मचारी एक लम्बी साँस खींच कर मौन हो गये। विकसित हृदय कमल की वह आभा संकुचित सी हो गई। मुखमुद्रा म्लान हो गई। मानों अनतर्हृदय की वेदना जाग्रत हो उठी है। कारण कि आज उनकी वह निधि लुट गई है जिसे वे अपने हृदय के अनतरतम में बड़ी सावधानी से सदा ही छिपा कर अब तक सम्भाले हुये थे। आज लोगों ने उन्हें विवश कर दिया कि वे स्वयं अपने मानस पट के रहस्यमय गोपनीय चित्रों को खुले आम सब के सामने प्रकट कर दें। जो कहने की वस्तु नहीं थी, वह उन्हें आज बरबस कह देनी पड़ी। वातावरण स्तब्ध हो गया। उपस्थित मण्डली का हृदय धड़कने लगा। नेत्र एक दूसरे को देख कर अपने पर लज्जित हो रहे हैं। जहाँ उन्हें केवल कोयले का भाण्डार समझ पड़ा था, वह तो चमकते हुये हीरों की खान निकली। जहाँ उन्होंने दिन में भी अंधकार देखा था वहाँ चिर प्रकाशित अखण्ड प्रभा का साम्राज्य

दृष्टिगोचर हुआ। सभी को अपनी अन्तरदर्शिता पर खेद हुआ। सभी ने अपने मलिन हृदय को ब्रह्मचारी जी के निर्मल भावों से धोकर पवित्र किया।

इधर गुरु जी के नेत्रों में प्रेमाश्रु छलक उठे, क्योंकि अब तक शिष्य के हृदय के आत्मसमर्पण का भाव उस हृदय में ही गुप्त था बाहर नहीं निकला था। गुरु जी के हृदय में भी वह सुरक्षित और गुप्त था। किन्तु जब एक हृदय से उसका विवरण बाहर निकला तब दूसरा हृदय भी उसे अपने में छिपाये रहने में असमर्थ हो उठा। गुरु जी के हृदय में प्रेम का समुद्र उमड़ आया। इस समय गुरु और शिष्य समाज के बीच केवल मौन का ही साम्राज्य रहा। किसी को स्मरण नहीं कितना समय इस भाव-समाधि में बीत गया। सहसा गुरु जी ने आदेश दिया, "सब लोग चले जाओ" एक के बाद एक उठ कर सब चले गये किन्तु अभी छोटे ब्रह्मचारी का आसन नहीं उठा। सबके साथ वे कैसे उठें। उन्हें तो अभी अपने अपराध की क्षमायाचना करनी है। एकान्त पा कर गुरु से जी बोले, "भगवन्, आज मुझे गोपनीय विषय का सबके समक्ष प्रकाश करना पड़ा है, इसके लिये क्या प्रायश्चित करना होगा? गुरु जी ने कहा, "है तो यह अपनी निष्ठा का विषय, अवश्य गोपनीय, पर तुमने तो हमारी आज्ञा से कहा है इसलिये इस विषय में अधिक विचार करने की आवश्यकता नहीं है। सुन तो लिया लोगों ने पर यह निष्ठा कोई बँटा नहीं सकता। संसार का प्रवाह ही ऐसा है कि सुन, जान कर भी विरलों की ही सत्य में प्रवृत्ति होती है।"

Saraswati – goddess of learning

Chapter 3
Allegiance to Guru

One time a great philosphical speaker came to Uttarkashi in order to explain aspects of Indian *Shastra*. All the *sadhus* and *mahatmas* were invited. As Guru Ji [Dandi Swami Krishnanand Saraswati Ji] seldom went anywhere and all the students engaged in spiritual practice at the ashram desired to hear his lecture, at Gurudeva's command the students were to lock and unlock on their return. When the time came all the *ashramites* went to listen to the lecture and they closed the lock on the outside.

The heart of the little *brahmachari* palpitated. He thought that, 'Of all the *pandits* showing aspects of the *Shastras*, that he has the greatest *acharya* (instructor), who is the best *tapasvi* (recluse), who has *tatvagyaana* (knowledge of the divine), that Shri Gurudeva has strength of kindness and he perceives God. So, he who is dedicated to life of Shri Charanon ('the feet' of the *guru*), who is leaving Shri Charanon, where is there to go? It would be foolish to leave the one whose word can bring happiness and by kind look can unfold the petals the covering of the heart, and light the divine knowledge. What substance will there be in the explanation of someone of mere book learning and who is just a worthless orator? Conversely, what might one receive in retribution for such terrible disrespect of the beloved one? What a great scandal that all the folk going and closing the lock in this way?'

Step after step the feeling became stronger and on going a little distance he decided that if all are going, then let them go, but it would be well that he himself returns. Now it was essential that he give his companions a reason for returning. But the disciples that are going away are of such long standing, how come they are disrespecting Guru Ji? *But he couldn't say that it is not proper to go and lock in Guru Ji because all would hear this as if you were really the great bhakta (devotee) of Guru Ji.* Therefore he said,

'Going to the lecture will be learned *mahatmas* of Uttarkashi and so the lecturer's speech will be difficult and I will not understand, therefore there is no purpose in coming. I will return.'

After a time he returned, taking with him the key. After walking back he saw two *dandi sannyasi mahatma* who were going to the ashram. Quickly he undid the lock.

He gave them a seat in the *kutiya* (cottage, hut) asking; 'Maharaj, have you not had *bhiksha* (food given as alms)?'

They said, 'This is the object of our coming here, for some *bhiksha,* then we will go to the lecture.'

Realising that it was nearly time for the lecture he hurriedly made some *halwa* as a light repast for them, then they went to hear the lecture.

There you stayed, engaging in your regular duties. In the evening all the folk returned from hearing the lecture. Both of the *dandi sannyasis* also came and Guru Ji looked at the *dandi mahatmas* and asked; 'Have you people had *bhiksha*?'

They said, 'Yes Maharaj, in this very *ashram,* whilst going to listen to the lecture we had been having *bhiksha.*'

Guru Ji considered that today the ashram was actually locked so where did they get the *bhiksha* here?'

He asked, 'Where in the ashram?'

The *sannyasis* informed him, 'In the end *kutiya* (hut) there was a little *brahmachari*. Very quickly he made *halwa* and gave us people *bhiksha*. From his doing that we arrived at the lecture on time.'

So, when the little *brahmachari* went to make *pranaam* to Guru Ji in the normal way the *guru* asked; 'Did you not go and hear the lecture?'

'No Maharaj. I imagined I would understand, so I didn't go

there.'

Asked to speak in respect of the *dandi sannyasi* guests, he told him what he had done. Guru Ji reasoned that at this stage it is natural for youngsters to be drawn to a magnificent assembly, so there must have been a special reason for someone not going. Giving some subtle thought as only a *yogi* is able, the circumstances became clear. It became known to him that of all the devotees in the ashram his allegiance to the Guru is the best. What was the future? An excellent path for one who has an excellent right.

The next day at nightime when he (the little *brahmachari*) came to do *pranaam* (salutations), the *guru* detained him. When all had made their *pranaam* and had gone, then the *guru* said; 'You have made enough study of the *Shastra*. Now I desire that you engage in *sadhana*. From your understanding of the description in the *Shastra*, take the experience thereof.'

[The child renunciate replied] 'If you command, Maharaj'

[The *guru*] 'Certainly for doing that *sadhana* (spiritual practice) you cannot do that with us in the ashram, because yours will be the way.... that very great *sadhana*. In this ashram are several people who have stayed twenty, twenty-five years, and not advancing with their *sadhana*. The reason being is that they are not possessed of the right to that *"adhyaatma vidyaa"* (spiritual knowledge) therefore I am not instructing any of them on this path. So if you stay here and you have an understanding presented to you, then these people's envy will become a hindrance in your way. Nearby to here, at a distance of three miles, you are to go to that very place... Do practise of this kind! Once every seven days come and spend the night here, and leave at daybreak. Tomorrow I will give you an order to go, but I will not say anything about your going there for this exercise. In front of all the people I will give you a forceful reprimand and tell you to get out and to go and stay there. You are not to be perplexed. Quietly take your possessions and go there. From your going the folk will understand that you have made a big error and the Guru Ji is displeased with you and is getting you to leave the ashram.'

The next day, for no reason, Guru Ji became enraged at everyone at the ashram. Something of an uproar occurred. All the people gathered together in the same place and as Guru Ji was displeased, everyone stood with heads bowed, filled with suffering. The little *brahmachari* came and appeared to accept all the blame so all assumed he would be got rid of,. They became centred on looking at Guru Ji.

He spoke. 'Get out! Disappear from here! This place is not for children. You don't have any business here. Storekeeper... get rid of him, cause the *kutiya* to be vacated right now. Go! You have no business here!'

'Where shall I go Maharaj?'

'Go and stay wherever you think is proper! Store-keeper, three miles away is a place.. tell him of it. Remain there if you want. You stay right there, or go elsewhere. Wherever you think proper.'

'Whatever you command,' he said prostrating, doing *pranaam*. He took his possessions. The storeman was to give him a supply of one week's food regularly. Taking everything he went and stayed there.

It came to pass he stayed for days and nights, going ahead on the course of *sadhana*. Every *guruwar* (Thursday) he took the benefit of *darshan* at the feet of *guru*, and after having related his perception of experiences which had occurred in the last seven days, he slept and then came to receive fresh instructions. From *darshan* at the feet of the *guru* he received fresh inspiration of heart, and he met with light on the path of *sadhana*. Having resolute faith, strong ability and the support of the grace of a *sadguru*, the wish came to be fulfilled. With the *gurukripa* (grace of the *guru*) the *brahmachari's* course of *sadhana* quickly grew to the highest point. He was peerless, praiseworthy and exemplarary.

One time Guru Ji sent a servant [said to be the eldest disciple whose name was Yoganand] who enquired:- 'I (the *guru*) wish to come. What place is empty there?'

He was met with the answer;

"स्थान बिलकुल खालि नहीं है । "

"sthaan bilkul khaali nahiin hai."
'There is no vacancy in the whole place.'

[*sthaan* = place. *bilkul* = all, full, whole. *khaalii* = empty, void, vacant, unoccupied. *nahiin* = not, no. *hai* = is.]

The servant explained, 'You should be very cautious in your behaviour with *gurus*. So, if I go and say according to what you have said, then Guru Ji will probably be displeased. It will be a disaster for us. With accuracy then, I will say that, "There are many empty caves. We have been to see. You can go".'

He got an answer; 'You should see that with devotion I do *namaskar* (pay obeisance) to your age, to your learning and to your devotion to Guru. You are bigger than me, I respect you. But this time you come in the status of messenger. I have heard Guru Ji's question from you. According to our reply you should announce to Shri Charanon that;

"यहाँ पर एक भी कमरा खाली नहीं है ।"

"yahaan para eka bhii kamaraa khaalii nahiin hai."
'There is not one *kamara* (room, chamber) empty here.'

[*yahaan* = here. *par* = on. *ek* = one. *bhii* = also. *kamaraa* = room. *khaalii* = empty, void, vacant, unoccupied. *nahiin* = no, not. *hai* = is.]

'After this you can say any thing from your own side, you can say any good thing. But you are telling my answer in my words. If Guru Ji becomes displeased then I will accept to undergo that displeasure. What is it to you? At this time you are just conveying the information.'

The messenger went and gave the reply. Having heard it Guru Ji stayed in *maun* (silence). But talk of the little *brahmachari's* impudence spread throughout the ashram. They felt that Guru Ji had been very dishonoured. Now, when *guruwar* (Thursday) came they wanted to settle the matter. This kind of feeling pervaded the entire ashram. The older devotees of the ashram were waiting for Thursday.

Thursday came and when it became evening the little *brahmachari* arrived there to be near Guru Ji. He watched as one after the other folk came to sit near Guru Ji. Now, in all of their eyes was a special seriousness directed towards the *brahmachari*. Among themselves, one another's eyes met saying, 'See, now he will get the fruit of his audacity'. Now all were fretting in the their minds for an occasion to present his own thoughts before Guru Ji.

One who thought himself to be a special recipient of the grace of Guru Ji spoke; 'Maharaj, what penance is escaped by the one who disrespects the will of the *guru*? Disrespect of the will then is a kind of contempt of the *guru*. From this then is a proven insubordination of the *guru*. Then, in this way with insubordination of the *guru*, what should be the treatment?'

Guru Ji was acquainted with the atmosphere of the ashram

really, but he said with some indifference; 'Clarify your question with any example. Your gist is not clear just now.'

Now then the questioner felt shy. How could he say it clearly? But the *guru* was commanding that he speak. He said, 'The news that one day it became clear that Maharaj wished to go to that place and someone enquired of the situation from the little *brahmachari* whether there were any empty rooms there. He said that there was no place empty. The insolence towards Shri Charanon is greatly unsettling all the folk in the *ashram* and we would like to know from Maharaj Shri how we should conduct ourselves with him?'

Guru Ji spoke (his words directed to the little *brahmachari*); 'What sir do you wish to tell in this connection?'

The little *brahmachari* said, 'As to what kind of conduct the inhabitants of the *ashram* are to have towards me, only Shri Charan is capable of giving this instruction. Yes, I can say this much that, that day, what I said was the very truth and also the situation is the very same now; that there is not any empty space for Guru Ji.'

From the side a voice came, 'Why *brahmachari*, what of the two rooms on the side and the two rooms at the front?'

He got this answer, 'There, you do not understand. I am being torn apart by you. Why do you do this?'

'Give understanding to these people. Tell them clearly the meaning!' said Guru Ji.

'Maharaj, What can I tell these people who are not informed about this thing? I can only say in the form of *"praarthanaa"* (prayer).'

'Good, then say to only us. These people want to hear, then let them hear.'

The little *brahmachari* said, 'As far as we understand Guru

Charanon's abode is not in rooms of stone and clay. There should be a room in the heart of devotees for him to dwell. Since a long time all the rooms of my *panchkoshon* (five *kosha*, the receptacles within the body according to the *Vedanta* system) were adjusted to be the abode of Shri Charanon. From the day we seized the water that washed Shri Charanon (the blessed feet) of the holy soul, really at that time the emptiness of the rooms of my own heart were filled, there you became seated. Now we do not have any empty room. Guru Dev then became an occupant of the finest hairs on the body. If we had known before that day that in future you would request a place sometime, then within the *panchkoshon* I would have set some, one or two empty places, but I was ignorant of this wish and had previously filled all the rooms.

And speaking of these rooms of earth and stone, then Maharaj Ji understands that all are empty. Had he desired to dwell at that place he would really have graced it by going there. It really is not necessary to inquire from me. Therefore, I gave the answer about which rooms Maharaj Ji was asking of.'

Having said so much, the *brahmachari* pulled a long breath and become silent. That splendour of the unfolding of the lotus heart became as if folded again. The countenance of his face became pale. He became aware of the ache of the weight of his heart inside and the reason was that today the treasure of the inner soul of his own heart which with great vigilance had been constantly hidden until now, had become looted,. Today he was helpless, as the screen that concealed the images in his heart, was opening and making them apparent, publicly in front of all. That was not a thing to tell. That today he had been forcibly made to say.

The atmosphere became dead. The hearts of those present pulsated. They looked each other eyeing each other bashfully. What they had understood to be only a coal-store, turned out to be a mine of brilliant diamonds. Where they had seen darkness in the day, an empire of perfect long lasting light became apparent. Every one of them was saddened by their own lack of foresight. All of their soiled hearts were washed clean by the pure feelings of the *brahmachari ji.*

Here the eyes of Guru Ji spilled with tears of love, because up to now the feeling of surrender of heart of the *shishya* (disciple) was a secret in his heart and was not visible outside. It was secure and hidden in the heart of Guru Ji too. But when an explanation appears from the one heart then the other heart becomes incapable of hiding within itself. In the heart of Guru Ji the ocean of love came to overflow. At this time, in the midst of the meeting of *guru* and *shishya,* only silence reigned. No one remembers how much time passed in this feeling of *samadhi* (meditation).

Unexpectedly Guru Ji gave a command, 'All you people get going!'

So, one after the other they all got up and went. But the little *brahmachari* did not get up from being seated, just now. How could he get up along with them? Just now then he has to ask mercy for his offence. Having obtained privacy with the *guru ji*, he said, 'Bhagwan, today I have brought to light, to all, a topic that is confidential, what will be the penance for this?'

Guru Ji said, 'Oh, the matter of one's allegiance is certainly confidential, but you spoke at my command therefore it is not necessary to give this matter any more consideration. On account of having heard of this allegiance, none can share it. Such is the stream of *samsara*, that even having heard, in truth, rarely is there the inclination of the mind.'

४

चौथा अध्याय

कुछ चमत्कारपूर्ण घटनाएँ

श्री महाराज जी ने उत्तरकाशी में गुरु जी के समीप रह कर तपश्चर्यापूर्वक शास्त्राध्ययन और योगाभ्यास पूर्ण किया। २५ वर्ष की अवस्था में आत्मनिष्ठ होकर हिमालय से नीचे उतरे। गुरु जी भी साथ चल दिये। कुछ दिन ऋषीकेश के समीप कजलीवन में निवास किया। यह अत्यन्त एकान्त और निर्जन स्थान है। घनघोर जंगल, जहाँ हिंसक जीव जन्तु साधारण ही विचरते हैं। ऐसे एकान्त स्थान में यदि कोई साधु महात्मा कुछ समय रुक जाता है, तो शीघ्र ही समीप व दूर के गाँवों में ख्याति हो जाती है और स्वभा इक ही लोग दर्शन के लिये दौड़ पड़ते हैं। दर्शनार्थियों में एक ब्रह्मण- महात्माओं की सेवा शुश्रूषा के निमित्त कुछ दूध लाया करता था। अपने गुरु जी की सेवा के लिये महाराज श्री उस ब्राह्मण से प्रतिदिन आधा सेर दूध ले लिया करते थे और रात्रि में गरम करके गुरु जी को पिला देते थे।

एक दिन ऐसा हुआ कि दूध लाते समय ब्राह्मण की स्त्री ने कहा, "आज दूध कम है, बच्चों के लिये कम पड़ेगा" किन्तु ब्राह्मण जैसे दूध रोज लाता था ले आया। महाराज श्री ने रोज की भाँति उस दिन भी दूध लेकर गरम करके गुरु जी के सामने रख दिया। गुरु जी ने कहा, "इस दूध में आज क्लेश है, हम इस दूध को नहीं पियेंगे। दूध वाले को उसे लौटा दो और उससे दूध लेना बन्द कर दो।" महाराज श्री ने वैसा ही किया। इसके बाद लगभग १५ दिन के पश्चात् उस ब्राह्मण

का पुत्र मर गया। सारी बस्ती में यह चर्चा होने लगी कि महात्मा
जी नाराज हो गये हैं। इसलिये इस ब्राह्मण का लड़का मर गया।
महाराज श्री ने यह बात अपने गुरु जी से कही। उन्होंने कहा कि
जब उस लड़के की अर्थी स्मशान में आवे, तो लोगों से कहना कि
उसको अभी न जलावें और पहिले हमको बुला लें। जब उस लड़के
की अर्थी स्मशान में आई तो उसको वहीं रख दिया। इतने में गुरु
जी भी आ गये। इन्होंने अर्थी की सब रस्सियाँ खोलवाईं और मृतक
के शिर पर अपने चरण से धक्का देते हुये कहा, "इतना क्यों सोता
है?" इस पर वह मृतक जी उठा। सबके सब आश्चर्य चकित हो
गये। वे सब महात्मा जी को बारी-बारी से प्रणाम करने लगे। अपनी
कुटिया पर वापस आते ही गुरु जी ने महाराज श्री से कहा, "अभी
यहाँ से चलो, नहीं तो यहाँ के सब मुर्दे हमारे सिर पड़ेम्गे।" इतना
कहकर उन्होंने वह स्थान छोड़ दिया और गुरु शिष्य एक दूसरे से
पृथक् हो गये।

एक बार महाराज श्री ने देखा कि गंगा जी में भीषण बाढ़ आ रही
है, प्रतिक्षण पानी ऊँचा उठता जा रहा है। किनारे पर बसे सभी
महात्मा विपत्तिजनक क्षेत्रों से हट चुके हैं। किन्तु दो साधु इस बाढ़
की तनिक भी चिन्ता न करते हुये अपने-अपने तखतों पर, जो पास
ही किनारे के कीकर के पेड़ों से बँधे निश्चिंत बैठे हुये हैं। आपको बड़ा
आश्चर्य हुआ कि जब सभी साधु अपनी-अपनी रक्षा के लिये सुरक्षित
स्थानों का चले गये हैं तो ये क्यों नहीं गये? एक पेड़ पर आप भी
चढ़ गये और उनकी गति विधि देखने लगे। तीन दिन बीत गये
परन्तु वह दोनों साधु तथा स्वयं भी अपने-अपने स्थान पर डटे रहे।
गंगा की बाढ़ से जल-प्रवाह के वेग का सहन करना उन पेड़ों के
लिये कठिन हो गया और एक पेड़ जड़ से उखड़ कर वह चला।

साथ ही साथ उस तखत पर बैठा हुआ वह साधु जो उस पेड़ से बँधा था बह चला। महाराज श्री ने देखा कि उस बहते हुये साधु के चेहरे पर कोई चिन्ता नहीं थी, उलझन नहीं थी, व्यग्रता नहीं थी, अपितु प्रसन्न मुखमुद्रा में मुसकराता हुआ दूसरे साधु से बोला, "नमो नारायण, अब तो हम चले।" दूसरे साधु ने भी उसी प्रकार की प्रसन्नमुद्रा में दृढ़ शब्दों में उत्तर दिया "नमो नारायणाय, जहाँ कहीं भी जिस परिस्थिति में रहना, भगवान का समरण करते रहना और प्रसन्न रहना।" बड़े मार्मिक थे साधु के यह शब्द, एक अमिट रेखा खींच गये महराज श्री के हृदय-पटल पर। महाराज श्री ने विचार किया कि कठिन से कठिन परिस्थिति में प्रसन्न रहना और भगवान् का चिन्तन करते हुये धीरज नहीं खोना चाहिये। सुनने में आश्चर्य होता है कि वह बहते हुये तखता पर बैठा हुआ साधु अनत तक सुरक्षित ही रहा – उसका तखत धारा प्रवाह में वेग से बहता हुआ थोड़ी दूर पहुँच कर किनारे लग गया। साधु जीवित सुरक्षित रहते हुये जल प्रवाह के बाहर आ गया।

कुछ दिन आपका निवास ऋषीकेश में ही रहा। एक दिन की बात है एक निर्जन स्थान में आप ध्यानस्थ बैठे थे। कलकत्ते का एक मारवाड़ी सेठ जो जाड़े के दिनों में इस प्रदेश में आकर साधुओं, महात्माओं, ब्रह्मचारियों को शाल बाँटा करता था, उधर आ निकला। इस समय भी महात्माओं को वितरण करने के लिये कुछ शाल ले आया था। देखा कि यह मैदानी बाबा ठिठुरते जाड़े में केवल एक उपरना शरीर पर डाले हुये ध्यानमग्न बैठे हैं। जाकर एक शाल ओढ़ा दी और सामने बैठ गये। थोड़ी देर में जब महाराज श्री ने आँखें खोलीं तो देखा कि सामने एक मारवाड़ी सेठ जी बैठे हुये हैं – पूछा, "यह शाल आपने ओढ़ायी है? आप क्या चाहते हैं? आपने

क्या समझ कर इसे मुझे ओढ़ायी है? यदि हमें गरीब समझ कर ओढ़ायी है तो यह बात ठिक नहीं है, क्योंकि कोई साधु महात्मा गरीब नहीं होते, और यदि आपका कोई दूसरा प्रयोजन हो, तो बताइये" सेठ जी दण्डवत प्रणाम करते हुये बड़ी नम्रता से बोले, "भगवन्, हम मारवाड़ी व्यापारी हैं, पंडितों के द्वारा शास्त्रों में सुना है कि महात्माओं को दान देने से एक का हजार मिलता है, इसलिये एक शाल देकर बदले में आपके आशीर्वाद से एक हजार पाने की आशा करते हैं। यह सुन कर महाराज श्री ने बड़ी ही शान्ति के साथ धीरे से उस शाल को उतारा, उतार कर तहाया और उसे वापस देते हुये कहा, "एक तो अभी ले लो; शेष ९९९ का प्रयत्न करूँगा, "इस गूढ़ उत्तर से सेठ जी चकित हो गये और भयभीत भी हो गये कि कदाचित् म्हात्मा जी रुष्ट हो गये। थोड़ी देर चुपचाप बैठे रहे। तब महाराज श्री उन्हें उपदेश् छेते हुये बोले, "भला यह बताइये कि यदि संसार की सारी सम्पत्ति वैभव आपकी हो जाय, संसार के सारे मकान, सुख-सामग्री आपकी हो जाय, तो क्या वह सब आपके काम आयेगा? जब यहीं सब कुछ छोड़ जाना है, पूर्व की कमाई खा रहे हो, आज आपको दान देने की भी सुविधा प्राप्त है, फिर भी आपकी दृध्हिट जगत् की ओर है। यदि पूर्व की कमाई खाते हुये आगे के लिये उन्नति नहीं करोगे तो क्या लाभ?" यह सुन कर सेठ जी ने क्षमायाचना की और प्रणाम करके यह विचार करते हुये चले कि कम से कम एक साधु ऐसा तो मिला जिसने वास्तव में साँसारिक सुखों का त्याग किया है। वस्तु के अऩाव में तो सभी त्यागी हैं, किन्तु वस्तु की प्राऩि में त्याग करना सच्चा त्याग है।

ब्रह्मचर्य्यावस्था में आपने कई बार बदरीनारायण की यात्रा की। एक बार इनके साथ तीन और ब्रह्मचारी साथ हो लिये। थोड़ी दूर

जाने के बाद आपने शेष तीन ब्रह्मचारियों से कहा "देखो मैं तो अपने पास रुपया पैसा द्रव्य आदि कुछ भी नहीं रखता और यदि आप लोगों में से किसी के पास कुछ हो तो या तो उस धन को अलग कर दो। या जिस किसी के पास हो वह स्वयं हम सब से अलग हो जाय, क्योंकि हम सब साथ के ब्रह्मचारियों को एक सा होना चाहिये, नहीं तो कष्ट होगा। जिसके पास रुपया पैसा होगा, वह यदि सब के साथ रहेगा तो संकोचवश उसका उपयोग नहीं कर सकेगा और यदि उपयोग न कर पायेगा तो उसे मन ही मन कष्ट होगा। इसलिये उसे या तो स्वयं अलग हो जाना चाहिये या उस द्रव्य को ही अलग कर देना चाहिये। एक ब्रह्मचारी के पास तीन अशर्फियाँ थीं। उसने बताया कि मेरे पास तीन अशर्फियाँ हैं, इन्हें आप जैसा चाहें वैसा करें। हमें तो साथ ही रहना है।"

निश्चय किया गया कि अमुक वृक्ष के नीचे उनको पृथ्वी में गाड़ दें और बदरीनारायण की यात्रा समाप्त होने पर लौटते समय इनको निकाल लिया जायगा। तीनों अशर्फियों को निश्चित स्थान में गाड़ दिया गया और चारों ब्रह्मचारी यात्रा में साथ-साथ चल दिये।

पैदल यात्रा तो थी ही। शारीरिक परिश्रम व स्थान-स्थान के जलवायु के कारण एक सप्ताह यात्रा करने के बाद उसी ब्रह्मचारी को जिसकी अशर्फियाँ पृथ्वी में गाड़ दी गई थी विशूचिका हो गई। दशा खराब हो गई और सुधार के लक्षण नहीं रहे। अनत में उसी में उनका शरीर भी शान्त हो गया। अन्त्येष्टि क्रिया करने के पश्चात् शेष तीनों ब्रह्मचारी आगे बढ़े और बदरीनारायण की यात्रा पूरी की। दर्शन लाभ मिला। वापसी यात्रा में जब वे उसी स्थान पर पहुँचे जहाँ शर्फियाँ गाड़ी गई थीं, महाराज श्री ने कहा कि उन अशर्फियों को निकाल लिया जाय और दान-दक्षिणा में वितरण कर दिया जाय।

उस स्थान पर पृथ्वी खोदी गई, देखा कि उन अशर्फियों के चारों तरफ अशर्फी के ही रंग का एक बहुत पतला सर्प लिपटा हुआ है। महाराज श्री ने कहा, "वेदशास्त्र में लिखा है कि मृत्यु के समय गड़े हुये धन पर मन लगा रहने से सर्प होना पड़ता है। इसका प्रमाण यहाँ प्रत्यक्ष है। ऐसा मालूम पड़ता है कि उस ब्रह्मचारी का मन मरने के समय इन्हीं अशर्फियों में लगा रहा। इसीलिये वे अब सर्प बनकर यहाँ अपने धन की रक्षा कर रहे हैं।" महाराज श्री ने उस सर्परूप ब्रह्मचारी को सर्पयोनि से शीघ्र छुटकारा दिलाने के लिये पकड़ लिया और गंगा जी में प्रवाह कर दिया और अशर्फियों को दान-दक्षिणा व ब्राह्मण-महात्माओं के भोजन आदि में खर्च करा दिया।

भ्रमण करते हुये व मार्ग में तीर्थों में निवास करते हुये आप प्रयाग आ गये। उन दिनों प्रयाग में मछली मारनेवालों का विरोधियों से वाद-विवाद चल रहा था। निर्णय के लिये : दोनों पक्ष के लोग महाराज श्री के पास आये। सब से महाराज श्री ने कहा "आप लोग कल आइये," आज्ञानुसार प्रात काल सब आ गये। किन्तु मछुओं ने आने के पहिले ही जाल लगा दिये। महाराज श्री ने विरोध करनेवालों से कहा, "जाओ चने के बराबर ५-७ कंकड़ उठा लाओ।" जब वह कंकड़ आ गये तब महाराज श्री ने उन कंकड़ों को विरोध करनेवालों के हाथ में देते हुये कहा कि जाओ इन कंकड़ों को गंगा जी में जहाँ मछली मारने वालों ने जाल लगा रखा है वहाँ फेंक दो, अपने-अपने घर जाओ और शाम को उस स्थान पर जाकर देख लेना।" उन लोगों ने वैसा ही किया और समय से पहिले ही वहाँ उपस्थित हो गये। मछली मारनेवालों ने समय आने पर जाल निकाले परन्तु देखा कि जाल में एक भी मछली नहीं फँसी। सब

लोग आश्चर्यचकित हो गये और विरोध करनेवाले उच्च स्वर से महाराज श्री का जय-जयकार करने लगे। इसका विशेष फल यह हुआ कि विरोध करनेवालों के साथ-साथ मछली मारनेवालों की भी महाराज श्री के प्रति अपूर्व श्रद्धा हो गई।

वर्षों व्यतीत हो गये। अनेकानेक रोचक एवं शिक्षाप्रद घटनायें घटीं और घटती रहीं, जिनका उल्लेख करना अत्यन्त कठिन है। संस्कारी प्राणी को सभी पदार्थ स्वयं सदैव प्राप्त् झोते रहते हैं। गुरुदेव की कृपा से आपको योग के अनेक विधि-विधानों व अनुष्ठानों की क्रियायें प्राप्त थीं। सदैव आप अपनी साधना में ही संलग्न रहते थे। निर्जन वनों के वृक्षमूल ही आपके निवास स्थान थे। वन्य फल, मूल, शाकादि ही आहार था। स्वभावतः आये हुये सिंह, व्याघ्र, मृग आदि जीव ही आपके सहवासी थे। कभी किसी से कोई याचना या प्रतिग्रह न करना, जन समाज से दूर रहना, नारीवर्ग को दर्शन तक न देना, धन-परायण कुबेर तक को तृण के समान समझना आपके स्वाभाविक गुण थे। इसी प्रकार गंगोत्तरी (हिमालय), नेपाल, कश्मीर, विन्ध्याचल, अमरकंटक आदि वनों में तपश्चर्यापूर्वक रह कर आत्मानन्द का अनुभव करते रहे।

Chapter 4

Some Perfectly Astonishing Occurrences

Shri Maharaj Ji stayed beside Guru Ji in Uttarkashi, perfecting penance, learning the *Shastra* and practising and living according to the rules of Yoga philosophy. At twenty-five years old, having become Self-realised he came down from the Himalayas. Guru Ji moved with him. For some days they stayed in Kajaliwan, near Rishikesh. This is an isolated and uninhabited place, a very dense jungle where it is commonplace for carnivorous creatures to stroll about. Thus if any *sadhu* or *mahatma* went to stop in this place for any time then it quickly became known in the villages near and far, and the inhabitants would run for his *darshan*.

Amongst those gaining the benefit of *darshan* was a Brahman who attended the *mahatmas* out of service, and brought them a little milk. Every day the Brahman took with him half a *seer* of milk as service to his *guru*, and in the night Maharaj Shri gave his Guru Ji hot milk to drink.

One day it was like this; that fetching milk, the wife of the Brahman said, 'Today there is only a little milk so there will be little milk for the children.'

But the Brahman who was daily bringing the milk came to take it anyway. That day too, according to the daily routine, Maharaj Shri heated the milk and put it in front of Guru Ji.

Guru Ji said, 'Today there is suffering in the milk, we will not drink this milk. Return it to the milkman and stop taking milk from him.'

Maharaj Shri did exactly that.

After this, about fifteen days later, the son of the Brahman died. Amongst all the local population this rumour spread, that the *mahatma* had become dissatisfied and for this reason the son of this Brahman had died. Maharaj Shri related this talk to Guru Ji. He said that, 'Tell the people that when the bier of the child comes to the cremation-ground, not to set it light just then and to summon us first.'

When the bier of that child came to the cremation-ground then it was kept at that very place. To this place Guru Ji also went. He then had all of the cords of the bier untied and with his foot he gave a jerk to the head of the dead one saying; 'Why do you sleep so much?'

At that the dead spirit got up. Everyone became amazed and puzzled. They all made a very great *pranaam* to the *mahatma*.

On returning to his *kutiya* (hut) Maharaj Shri said, 'Now, if I do not go from here all the carcasses will fall on my head.'

Having said as much, he left that place, and the *guru* and *shishya* became separated from one another.

*

One time Maharaj Shri saw a formidible obstruction coming in Ganga Ji, at every moment the water was rising higher. All the *mahatmas* within the area of the disaster area had already got out of the way. But thinking it only a small obstruction two *sadhus* were sat on a seat attached to two acacia trees near the bank, unconcerned.

It had been a big surprise to you. 'When all the *sadhus* left to go to places for their own protection then why did they not go too?'

You climbed a tree and watched the movement of fate. Three days passed, but of their own accord both those *sadhus* stayed in there place. With the obstruction of the Ganga it became difficult for these trees to endure the current of the stream of water and one immovable tree became uprooted and moved, together with that seat attached to the tree with that *sadhu* sitting upon it, which floated away.

Maharaj Shri saw that was no care on the face of the *sadhu* as he floated away, he was uninvolved, he wasn't anxious, but upon his satisfied countenance was a smile.

The second *sadhu* said, *"Namo Naaraayana"*, 'Now then, we [also] go!'

The other *sadhu,* also with an expression of pleasure answered *"Namo Naaraayanaaya"*, 'Wherever, whatever the circumstances are anywhere, stay remembering Bhagwan and be happy!'

The words of the *sadhu* were very moving, making an indelible mark on a layer of Maharaj Shri's heart. Maharaj Shri considered, 'In difficult circumstances be happy and thinking of Bhagwan you should not lose your patience.'

It is astonishing to hear that seated on a floating log, the *sadhu* stayed strong up to the end. With speed on the stream of water he arrived at the bank a little further on. Going beyond the current of the water the *sadhus* remained alive and safe.

*

For some days you made your abode in Rishikesh. The word is that you were sat one day in an uninhabited place, musing. A Marwari *seth* (businessman) of Calcutta, had appeared on that side [probably across the river from Rishikesh, in the area now known as Swargashram]. Having come to spend the winter days in this region, he was distributing shawls to *sadhus, mahatmas* and *brahmacharis*. On this occasion too he had come to make gifts to *mahatmas*. He saw that this ascetic of the plains was sitting sunk in meditation and had only a single covering on his body in the chill winter. Having gone and draped a shawl on him he sat before him. After a little while Maharaj Shri opened his eyes, and seeing the Marwari businessman in front of him, he asked, 'Why did you wrap this shawl? What do you want? What do you think by covering me with this? If you are covering because you think I am poor, then this is not proper, because no *sadhu* or *mahatma* is poor, and if you have any other motive then you ought to explain it.'

Seth Ji prostrated and did *pranaam*. With great courtesy he said; 'Bhagwan, I am a Marwari merchant. From *pandits* I have heard that by giving one to *mahatma* a thousand is got, therefore in exchange for giving one shawl, with your blessing I hope to get a thousand.'

Having heard this, Maharaj Shri with great silence indeed, slowly cast off that shawl. Having cast it off, he folded it and gave it back. He said, 'Just now take this one; then I will attempt the balance of the nine-hundred and ninety-nine.'

Seth ji became perplexed with this obscure answer and also became alarmed that possibly the *mahatma* had become angry.

For some time they sat quietly. Then Maharaj Shri gave a lecture, saying, 'Well, you should tell this, that if you had all the wealth of *samsara* (worldliness), if you became great, if your abode was the entire *samsara*, and the materials of pleasure became yours, then how will all your desire become fulfilled? When you are to go and leave everything, you are going to live on former earnings. Today you the comfort of giving charity, but your sight is still in the direction of the world. If you are living on previous earnings, but you are not advancing afterwards, then what is the gain?'

Having heard this, Seth Ji asked his mercy. Doing *pranaam* he left thinking little by little that he had met with a *sadhu* who had truely abandoned worldly pleasures. Not having something then anyone can have unattachment, but to forsake a thing which one has acquired, that is true surrender.

*

[In a sound recording of a lecture some given many years later Guru Dev made brief mention of this period.

'One time, we were in Punjab, then at that time we were a *brahmachari*. Then it was the custom there for people to drink a lot of *chaay* (tea). Then it came in a *kulhara* (a small earthenware pot). Then we never drank *chaay*.'

During the stage of brahmacharya, several times you made a yatra (pilgimage) of Badri Naryayana (the god of Badrikasharam at Badrinath). One time three other monks accompanied him. After going a short distance he told the other three *brahmacharis*, 'Look, I do not carry any *rupees*, *paisa* or any other wealth, and if any of you folk have anything, then he should separate himself from that wealth. Or if is having any, then he is going to separate from us, because we *brahmacharis* should all be alike, then there will be no suffering. Whoever will have *rupees* and *paisa*, will be reluctant to use it if he remains with us all, so there can be no use for it and if it does not get used then his mind will be suffering. Therefore, either he should go separately or he should become separated from the wealth.'

One *brahmachari* had three *ashrafi* (gold sovereign coins). He said that, 'I am having three *asharphi*. You can do what you wish with these. We will all stay together.'

It was decided for the coins to be buried in the earth close to a particular tree, and once the *yatra* (pilgrimage) to Badri Narayana (Badrinath) had been accomplished, at that time they would return and go to unearth them. So the three sovereigns were buried in a safe place and the four *brahmacharis* travelled together.

The travel was on foot. [Unlike today when most people travel to the pilgrimage shrine at Badrinath using road transport] After one week of *yatra* (pilgrimage) the combination of physical fatigue and the change of climate moving from place to place caused the *brahmachari* who had gone and put those sovereigns under the ground to become ill with cholera. The condition became worse and there was no sign of improvement. In the end his body became dead. After performing the funeral rites, the three *brahmacharis* went on further and fulfilled the entire *yatra,* obtaining *darshan* of Badri Narayana. When they returned from the *yatra* and arrived at where the sovereigns had been buried, Maharaj Shri said that, 'Those *asharphi* (sovereigns) should be unearthed and given as charitable donation.'

So they dug up the earth at that place, they saw that to all four sides of the sovereigns there was a very thin serpent the colour of the gold coins coiled there.

Maharaj Shri said, 'In the *Veda Shastra* it is written that if at the time of death the mind is attached to buried treasure then he becomes a serpent. Here is this proof.! It is apparent that at the time of death the *brahmachari's* mind was attached to these *asharphi* (sovereigns). There, now he has become a serpent he is protecting his wealth.'

Maharaj Shri quickly got rid of the form of a snake that the *brahmachari* had become and gave it to the flow of Ganga Ji and the sovereigns he gave as charitable donation for food etc for Brahman *mahatmas.*

*

Having been roaming about and staying at the sacred places on the way, you came to Prayag (Allahabad). In those days in Prayag a dispute was going on there with those people who objected to the killing of fish. Hoping for a settlement, the people from both sides came to Maharaj Shri.

Maharaj Shri said to them all, 'You folk should come back tomorrow.'

According to the order they all came at daybreak. But the

fishermen had come earlier, laying a net.

Maharaj Shri said to those people who were in opposition, 'Go bring five to seven small stones, the equivalent of *chana* (gram, which is about the size of peas).'

When this gravel was brought, Maharaj Shri put them into the hands of those people who objected, saying; 'Go, throw these pebbles into Ganga Ji wherever those who kill fish have placed the net. Go to your own home and in the evening return and look at that place.'

Those people did exactly as he said and were ready before time. The killers of the fish came to take out the net, but found that no fish had been caught in the net. All the folk were surprised and astonished, and the opponents raised their voices to cheer Maharaj Shri. The remarkable upshot of this incident was that both those people who opposed the killing of the fish together with the fishermen all became equally reverential of Maharaj Shri.

'Landscape at the Foot of the Vindhya'
[*'Vedic India'*, Z A Ragozin, T. Fisher Unwin, 1895]

Years passed together with various interesting and instructive events, which are inordinately difficult to mention. *Everything for the improvement of your life occurred automatically. By the grace of the Gurudeva you obtained many sorts of yoga and gained actions of rituals (spiritual powers). Always you remained in your own sadhana. Really, at the roots of trees in uninhabited forests were the places you dwelt. Wild fruits, roots, vegetables etc were really his food. Naturally the lion, tiger, deer etc came to be the fellow inhabitants of your life.* Never did he beg donations but lived far away from the society of mankind, not keeping company with women. *Your natural quality was to understand equality, from the blade of grass up to Kubera devoted to wealth.* In this way, doing *tapasya* in Gangotri (Himalyas), at Nepal, Kashmir, the Vindhya (mountains), the Amarakantaka (the source of the Narmada river) he was experiencing *"aatmaananda"* (bliss of oneness with the Supreme Soul).

' "Living Bridge" formed of the aerial roots of the India-rubber and other kinds of figs.'
[*'Hooker's Himalayan Journals'*, 1855]

५

पाँचवाँ अधयाय

पुनः गुरु – मिलन और संन्यास

प्रयाग में कुम्भ पड़ा। सम्पूर्ण भारतवर्ष के महात्मा-गण, साधु-संन्यासी एकत्र हुये। आप भी प्रयाग आ गये। गुरुदेव का समागम हुआ। ऐसे शुभ अवसर को पाकर आपने गुरुदेव से प्रार्थना की कि भगवन्, अब यदि योग्य समझें तो संन्यास दीक्षा प्रदान करें। गुरु जी ने सर्वथा अधिकारी समझ कर आज्ञा दे दी।

त्रिवेणि संगम की सितासित धारा पर संन्यास का कर्म काण्ड हुआ। समष्टि भण्डारा हुआ और समस्त ब्रह्मचारी साधु, दण्डी स्वामियों को वस्त्रादि देकर सम्मानित किया गया। गुरुदेव ने आपको ३६ वर्ष की आयु में संन्यास दीक्षा देकर दण्ड-कमण्डलु और कौपीन प्रदान किया। आज से आप का नाम "श्री स्वामी ब्रह्मानन्द सरस्वती महाराज" हुआ। सभी साधु महात्मा धार्मिक जन अब तो और भी आपके दर्शन तथा आशीर्वाद के लिये आकुल हो उठे। किन्तु आप विशेषतया निर्जन वन-स्थानों में ही विचरण करते रहे। जनता जहाँ कहीं आपका पता लगा पाती, दर्शनों के लिये वहीं पहुँच जाती। कदाचित् पर्व समयों में आप काशी, प्रयाग, अयोध्या आदि नगरों में आ जाते तो आपके समीप दर्शनार्थियों का मेला ही लग जाता था।

महाराज श्री एकान्तप्रिय थे। जहाँ भी रहते एकान्त में ही निवास करते। भक्तों को यह बात पूर्णतया विदित थी। इसलिये आपके निवास के लिये विश्राम के लिये प्रत्येक स्थान में भक्त लोग ऊपर के ही भाग में प्रबन्ध करते। ऊपर के स्थान को महाराज श्री ऊपर से

ही बन्द कर लेते और इस प्रकार उनका स्थान सर्वथा एकान्त बन जाता। आपका दर्शन असम्भव तो नहीं, पर दुर्लभ और कठिन अवश्य था। आपके विश्रामस्थान में दर्शन करने के लिये भक्तों को पर्याप्त समय खर्चना पड़ता था। दर्शन के निमित्त भक्तों का एकत्रित होना प्रायः ४ बजे शाम से प्रारम्भ होता और इसका क्रम १०-११ बजे रात्रि तक चलता रहता। दर्शनार्थी उस स्थान के निचले भाग में एकत्र होते रहते और महाराज श्री के दर्शन के समय तक जो लगभग ८॥-९ बजे रात्रि में था, बैठे प्रतीक्षा भी ले लेते थे। रात्रि ९ बजे महाराज श्री के आज्ञानुसार समीप का ब्रह्मचारी सेवक सब दर्शनाथ भक्तों की सूची तैयार करता और उसे महाराज श्री के समीप रख देता। उस सूची को दे देखकर महाराज श्री प्रायः कहीं देते, "जाओ, कह दो, आज नहीं मिलेंगे।" ऐसा अवसर बहुधा आ जाता, जब कि महाराज श्री को यह कहलाना पड़ता कि सब से कह दो, "आज नहीं मिलेंगे।" इसलिये आपने इन्हीं शब्दों का एक साइनबोर्ड भी बनवा लिया था "आज नहीं मिलेंगे" और ऐसा अवसर आने पर यह साइनबोर्ड दरवाजे पर ही टाँग दिया जाता था। भक्त लोग निराशा में भी प्रतीक्षा करके एक-एक उठ कर वापस होने लगते। वापस होने का क्रम भी इसी प्रकार धीरे-धीरे चलता जैसा आने का और इस प्रकार रात्रि के १०-११ बज जाते। उस समय महाराज श्री की आज्ञा होती, "देखो, कोई दर्शनार्थी नीचे बैठा है" देखा गया तो मालूम पड़ा कि अब भी २-३ भक्त लोग बैठे हैं। आज्ञा हुई "बुला लो उन दर्शनार्थियों को" ऐसे समय में महाराज श्री के मुख से यह शब्द निकल पड़ते, "यही हैं दर्शनार्थी; शेष तो ऐसे ही सोच समझ कर आ जाते हैं कि चलो इधर-उधर शाम को टहलने नहीं जायेंगे, महात्मा जी का दर्शन ही कर आवें "इन दो तीन भक्तों को दर्शन देते समय महाराज श्री बड़ी ही प्रसन्न मुद्रा में मिलते,

अधिक समय तक उपदेश भी करते और अपने वचनामृत से भक्तों को ऐसा तृप्त कर देते कि उनको अधिक देर तक प्रतीक्षा का कष्ट परिणत होकर प्रसन्नता की लहरों में हिलोरें लेने लगता और लौटते समय वे यही समझते कि मानो उन्हें कोई निधि मिल गई हो । सच भी तो है निधि अवश्य मिल गई, ऐसी निधि जो संसार के किसी कोने में लाख प्रयत्न करने पर भी नहीं मिला करती ।

'Shri 108 Shri Dandi Swami Ji Krishnanand Saraswati'

Chapter 5

Meeting the Guru Again, & Sanyas

The Kumbha occured in Prayag (Allahabad) [this would have been in 1906. The festival of the Maha Kumbh Mela at Prayag (Allahabad) is a religious event that occurs every twelve years where an immense gathering of Hindu pilgrims congregate. Many go to bathe in the confluence of three sacred rivers of Saraswati, Ganga and Yamuna. In the last century such festivals occurred in 1906, 1918, 1930, 1942, 1954, 1966, 1977, 1989 & 2001. Numbers increase with each successive Kumbha Mela, for instance at the 1906 Kumbha approximately three million people attended whereas in 2001 the numbers were estimated at seventy million.]

*

The entire community of *mahatma*, *sadhus* and *sannyasis* of India all meeting in the same place. *You came to Prayag too and became reunited with Gurudeva. Thus at such an auspicious opportunity you requested your Gurudeva that,* 'Bhagwan, if you consider me suitable then make the gift of *sannyas diksha* (initiation into *sannyas*).'

*

Guru Ji considered that you altogether possessed the right and so he gave his permission. At the *sangam* (confluence) at Triveni, where the rivers of Ganga, Yamuna and Saraswati appear clearly as black and white, the passage of *sannyas* occurred. A feast for mendicants was arranged for all the *brahmacharis*, *sadhus* and *dandi swamis* who were honoured by being given garments. *Gurudeva gave you diksha (initiation) into sannyas at thirty-six years old* [more likely thirty-four years old], *giving you a gift of danda (a staff), kamandalu (water-pot) and kaupeen (loincloth).*

From that day on your name became Shri Swami Brahmanand Saraswati Maharaj. The sadhus, mahatmas and other devout people queued for your darshan and for your ashirvad (blessing).

Your habit was to wander about in uninhabited wooded places, but whenever folk got to hear where you were, they would arrive for darshan. At festival times you might go to the cities, to Kashi (Varanasi), Prayag (Allahabad), Ayodhya etc, then crowds would come for the benefit of darshan.

Maharaj Shri loved privacy and wherever he stayed he dwelt alone. His devotees understood this issue entirely, therefore, for his comfort, devotees made arrangements for there to be an upper storey for him at every place he stayed. Maharaj Shri locked the upper place from within and in this way his place became altogether secluded. *At such time, if it was not impossible to get your darshan it was certainly difficult. But you did find time for devotees wanting darshan at your place of rest.*

For the purpose of obtaining *darshan* devotees would begin to gather at 4 o'clock and continue to come in this way until ten or eleven o'clock at night. Those who wanted the benefit of *darshan* would collect together in the lower area up to about eight-thirty or nine o'clock at night sitting waiting. At Maharaj Shri's behest, at nine o'clock at night, the attendant *brahmachari* made ready a list of those devotees coming for the benefit of *darshan*, and gave this to Maharaj Shri. Looking at the list Maharaj generally he said, 'Go say this, *"Aaj nahin milenge"* – 'Today we will not meet'.'

Thus in most cases there came a time when Maharaj Shri had said to all, *"Aaj naiin milenge"* – 'Today we will not meet.' *For this purpose you had a signboard made with these words, "Aaj nahin milenge" – 'Today we will not meet' and so the hour would come when this signboard would be placed at the foot of the door.* Out of despondency, one-by-one devotee folk who had been waiting got up to return home. They left slowly, slowly as in the manner that they came. In this way ten-thirty and eleven o'clock came. At which time Maharaj Shri would give the order, 'Look if there are any *darshan* seekers sitting below?'

Having looked then it became known that just two or three devotee folk were still sitting.

He commanded, 'Call to those *darshan* seekers.'

At this time these words fell from the mouth of Maharaj Shri, 'These are really *darshanarthi* (seekers of *darshan*); the rest are just coming to think and reflect, they won't roam here and there in the night to come for *darshan* of a *mahatma*.'

To those two or three devotees who waited Maharaj Shri gave *darshan* time, giving the impression of great delight to meet with them. With his nectar speech he counselled them for a long time and he gave so much satisfaction to the devotees that to them the discomfort of the long wait turned into wave upon wave of happiness, and later they considered that they had gained some treasure. Certainly, it is true also that naturally they got treasure, such treasure which don't receive in *samsara* (mundane existence) even after a hundred thousand fold effort.

६

छठवाँ अध्याय

स्वच्छन्द विचार और संसार

सन् १९३० ई० के प्रयाग कुम्भ के अवसर पर महाराज श्री के दारागंज में निवास करने की पूर्व व्यवस्था हो चुकी थी। गंगागंज, प्रयागनिवासी एक भक्त ने अपने दारागंज स्थित क्षेत्र को जिसमें लगभग १० कमरे थे खाली कराकर सुरक्षित रख छोड़ा था। महाराज श्री के आगमन की प्रतीक्षा की जा रही थी। महात्माओं की विचारधारा स्वतन्त्र तो हुआ ही करती है। महाराज श्री का विचार हुआ कि प्रयाग कुम्भ-मेले में जहाँ सब जा रहे हैं, वहाँ नहीं जायँगे और प्रयाग से १०-१२ मील दूर पश्चिम में गंगा-तट पर कौरवेश्वर महादेव के मन्दिर में जिसमें एक अत्यन्त छोटी कोठरी है उसी में ठहर गये। परन्तु इधर यह भी सोचा कि किसी भक्त ने प्रयाग क्षेत्र में एक विशाल भवन खाली रख छोड़ा है, उसे भी अपने ही काम में ले लेना चाहिये, ताकि भक्त के हृदय में यह ठेस न लगे कि उसकी सेवा बेकार हो गई। इसलिए उसमें अपने कुछ दण्डी संन्यासी शिष्य मेला भर के लिये ठहरा दिये। भक्त को जब मालूम पड़ा कि महाराज श्री प्रयाग नहीं आवेंगे, तो उन्हें कष्ट हुआ; किन्तु यह जान कर कि महाराज श्री की आज्ञा से उन्हीं के ही दण्डी संन्यासी शिष्यगण उसमें ठहराये गये हैं, उन्हें सन्तोष हुआ; फिर भी "श्रेयांसि बहु विघ्नानि भवन्ति महतामपि" के अनुसार एक विघ्न आया। व्यापारिक सम्बन्ध से सम्बन्धित एक कलकत्ता निवासी धनी मानी प्रेमास्पद मित्र ने उस भक्त से यह इच्छा प्रकट की कि वह उन्हें दारागंज स्थित मकान मेले भर के लिए दे दें, क्योंकि उनके परिवार के लोग मेले में

प्रयाग निवास करना चाहते हैं। भक्त ने यह जानते हुये कि मकान खाली नहीं है, किन्तु यह सोच समझ कर कि महाराज श्री तो उस मकान में ठहरे हैं नहीं, खाली कराया जा सकता है। भक्त ने सेठ जी की बात को टाला नहीं। उन्होंने महाराज श्री से प्रार्थना की, "आप तो उस मकान में ठहरे नहीं हैं यदि, उचित समझें, तो सेठ जी जो उनके घनिष्ठ मित्र हैं उनके परिवार के लिये संन्यासी महात्माओं से कह कर मकान खाली करा दें।" मर्यादा के विषय में महाराज श्री का विचार अत्यन्त उत्कृष्ट था। सेठ जी के परिवार के लिये महात्माओं साधु-संन्यासियों से मकान खाली कराया जाय, ऐसा नहीं हो सकता, क्योंकि इसमें महात्माओं का अपमान होगा। उत्तर दिला दिया, कि अब उस मकान में दण्डी-संन्यासी वर्ग ठहराये जा चुके हैं, उनसे यदि कहा जायगा कि सेठ जी के बाल-बच्चों के लिये मकान खाली कर दें तो उनका बड़ा अपमान होगा। इस लिये मेला भर मकान खाली नहीं किया जा सकता। आप उनके लिये कोई दूसरा प्रबन्ध कर दें।" भक्त ने सोचा कि साधु महात्मा ही लोग तो ठहरे हैं कुछ बल प्रयोग करके मकान खाली करा लिया जाय। यह बात महाराज श्री को मालूम पड़ी, तो उन्होंने अपनी आज्ञा को अधिक दृढ़ कर दिया कि किसी भी प्रकार से तिवारी जी अपने मकान को खाली न करा सकें। वैसा ही किया गया। तिवारी जी निराश हो कर चुप रहे और मेले भर मकान नहीं खाली किया गया। किन्तु महाराज श्री फिर उस मकान में कभी नहीं ठहरे और अपनी तरफ से सदा के लिए उसे खाली कर दिया।

महाराज श्री का निवास इस समय कौरवेश्वर में हो रहा था। आपके एक परम भक्त कुबेरदत्त ओझा ने सुना कि महाराज श्री कौरवेश्वर में आ गये हैं तो वहीं गये और दर्शन किया। उनका नियम

था दिन में प्रयाग में अपनी जीविका के लिये दफ्तर में नौकरी करते और शाम को ४ बजे साइकिल द्वारा महाराज श्री की सेवा में कौरवेश्वर पहुँच जाते। कुबेरदत्त दारागंज में ही रहते थे। उन्हें मालूम पड़ा कि दारागंज-स्थित गंगा-भवन में महाराज श्री के गुरु देव पधारे हैं। वहाँ गये; दण्डवत प्रणाम किया और चले आये। सायंकाल जब वह महाराज श्री के दर्शन करने कौरवेश्वर गये, तो वहाँ भी गुरुजी के प्रयाग पधारने की बात बतलाई। इस प्रकार नित्य वह गुरुजी का तथा महाराज श्री का दर्शन करते और एक दूसरे के यदा-कदा के शब्द इधर-उधर पहुँचा दिया करते। एक दिन गुरु जी ने कुबेरदत्त से कहा कि क्या स्वामी जी इधर कुम्भ के अवसर पर प्रयाग नहीं आवेंगे? यह बात कुबेरदत्त के द्वारा महाराज श्री के पास पहुँची। महाराज श्री ने कहा कि हमारा विचार मेले में जाने का नहीं है। गुरुजी को जब यह मालूम हुआ कि महाराज श्री प्रयाग आने वाले नहीं हैं तो कहा, "मेला क्या व्याघ्र है? अच्छा, हमी उनसे मिलने किसी दिन चलेंगे"। गुरुजी की यह बात कुबेरदत्त ने जाकर महाराज श्री को बतलाई। महाराज श्री एकाएक चिंतित हो उठे और बोले, "अनर्थ हो जायगा, कहीं गुरुजी ही मेरे लिये किसी दिन न चल प.दें। जाओ, अभी जाओ, प्रातःकाल ४ बजे तक कोई न कोई मोटर लेकर यहाँ आ जाओ। हम चाहते हैं कि कल प्रातः काल सूर्योदय से पहिले ही गुरु जी के दर्शन के लिये प्रयाग पहुँच जायँ।" ऐसा ही हुआ। दूसरे दिन प्रातःकाल ४ बजे से पहिले कुबेरदत्त एक मोतोर लेकर कौरवेश्वर पहुँच गये और ६॥ बजे के लगभग महाराज श्री गुरु जी के समीप पहुँच गये। दण्ड उठाकर मर्यादापूर्वक प्रणाम करना चाहा। परन्तु गुरु जी ने उन्हें प्रणाम नहिं करने दिया। दण्ड हाथ से लेकर छाती से चिपटा लिया और समीप में आसन पर बैठा लिया। कहा, "महाराज, मर्यादा है, प्रणाम कर लें।" गुरु जी ने

कहा, "बैठ जाओ, हमारी इच्छा ही यहाँ मर्यादा है।" गुरु जी के पास उस समय पचासों व्यक्ति इकट्ठे थे। यह देखकर सभी को आश्चर्य हुआ कि स्वामी जी को उनके गुरुजी भी इतना अधिक आदर देते हैं। किसी ने कहा, "क्यों न हो, अपनी स्थिति में पहुंचा हुआ देखकर गुरु जी व्यवहार में भी समानता करें, तो कोई अनुचित नहीं।" परन्तु इस ओर तो देखो कि गुरु जी को नमन के लिये वही उत्सुकता, मर्यादा पालन श्रेष्ठता और आदर्श है। गुरु जी ने इसी समय आज्ञा दी, वन-पर्वतों में बहुत रह लिया। अब नगरों के समीप भी रहा करो, जिससे लोगों का कुछ उपकार हो सके।" इसके पश्चात् नगरों के निकट भी निवास होने लगा। गुरुजी आपका इतना अधिक आदर सम्मान करते थे कि कभी-कभी कह देते थे, "वह तो हम से भी अधिक योग्य एवं विद्वान हैं और प्रश्नों का उत्तर देने में तथा शंका समाधान करने में अद्वितीय हैं।"

किसी समय शिवकोटि महादेव के समीप श्री महाराज जी का चातुर्मास्य व्रत चल रहा था। एक साधु वेशधारी मनुष्य उस स्थान में आकर महाराज श्री का नाम ले लेकर गालियाँ बकने लगा। आश्रम निवासी सेवकगण जब गालियाँ बकनेवाले उस साधु की बकवास रोकने और न मानने पर उसे मार भगाने को उद्यत हुये, तब महाराज श्री ने सबको तुरन्त अपने पास बुलाकर कहा, "हम तुम लोगों को छोटी छोटी बातों से लेकर योग समाधि तक सब सिखा सकते हैं। पर गालियों पर सहनशीलता का पाठ शायद नहीं पढ़ा सकते। ईश्वर की कृपा है कि आज यह अवसर उपस्थित हो गया है। तुम्हें सहनशील बनने का अभ्यास करना चाहिये।" एक ब्रह्मचारी बोले, "क्षमा हो, स्वायंभुव मनु की आज्ञा गुरु निन्दा श्रवण का स्पष्ट निषेध करती है।" महाराज ने कहा, "ठीक है, इस पर

विचार कर डालो कि निन्दा से क्या हानि-लाभ है? यदि निन्दा से
लोक में हानि समझते हो, तो यह स्मरण रखो कि सम्पत्ति विपत्ति
एवं समस्त लौकिक कार्यों की सफलता विफलता प्रारब्ध के अधीन
रहती है। निन्दायें प्रारब्ध को स्पर्श तक नहीं कर सकतीं। जो
प्रारब्धाधीन पूर्व निश्चित है, वही होगा। निन्दा उसमें किंचिन्मात्र भी
अन्तर नहीं डाल सकती। इधर शास्त्रकारों का मत है कि निन्दक-
जन महात्माओं का पाप बँटा लेते हैं। इसलिये वे पारलौकिक उन्नति
में सहायक ही होते हैं। संतगणण् निन्दकों को उत्कृष्ट भक्तों की
श्रेणी में रखते हैं, क्योंकि श्रद्धालु भक्त तो पूजन आरती सेवा शुश्रूषा
द्वारा महात्माओं का संचित पारलौकिक शक्ति उनकी कृपा के द्वारा
बंटाते हैं; किंतु निन्दक लोग अपने लिये कुछ नहीं चाहते, प्रत्युत
निन्दा करके उनका पाप ही बँटाते हैं। इसलिये वही उत्कृष्ट भक्त हैं
और उन्हीं के द्वारा लाभ होता हैं। उनके द्वारा निन्दा रोकने का
प्रयास नहीं करना चाहिये। वरन् अपना कार्य करते जाना चाहिये
और उन्हें अपना कार्य करने देना चाहिये।” इस प्रकार समझाकर
अपनी सेवक-मण्डली को रोक लिया। इधर वह साधुवेशधारी दुष्ट
लगभग एक घन्टे तक गालियाँ बक कर पास ही वृक्ष के नीचे
विश्राम करने के लिये बैठ गया। तब श्री चरण ने उसे बुलाकर कहा,
“बहुत देर गाली का पाठ करते-करते आप थक गये होंगे, कुछ
जलपान कर लीजिये।” आश्रम के सेवकों ने उसे मिष्टान्न आदि से
तृप्त किया और चलते समय उसे महाराज श्री की आज्ञा से दो रुपये
इक्कागाड़ी के लिये भी दिये। बाद में पता चला कि वह अपने साथियों
की गोष्ठी में जाकर इतने बड़े महात्मा के प्रति अपशब्द बकने पर
बहुत पछताया। दूसरे दिन आश्रम के सामने आकर “स्वामी जी की
जय हो, स्वामी जी, क्षमा करें, हमसे बहुत बड़ा अपराध हुआ” आदि
आदि प्रायश्चित वचन बहुत देर तक बोलता रहा और क्षमा याचना

कराता रहा ।

ऐसी अनेक आदर्श घटनायें प्रकाश में आईं । उनसे शिक्षा मिलती है और श्री चरण के उत्कृष्ट आदर्शमय, त्यागपूर्ण, तपश्चर्यामय जीवन की झाँकी मिलती है । इसलिये आपके जीवन की कुछ घटनाओं का संक्षेप उल्लेख किया जा रहा है जिससे पाठकों को आपकी पुण्य-जीवनी का साधारण दिग्दर्शन हो जाय ।

एक समय महाराज श्री का निवास प्रयाग में राजा ढिंगवस की कोठी में हो रहा था । समीप ही एक भक्त वकील साहब रहते थे । उन्होंने सुना कि महाराज श्री रात्रि भर आसन जमाकर बैठे-बैठे भजन करते रहते हैं । इच्छा हुई कि महाराज श्री का यह दृश्य देखा जाय । प्रार्थना करूँगा कि मैं यह दृश्य देख सकूँ । अतः उन्होंने प्रार्थना की, "महाराज जी मैंने सुना है कि आप रात्रि भर आसन में बैठे रहते हैं । मैं देखना चाहता हूँ ।" महाराज जी हँस कर बोले, "क्या तुम रात्रि भर जाग सकोगे?" उत्तर दिया, "अवश्य, कोशिश करूँगा ।" महाराज जी ने कहा, "मेरा तो कोई हर्ज हैं नहीं, परंतु ध्यान रहे, कोई शब्द उच्चरण नहीं करना ।" वकील साहब रात्रि भर बैठे रहे और सारी रात्रि समाप्त हो गई ।

थोड़े ही समय में इस प्रकार की बात इधर-उधर फैली । कुछ दुष्ट-हृदय ईर्ष्यालु और विरोधी भी हो जाते हैं । सबने एक षड़यंत्र रचा । एक वेश्या को द्रव्य देकर समझा-बुझा कर तैयार किया कि रात्रि में महाराज जी के पास जाकर उन्हें डिगाने की वह कोशिश करे । वेश्याएँ लोभी तो होती ही हैं । पुरुष के वेश में और लोगों के साथ-साथ १०-११ बजे रात्रि में दर्शन के बहाने वहाँ तक पहुंच गई । सत्संग चलता रहा । सत्संग हो जाने के बाद सब लोग तो वहाँ से

चल दिये और नीचे उतर आये। परन्तु वेश्या वहीं बैठी रहो।
महाराज जी के भय व तेज के कारण कुछ बोल नहीं सकी। परन्तु
वह कुछ देर बैठी रही। इधर सब लोग, जिन्होंने यह षड्यंत्र रचा था,
नीचे उतर कर यह प्रतीक्षा कर रहे थे कि क्या होता है। उधर उस
वेश्या के शरीर व पेट में इतनी अधिक पीड़ा हुई कि चीख मार कर
भागी। नीचे धूर्त लोग जो प्रतीक्षा में खड़े थे पूछा, "क्या हुआ?"
उसने अपनी पीड़ा का समाचार कह सुनाया। सब लोग सुनकर
अत्यंत दुखी हुए और पश्चाताप करने लगे कि व्यर्थ ही में हम लोगों
ने महाराज जी को कष्ट दिया। जब यह बात इधर-उधर साधारण
लोगों में फैली तो महाराज श्री के प्रति अत्यधिक श्रद्धा चारों ओर से
उमड़ पड़ी।

महाराज श्री की आज्ञा थी शूद्र अथवा स्त्री आश्रम में उनके
निवास स्थान में आकर दर्शन-प्रणाम अथवा सत्संग करने की चेष्टा
न करें। यदि कोई शूद्र या स्त्री उनका प्रणाम या दर्शन करना चाहती
है तो जब कभी वह कहीं की यात्रा के लिये बाहर निकलें या बाहर से
निवास स्थान पर लौटें तो फाटक पर प्रणाम दर्शन हो सकता है।
एक समय की बात है जब प्रयाग में गंगातट पर एक मकान में आप
ठहरे हुये थे, तो महमना मदनमोहन मालवीय के परिवार की एक
विधवा स्त्री ने महाराज श्री से उनके निवास स्थान में दर्शन करने की
आज्ञा माँगी। उत्तर वही साधारण था कि शूद्र अथवा स्त्री वर्ग उनके
ठहरने के स्थान पर दर्शन सत्संग नहीं कर सकते वह स्त्री विदुषी थी
और सत्संगिनी भी। उसने महाराज श्री को पत्र लिखा कि हमारी
किसी बहिन के ही उदर से आपका जन्म हुआ है। जिस माता से
आपकी उत्पत्ति है उसी स्त्री-जाति से इतनी घृणा क्यों? पत्र को
महाराज श्री के पास किसी सेवक के द्वारा भेज दिया और कहा कि

इसका उत्तर ले आना। महाराज श्री ने थोड़ी उपेक्षा कर दी और सेवक से कहला दिया कि इसका उत्तर फिर मिल जायगा। इस समय अवसर नहीं है। दूसरे दिन उसने फिर उत्तर के लिये आग्रह किया और कहला भेजा कि आज इसका उत्तर अवश्य मिल जाना चाहिये। महाराज श्री यह सब सुनकर कहने लगे कि इसने प्रश्न का तो अन्त ही कर दिया है, उत्तर भी असाधारण ही देना चाहिये। प्रश्नोत्तर इस प्रकार लिखा दिया

"मैं आप लोगों के संसर्ग में नौ महीने रहा। उस समय मेरी कैसी दशा थी! उलटे टँगे थे, बन्धनों में जकड़ा था कष्ट का पारावार न था। इस प्रकार मलमूत्र के भाँड में नौ महीने बीत गये। वे दिन मुझे आज भी नहीं भूलते। यही कारण है कि आप लोगों के सम्पर्क की इच्छा नहीं करता।" इस विषय में और आगे इस प्रकार लिखा था –

"कुम्हार घट बनाता है। उसे जन्म देता है। वह घट पक जाने पर यज्ञमंडल में पहुंच जाता है। परन्तु उसका बनाने वाला कुम्हार यज्ञमण्डप के बाहर ही खड़ा रहता है। उसे यज्ञमंडल में जाने की आज्ञा नहीं होती।"

यह पत्र उस विधवा स्त्री के पास पहुंचा दिया गया। पत्र पढ़ कर उसे और अधिक श्रद्धा उत्पन्न हो गई और ऐसे अवसर पर के ताक में हो गई कि महाराज श्री गंगा-स्नान के लिये अथवा अन्यत्र कब जायेंगे। पता लगा कि कल प्रातःकाल ४ बजे नाव द्वारा संगम स्नान करने जायेंगे। वह भी उसी समय स्नान के लिये से चल पड़ी। गंगा-स्नान के समय दर्शन-प्रणाम कर आनन्दमग्न होकर कह पड़ी, "यहाँ तो सभी को दर्शन करने का अधिकार है।"

महाराज श्री का निवास दारागंज (प्रयाग) में हो रहा था।

कलकत्ते के एक सेठ जी, जिनका मुकदमा हाईकोर्ट में चल रहा था, प्रयाग आये। कभी-कभी जब वह गंगा-स्नान करने जाते, तो दारागंज में महाराज श्री का दर्शन भी करते। महाराज श्री के दर्शन में एक विचित्र आकर्षण था। जो एक बार भी दर्शन कर लेता, वह फिर बार-बार हुई। एक बार दर्शन करने के बाद बार-बार दर्शन करने जाने लगे। लोगों से ख्याति भी सुन चुके थे कि बड़े उच्चकोटि के महात्मा हैं। इनके दर्शन और आशीर्वाद से सभी के कार्य सफल हो जाते हैं। सेठ जी भी अपने मुकदमें की बात महाराज श्री को सुना दी और प्रार्थना की कि कृपा हो जाय तो मुकदमे में सफलता मिल जाय। ऐसे अवसर पर महाराज श्री कुछ उत्तर तो नहीं देते थे; किन्तु उस प्रार्थी को उनका मूक आशीर्वाद अवश्य मिल जाता था। कुछ दिन बाद सेठ जी को मुकदमें में सफलता मिल गई। तब तो सेठ जी बहुत ही प्रसन्न हुये और जब महाराज श्री का दर्शन करने गये, तो एक दोना भर अशर्फी बेले के फूलों से ढक कर लेते गये और उसे महाराज श्री के चरणों के समीप रख कर दण्डवत प्रणाम करके बैठ गये। सत्संग होता रहा और रात्रि आने पर सेठ जी घर चले गये और महाराज श्री भी उठ कर अपने विश्रामवाले कमरे में चले गये। प्रातःकाल जब महाराज श्री का ब्रह्मचारी सेवक उस बैठने के स्थान को झाड़ू से साफ कर रहा था, उस अशर्फी वाले दोने को भी यह समझ कर कि इसमें केवल फूल ही है झाड़ू से ठोकर देकर हटाने का प्रयत्न किया परन्तु जब वह दोना नहीं हटा तो उसे उठाकर देखा। मालूम पड़ा कि उसमें अशर्फियाँ हैं। उसने उन्हें ले जाकर महाराज श्री के समीप रख दीं। महाराज श्री को मालूम हो गया कि इसको लानेवाले वही सेठ जी ही हैं। आज्ञा दी कि यदि आज सायंकाल सेठ जी दर्शन के लिये आवें, तो उन्हें फाटक पर रोक देना और ऊपर हमारे पास दर्शन के लिये नहीं आने देना। रोज की भाँति सायंकाल

जब सेठ जी दर्शन करने आये, तो ब्रह्मचारी जी ने उन्हें फाटक पर ही रोक दिया। सेठ जी दो-ढाई घण्टे फाटक पर बैठे रहे। इसके बाद आज्ञा हुई कि बुला लो सेठ जी को। सेठ जी के दर्शन प्रणाम करने के बाद महाराज श्री ने कहा,

"ये अशर्फ़ियाँ आपने यहाँ चढ़ाई हैं? जो इनकी इच्छा करता है, जो इन्हें आपसे माँगता है, उसे तो आप देते नहीं। हमारे पास क्यों रख गये? क्या मुझे किसी बेटे-बेटी का विवाह रचाना है? ......, जाओ, ले जाओ, इन्हें उन लोगों को दो, जो इनके लिये लालायित हैं।"

ऐसा कह कर अशर्फ़ियाँ लौटा दीं और कहा,–

"हमारे यहाँ धन नहीं, अपने दुर्गुण चढ़ाओ जिससे तुम्हारा कल्याण हो जाय। यहाँ धन की आवश्यकता नहीं।"

स्वच्छंद विचार थे। जिधर की इच्छा होती चल पड़ते। मार्ग या सड़क के सहारे ही नहीं चलते, अपितु सीधे ही खेत-बारी, ऊँचा-नीचा कूदते फाँदते सीधे चले जाते। पीछे से खेत बारी वाले लोग चिल्ला पड़ते, "खेत से होकर क्यों जाते हो? सीधे मार्ग से चलो।"

उत्तर मिलता – "हम तो सदैव के कुमार्गी हैं, अर्थात् सांसारिक मार्ग का अनुसरण न करते हुये गृहस्थ व वानप्रस्थ आश्रमों के मार्ग से न जाकर सीधा मार्ग संन्यास का पकड़ कर ही विचर रहे हैं।"

एक बार महाराज श्री के पीछे कुछ अधिक कोलाहल सुनाई पड़ा। पीछे मुड़कर देखा कि कुछ लोग धूलि में कुछ बीनते से बढ़े आ रहे हैं।" समीपवर्ती एक व्यक्ति से पूछा, "ये लोग क्या कर रहें हैं?" उसने बताया, "पद चिह्न देख कर महाराज श्री की चरण-धूलि उठा

रहें हैं।" "कितने ही साधक तपस्वी अनुष्ठान करते हुये जंगलों में अनुमान से इन चरणों को ढूंढ़ते हुये विचरते थे। कितने भक्तगण इनके दर्शन के लिये संकल्प लेकर देवी देवताओं के अनुष्ठान करते थे। इनके अंतर्यामित्व की ऐसी विचित्र घटनायें हैं कि जिनसे सिद्ध होता है अवश्यमेव उन यजमानों के संकल्प की पूर्ति होती थी। उनका अनुष्ठान सफल होता था और उन्हें अभीष्ट दर्शन प्राप्त होते थे। इसका रहस्य जानने के लिए श्री चरणों से उत्सुकता प्रकट करने पर यही उत्तर मिलता, "जैसी स्वच्छंद चित्तवृत्ति हो जाती है, उसी का अनुसर करके स्वच्छंदतापूर्वक नवीन दिशा में चल पड़ते हैं।" धन्य है भगवान् की महिमा।

एक बार मानिकपुर के पास विचरण करते हुये एक गांव में पहुंच गये। लोगों ने महाराज श्री के तेजस्वी स्वरूप का दर्शन किया और आकर्षित होकर उनके समीप आये। जलपान आदि कराकर सेवा की और कुछ समय तक सत्संग किया। महाराज श्री ने पूछा, "क्या भजन करने लायक कोई एकान्त स्थान आप लोग जानते है?" लोगों ने बतलाया यहाँ से लगभग ५ मील दूर एक गुफा है, जो घनघोर जंगल में है। सिंह, व्याघ्रादि जंगली हिंसक जीव-जन्तु अधिकता से रहते हैं।" इस प्रसंग में उन्होंने गुफा की एक घटना भी सुनाई – कहा कि गाँव के जमींदार के लड़के को एक बार वैराग्य हुआ। उसने विचार किया कि जंगल की अमुक गुफा में जाकर भजन जप तप करेंगे। ऐसा ही निश्चय करके उसने अपने कर्मचारियों से कहा कि तुम लोग बन्दूक आदि लेकर हमारे साथ चलो और हमको गुफा में पहुंचा कर चले आना। इस प्रकार वह अपने सब साथियों के साथ गुफा में पहुंचा तब अपने साथियों को घर लौट जाने की आज्ञा दे दी और स्वयं गुफा में रह गया। साथी लोग गुफा से कुछ दूर जाकर

एक जंगली झाड़ी के नीचे में रात्रि में रह गये। रात्रि के समय गुफा की वन-योगिनियों ने किलकारी मार-मार कर गुफा की दीवालों पर थपेड़ी मारी और उस जमीन्दार के लड़के के गालों पर खूब तमाचे लगाये। सब लोग बाहर से रात भर गुफा के भयानक शब्द सुनते रहे। किन्तु भयवश किसी को गुफा में प्रवेश करने का साहस नहीं हुआ। प्रातःकाल जब लोग गुफा में गये तो देखा कि जमींदार का लड़का बेहोश पड़ा है और उसके शरीर पर हथेलियों की रक्तिय छापें बनी है। यह देख कर लोग बेहोशी की हालत में उस लड़के को उठाकर घर ले आये।

वन-योगिनियों के ऐसे कृत्य सुन कर महाराज श्री ने विचार किया और कहा, "देख लिया जाया" बिना किसी से कुछ कहे सुने उधर ही चल दिये। ५ मील कोई ज्यादा दूर नहीं था। दो घण्टे में पहुँच गये। देखा सुन्दर रमणीक स्थान। एकान्त-प्रिय थे ही; एक वृक्ष के नीचे बैठ गये।

यह ऐसा घनघोर जंगल है, जहाँ दिन में भी लोग गिरोह बना कर सशस्त्र जाने में भी घबराते हैं, वहाँ महाराज श्री बैठ गए। रात हो गई। अंधकार छा गया। इसी स्थान में एक दूसरी घटना घटी। यहाँ जंगल में एक पुराना सिद्ध अघोरी रहता था। देखा कि जप-तप में निमग्न एक सिद्ध महात्मा यहाँ पधारे हैं और सोचा कि इनको अपना कुछ चमत्कार दिखा कर प्रभावित किया जाय। अचानक दिन के समान शुभ्र प्रकाश हो गया। एक दो फलांग की सीमा के भीतर वनस्थली जगमगा उठी। महाराज श्री ने ने यह देखकर अपने आसन के चारों ओर एक रेखा खींच दी और निश्चिंत बैठ गये। धीरे-धीरे वह प्रकाश बदल कर नीले रंग का सुन्दर प्रकाश हो गया। इस नीले प्रकाश में अनेक ऋषि महर्षि उधर-उधर जाते दिखलाई। राम-

लक्ष्मण सीता की त्रिमूर्ति की मनोहर छवि वन-विहार करती हुई इधर उधर आती जाती दिखाई दी। मधुर मनोहर बालरूप में घनश्याम का भी दर्शन हुआ। लगभग आध घण्टे तक यह नाटक होता रहा। थोड़ी देर में घनघोर घटा छा गई। वर्षा होने लगी। ओले पड़ने लगे। हड्डियाँ तथा रक्त की भी वर्षा होने लगी। इस प्रकार की दुर्घटनायें होती रहीं। महाराज श्री मौन होकर स्वप्नवत सब दृश्य देखते रहे। परन्तु महाराज श्री की रेखा के अन्दर कोई विक्षेप नहीं हुआ। इस प्रकार महाराज श्री की दृढ़ता को देख कर कि इतना उत्पात करने पर भी विचलित नहीं हुये। वह अघोरी सिद्ध इस प्रतीक्षा में बैठा रहा कि सम्भवतः उसकी सिद्धि देख कर महाराज श्री उसके समीप आएँ। वहाँ तो परम सिद्ध का आसन लगा था। वह कब डिगनेवाला था।

जब उसने देखा कि वे तो अपने आसन से नहीं डिगे तो अपनी माया द्वारा निर्मित एक शेर पर बैठ कर स्वयं आया और बोला, ''आप कौन हैं और किस लिये यहाँ आये हुये है?'' महाराज श्री ने देखा एक बड़ा ऊँचा आदमी जिसकी जटायें जमीन पर दो हाथ लटक रही हैं, भौंह के बाल भी बहुत बड़े-बड़े हैं, सामने खड़ा है। यह देख कर महाराज श्री ने हँस कर पूछा, ''यह नाटक किसको दिखा रहे हो? उस अघोरी महात्मा ने बड़ी नम्रता से प्रार्थनापूर्वक कहा, ''यहाँ रहकर जो कुछ आप चाहते हों वह हम अभीक् पूरा कर सकते हैं। अपना परिचय तो दीजिये।'' महाराज श्री ने उत्तर दिया, ''जो अभिलाषा पूर्ति करने में समर्थ हो सकता है वह अवश्य जान सकता होगा कि हम कौन हैं और किस लिये यहाँ आये हैं? - हमें कुछ चाहिये नहीं, गुरुकृपा से सब पूर्ण है।''

जब उस ओर से विशेष आग्रह हुआ कि कुछ तो आप मांग ही

लें, तो महाराज कहा "क्या आप हमारी प्रवंचना करने आये है? ठगना चाहते हैं क्या?" इस पर अघोरी बहु प्रसन्न हुआ और समझ गया कि ये स्वयं पूंजीवान हैं। अघोरी ने कहा, "क्षमा करें। मैंने बहुत उपद्रव किया। आज तक इतना उत्पात' करने पर कोई यहाँ टिक नहीं सका। २५० वर्ष हो गये इस जंगल में मुझे आये हुये, किन्तु कोई ऐसा पूंजीवान नहीं मिला। क्षमा किया जाय।" इतना कहते कहते किंचित मौन के पश्चात् बोला, "जब तक आप यहाँ चाहें रहें और मेरे योग्य जो भी सेवा हो बताएं।" महाराज श्री ने उत्तर दिया कि हमें किसी चीज की आवश्यकता नहीं है। यह तुम स्वयं जान सकते हो। भ्रमण करते हुये इधर आगये, स्वयं चले जायंगे। कुछ दिन निश्चिंतता से महाराज श्री वहाँ रहे। इस बीच वह सिद्ध अघोरी भी कभी-कभी आपके समीप आता रहा। किन्तु आपने विचार किया कि हमारे यहाँ रहने में इस अघोरी की स्वतंत्रता में बाधा पहुंचती होगी। अतः आपने स्थान परिवर्तन कर दिया और अन्यत्र चले गये।

घनघोर जंगल में भ्रमण करते हुये एक पगडंडी से जा रहे थे। उसी पगडंडी पर खड़ा हुआ एक सिंह दिखाई पड़ा। परम योगी ध्याननिष्ठ महात्मा के समीप आने पर वैर भाव वाले हिंसक जीव जंतु भी अपने स्वभाव को त्याग देते हैं। यह बात यहाँ प्रत्यक्ष घटित हुई। महाराज श्री प्रसन्न मुद्रा में उसी पगडंडी पर आगे बढ़ते चले जा रहे हैं। कुछ ही कदम पर सिंह को सामने खड़ा देखकर महाराज श्री के मुख से ये शब्द निकल पड़े "राजाओं का यह धर्म नहीं है कि किसी के रास्ते पर खड़े हों "इन शब्दों की झनकार सिंह के कानों में जाते ही, उसने अपनी पूंछ हिलाई, और रास्ते को छोड़कर एक तरफ धीरे से चल दिया। ठीक है जिस समय योगी यथार्थ अहिंसा के

उच्चतम स्तर पर पहुँच जाता है, उस समय उसके समीप में आने वाले हिंसक जन्तु भी हिंसक स्वभाव त्याग कर उसके प्रभाव से अहिंसक बन जाते हैं। महाराज श्री अपनी जिस चाल से उस पगडंडी पर जा रहे थे उसी चाल से आगे बढ़ते गये और आगे चले गये।

थोड़ी दूर पर देखा एक विशाल बरगद का पेड़ है। उसी के बगल में पास ही अति नीची खाईं है। खाईं इतनी नीची है कि कोई भी बिना किसी सहारे के नीचे नहीं जा सकता। नीचे खाईं से कुछ ही दूर पर जलस्तोत है। स्थान चारों ओर से घने वृक्षों से घिरा हुआ है। समीप जाने पर देखा कि बरगद की जटायें नीचे तक लटक रही है। देखा कि यहाँ परम एकान्त और रमणीक स्थान है। बरगद की जटायें पकड़ कर आप नीचे उतर गये। वहाँ एक सुन्दर गुफा भी दृष्टिगोचर हुई। घनघोर जंगल में जलस्तोत के समीप सुन्दर शीतल रमणीक गुफा देखकर विचार हुआ कि यहीं रहकर कुछ दिन योगाभ्यास किया जाय। यह स्थान इतने सघन वृक्षों के बीच है कि सूर्य का प्रकाश ६-६ महीने नहीं प्रवेश कर पाता। महाराज श्री आनन्द से यहीं निवास करने लगे। कंदमूल फल से जीविका निर्वाह होता और सदैव अहर्निश परमात्म-चिंतन में संलग्न रहते। लकड़ी काटने के निमित्त कभी-कभी यदि कोई ग्रामीण आ जाते तो उनके द्वारा कच्चा बना मंगा कर रख लेते और एक दो मुट्ठी खाकर अपनी जठराग्नि शान्त कर लेते। इस प्रकार आपको इस स्थान में निवास करते कुछ समय व्यतीत हो गये।

उस समय अंग्रेजों का राज्य था। अंग्रेज लोग कभी-कभी उधर शिकार खेलने आ जाया करते थे। एकान्त स्थान में जलस्तोत होने के कारण एक अंग्रेज शिकारी ने देखा कि यहाँ शेर का शिकार

सफलता पूर्वक अच्छा हो सकता है। उसकी आज्ञा पाते ही ग्रामीण लोग एक भैंसा ले आये और उसी स्तोत के पास ले जाकर बाँस की कमची (रस्सी) से बाँध दिया और सब चले गये। दूर एक निश्चित स्थान पर अंग्रेज शिकारी बैठ गया। सूर्यास्त होने के बाद से वह भैंसा चिह्लाने लगा। भैंसे की चिह्लाहट का शब्द कई घण्टे तक महाराज श्री को सुनाई पड़ता रहा। अधिक रात बीत जाने पर भी जब वह चिह्लाहट बन्द नहीं हुई, तो महाराज श्री ने विचार किया कि समीप में ही किसी प्राणी को अत्यन्त कष्ट है। उस कष्ट का निवारण करना चाहिये। आप उस भैंसे के समीप गये और उस बाँस की रस्सी के नीचे एक पत्थर रख कर दूसरे पत्थर को जोरों से उस रस्सी को काट दिया। भैंसा स्वतंत्र हो गया और भाग गया। इधर रस्सी काट कर वे अपनी गुफा में आकर फिर ध्यानमग्न हो गये। रात्रिभर शिकारी लोग अपने शिकार्र की प्रतीक्षा में बैठे रहे प्रातःकाल उन लोगों को मालूम पड़ा कि भैंसे की रस्सी को किसी ने रात्रि में काट दिया था, तब तो उस अंग्रेज को बहुत क्रोध आया। आवेश में वह अनाप-शानाप बकने लगा। ग्रामीण लोगों ने कहा, "यहाँ एक महात्मा रहते हैं। आप कोई अपशब्द यहाँ न कहें।" शिकारी के साथ उसकी मेम भी थी। अंग्रेजी राज्य था। उस समय सफेद चमड़ीवाले साहबलोग मदान्ध थे। उस मेम ने कहा, "महात्मा हमारा क्या कर सकता है? क्या हमारा रास्ता बन्द कर देगा? हम लोग इस जंगल के मालिक हैं, अधिकारी हैं, हमारा राज्य है।" इस प्रकार के अभिमान से भरे शब्दों के निकलने के बाद, उस मेम का मलमूत्र बंद हो गया। उसका पेट फलने लगा, कष्ट बढ़ गया। उपचार की सम्भावना कठिन थी। बहुत घबड़ाई। ग्रामीणों ने कहा "घनघोर जंगल में जो ये महात्मा भजन-तप करते हैं, उनके प्रति अपराध हो गया है, ऐसा मालूम पड़ता है। नहीं तो इस प्रकार

सहसा कष्ट नहीं होना चाहिये था । उस अंग्रेज ने कहा, "हो न हो, यही कारण हो; तब तो पता लगाओ उन महात्मा का । उनसे मिला जाय ।" सब लोग महाराज श्री का पता लगाते हुये वहाँ पहुँच गये और देखा कि एक महात्मा ध्यानावस्थित बैठे हुये हैं । दूर से ही हाथ जोड़ कर सब वृतांत कह दिया और कष्ट दूर होने की प्रार्थना भी की । नेत्र खोलकर महाराज श्री ने देखा कि सामने एक अंग्रेज और उसकी महिला तथा कुछ ग्रामीण खड़े हैं और प्रार्थना कर रहे हैं । श्री महाराज जी ने उनकी प्रार्थना सुन कर कहा, "इतना बड़ा जंगल पड़ा है, आप लोग मेरे नेत्रों के सामने ही हिंसा करने के लिये उद्धत हो गये । लगभग १२ बजे अर्द्ध रात्रि में मुझे वहाँ जाकर उस भैंसे को छुड़ाना पड़ा ।" तब तो उस अंग्रेज साहब ने कहा कि "मुझे यह कदापि ज्ञान नहीं था कि कोई इतना प्रभावशाली महात्मा इस घनघोर जंगल में तप कर रहे हैं । क्षमा किया जाय । अब कभी इस तरफ आपके समीप शिकार खेलने नहीं आऊँगा ।" महाराज श्री ने कहा, "अच्छा, अब आप लोग जाइये ।" वे सब लोग वहाँ से चले गये और तुरन्त ही उस अंग्रेज महिला का कष्ट दूर हो गया । इसके बाद वह अंग्रेज फिर कभी भी उस तरफ शिकार खेलने नहीं गया ।

लगभग ६ महीने बाद उस गुफा से महाराज श्री निकले और भ्रमण करते हुए पास के किसी गाँव में पहुँच गये । सिद्ध महात्मा होने की ख्याति उधर दूर तक फैल चुकी थी । लोगों की बड़ी श्रद्धा हुई और दर्शन के लिये उमड़ पड़े । सत्संग होता रहा । कभी-कभी प्रसंग आने पर महाराज श्री उस गुफा के सौन्दर्य और वहाँ अपने एकान्तिक जीवन का संक्षेप में वर्णन कर दिया करते थे । आप यह कहा करते थे कि अपने लिये भोग की क्या चिंता – वह तो स्वयं ही भोक्ता को ढूँढ़ता हुआ आ जाता है । एक समय रींवा जंगल की तरफ

किसी गाँव में महाराज श्री रुके हुये थे। श्री कुबेरदत्त ओझा, जो उनके अनन्य भक्त थे, दर्शन के लिये ढूँढ़ते हुये वहाँ पहुँच गये। सायंकाल का समय था। महाराज श्री ने अपना दंड-कमंडलु उठाया और चल दिये जंगल की ओर। कुबेरदत्त भी पीछे-पीछे हो लिये। लगभग दो मील जंगल में चले गये। कुबेरदत्त के के मन में यह बात आई कि अब हम लोग जंगल में यहाँ दूर आ गये हैं लौटना तो होगा नहीं, मालूम पड़ता है आज रात्रि में भूखे ही रहना पड़ेगा। थोड़ी देर बाद महाराज श्री एक पेड़ के नीचे रुक गये। कुबेरदत्त से कहा कि थोड़ी देर आप यहीं बैठिये; मैं उधर शौच को जाता हूँ। कुबेरदत्त एकाकी उस घनघोर जंगल में बैठे थे कि इतने में एक पुरुष उनके पास आया। वह एक हंडी में कुछ सामान लिये था। उसने कुबेरदत्त से कहा, "इसे रख लो, अपने काम में लाना"। कुबेरदत्त ने कहा, "आप कौन हैं? कहाँ से और क्या लाये हैं?" उसने उत्तर दिया, "इसे आप रख लीजिये और महाराज श्री से बतला देना, बस इतना ही प्रयोजन है।" ऐसा कह कर वह चला गया। जब महाराज श्री आये, तो कुबेरदत्त ने सारा वृत्तांत कह सुनाया। महाराज श्री ने कहा, "ठीक है, देखो तो उसमें क्या है?" देखा गया तो मालूम पड़ा कि उसमें हंडी भर भर मलाई थी। महाराज श्री ने कहा, "इसे काम में ले लो, खाओ, पियो, परन्तु ध्यान रहे कि इस प्रकार एकान्त में जब कभी कोई सामग्री लावे, तो उससे अधिक प्रश्न नहीं करना चाहिये। यह नहीं पूछना चाहिये कि कौन हो, कहाँ से लाये हो आदि-आदि।"

इसी प्रकार स्वच्छंद विचरण-काल में अनेकानेक घटनाएँ घटती रहीं। एक बार नीवा घाट (प्रयाग) की तरफ एक गाँव में पहुँच गये। महाराज श्री के साथ सेवा में एक ब्रह्मचारी भी था। एकान्त स्थान

था। अन्य गाँव वहाँ से मीलों दूर थे। थोड़ी रात्रि बीत चुकी थी। इतने में एक मनुष्य कुछ अन्न आदि भोजन सामग्री लेकर आया। उस समय महाराज श्री वहाँ मौजूद थे। ब्रह्मचारी ने सूचना दी कि महाराज एक मनुष्य कुछ खाने पीने की सामग्री लेकर आया है। महाराज श्री ने कहा, "बुलाओ उस मनुष्य को हमारे समीप।" आने पर महाराज श्री ने स्वयं उससे पूछा, "यह सामग्री किसने भेजी है? उसने उत्तर दिया, अमुक मनुष्य जो अमुक गाँव में रहता है, उसने।" आज्ञा हुई – ब्रह्मचारी, देखो, जो-जो यह बोलते हैं उसे नोट कर लो। ब्रह्मचारी जी ने उस सामग्री भेजनेवाले का नाम, ग्राम आदि नोट कर लिया। वह मनुष्य सारी सामग्री वहीं रख कर चला गया। दूसरे दिन प्रातःकाल महाराज श्री ने आज्ञा दी कि आओ उस सामग्री भेजनेवाले का पता लगाओ, और उससे पूछो कि उसने वह सामग्री कल भेजी थी। ब्रह्मचारी जी ने पता लगाया तो मालूम पड़ा कि अमुक ग्राम में उस नाम का व्यक्ति रहता तो है। परन्तु उसने कोई सामग्री महाराज श्री के यहाँ नहीं भेजी। उस प्रकार से अनेकानेक घटनायें नित्यशः होती रहीं।

आपका निवास अधिकतर विन्ध्यगिरि और अमरकंटक के घनघोर वन-पर्वतों की एकाकी गुफाओं और कंदराओं में होता रहा। वह जन-संसर्ग से सदा असंग थे। और उनके संगी थे बनचर, व्याघ्र, सिंह आदि हिंसक जंतु और कोल-भिल्ल आदि मानव एवं पशु। किन्तु ये वनचर प्राणी उस तेजोमय महात्मा को सदैव अपनी कंदराओं में न छिपाये रख सके। यहाँ-वहाँ कभी-कभी संसार की दृष्टि में आने लगे। मुग्ध होकर संसार ने देखा, समझा और कसौटी पर कसा। विशुद्ध तत्व थे वह। जिस कसौटी पर चढ़ाये गये, वही आभावान हो गई। जिसको उनका सम्पर्क मिला, वही चमक उठा।

सब प्रकार से पूर्ण थे वह। उन्हें कुछ आवश्यकता न थी। ऐसी कोई वस्तु न थी जो उन्हें प्राप्त न थी। जिससे सब कुछ जाना जाता है, आपको वह ज्ञान हो चुका था। सब लोग अपनी-अपनी दृष्टि से उन्हें देखते थे। अज्ञानी संसारियों की दृष्टि में वे एक साधारण साधु, साधुओं की दृष्टि में एक ज्ञानी महात्मा और महात्माओं की दृष्टि में एक सिद्ध पुरुष थे।

Chapter 6
Independence & Samsara

He was independent-willed, spontaneous – On the one hand he would go wherever the desire moved him for he did not depend of a road or highway. On the other hand he leapt and jumped the straight edges of fields high and low, going straight. The man that owned the field cried out afterwards, 'Why do you come by the field? Go by the straight road!'

He was met with the reply, 'We are always a *kumargi* (one who takes the 'bad path'). That is to say we are not following the *samsarik* (worldly) path, not going by the path of the stages of *grihastha* (householder) or *vanaprastha* (living the 'forest' stage of a twice-born), but we are strolling, having taken the straight path of *sannyas* (renunciation).'

*

One time Maharaj Shri heard a lot of noise behind him. Turning back he saw that some people were coming to pick up something in the lane. He enquired from a nearby individual, 'What are these people doing?'

He informed, 'Having seen the mark of the footstep of Maharaj Shri they are picking up the dust of his feet.'

Really, how many *sadhakas* (those practising a spiritual path) have been doing *tapasvi* (penance) in the jungles? By inference they were strolling in search of these feet. How many devotees of the spiritual community who vowed to take *darshan* of them were undertaking a celebration of the goddesses and gods? The curious incidents necessarily fulfilled the vows of the ones who performed sacrifices to the Supreme Being who controls living beings. Their religious performance yielded fruits and the desired *darshan* was obtained.

For those evidently keen to understand this mystery, this is the reply he gets from Shri Charanon ('the blessed feet' – one of the many names used to refer to Guru Dev, Swami Brahmanand Saraswati):- 'Just as *chittavritti* (mental activity) occurs spontaneously, really follow that, spontaneously go in a new direction. Blessed is the greatness of Bhagwan.'

*

One time, wandering near Manikapur (Nepal), he arrived at a village. The people were attracted to come closeby and have *darshan* of the lustrous self of Maharaj Shri. Having been served some *jalpan* (snack, refreshment) etc and for some time given *satsang* (inspirational spiritual meeting), Maharaj Shri asked, 'Do you people know of any isolated place suitable to do *bhajan* (prayer)?'

The people told him, 'Five miles away from here is a cave, although it is in very dense jungle where lions, tigers and other wild carnivorous creatures live.'

He heard of an incident in connection with the cave:- It is said that one time the son of a *zamindar* (land owner) of the village became an ascetic. He imagined going to a particular cave in the jungle to do *bhajan* (prayer), *japa* (silent repetition of *mantra*) and *tapa* (penance). He decided to tell his own employees, 'You people go with me, taking guns etc and we will go to the cave.' In this way they all went together with him arriving at the cave. Then he gave the order for them to return to house together, and he alone went into the cave. Having moved some distance away from the *gupha*, the companions settled down to spend the night in a jungle thicket.

In the night-time there came sounds from the cave, sounds of joy, of *vana yogini* (female forest ascetics) slapping and beating on the walls of the cave and the friendly slapping of the cheeks to the son of the *zamindar*. The whole night all the men heard hideous sounds from the cave. Out of fear none had the nerve to enter into the cave.

At daybreak, when the men went to the cave they saw the son of the *zamindar* had fallen senseless and that there were bloody handprints on his body. Seeing him in this condition, they carried the boy home.

Having heard of the *vana yoginiyon* (female forest ascetics) in this right way, Maharaj Shri thought, and then said, 'We will see.' Without saying anything more he went in that direction for about five miles and in two hours he arrived there. It looked to be a beautifully pleasing place, so, as a lover of seclusion, he sat beneath a tree.

This is such dense jungle that even in the daytime parties equipped with arms are perturbed about going there. But there Maharaj Shri went and sat and it became night. The darkness spread. Actually, just in this one place the darkess chanced to diminish!

Here in the jungle lived an old *Siddha Aghori*. He saw that a *Siddha Mahatma* had arrived here and was engaged in *japa-tapa* (prayer and devotion). So he thought he would impress him by showing some surprises. Suddenly it became brightly lit as if it were daytime. An area of one or two furlongs of heath glimmered with light. Having seen this, Maharaj Shri drew a line around his resting place and sat unconcerned. Slowly, slowly the light changed, the light becoming a beautiful blue. In this blue light several rishis and maharishis were seen going this way and that. The beautifully brilliant faces of Rama, Lakshman and Sita were to be seen as they wandered here and there in the forest. Also he had *darshan* of Ghana Shyama (having the complexion of 'dark rain clouds'), the sweet beautiful Krishna is his youthful form. This performance lasted for about half an hour.

After some time dense clouds spread, and it rained, and it hailed. Then it rained blood and bones too. In this way calamities continued to occur.

Maharaj Shri silently watched all the dreamy sights, however there was no disturbance within the line around himself. In this way Maharaj Shri was seen to be strong, for even with so much disturbance he still did not become unsteady. That *Aghori Siddha* was sitting waiting, thinking that that Maharaj Shri, having seen the *siddhi* (supernatural power, or success), would come near. But there then, still seated, was the best *siddha*. When would he be shaken? But the *aghori* saw that he was not be shaken from his seat, so by way of *maya* (illusion) created a tiger, seated himself on it and said, 'Who are you? What have you come here for?'

INDIAN FAKIR,

['*Indian Pictures*', The Religious Tract Society, 1891]

Maharaj Shri looked at him as he stood face-to-face before him, a very tall man with long tresses of hair trailing along the ground, and the hair of his eyebrows had grown long too.

Having seen him, Maharaj Shri laughingly asked, 'Who is coming to see this drama?'

That *aghori mahatma* then said, with great courtesy, 'I can fulfil any of your wishes while you are staying here. Introduce yourself then.

Maharaj Shri gave this reply, 'He who can fulfil desires would certainly be able to know who we are and why we want to come here. We do not desire anything. By *guru kripa* (grace of the *guru*) all is accomplished.' And as the *aghori* had been somewhat pressing to persuade him, Maharaj said, 'Why are you coming to cheat us? Do you wish to swindle?'

At this the aghori became very pleased, as he now understood that you are poona jivaan (have the 'wealth of the Self' – are Self-realised). He said, 'Give forgiveness, I was very annoying. Until today none could stay here. For two hundred and fifty years I have been coming to this jungle but I have never met anyone who is *poona jivaan* (Self-Realized). Please forgive me. Stay here as long as you wish and also please inform me if I can be of any service.'

Maharaj Shri answered that, 'We are not needing anything. This you should understand, I have been roaming here, and I will go of my own accord.'

Maharaj Shri stayed some days at leisure there, but in the middle of this, the Siddha Aghori also used to come near you sometimes. So you thought that, 'In our staying here this *aghori's* independence would come into question. Therefore, we will change place and go elsewhere.'

*

He walked in the dense jungle, going by a track, he saw a lion standing on the path. On approaching the *param yogi* who was engrossed in contemplation of the divine, the carnivorous creature abandoned its natural feeling of hostility. It is clear what happened, Maharaj Shri appeared to be in a comfortable state as he went ahead on the path treading the path some more he found himself standing before a lion. From the mouth of Maharaj Shri appeared these words, 'It is not the *dharma* of kings to stand on the path of anyone.'

As the words entered the ears of the lion they resonated. He wagged his tail and left the path slowly going off to one side.

It is as well that at that time the *yogi* had arrived at the highest level of *ahimsa* (non-violence, harmlessness) for on coming near the carnivorous creature at that time he had influenced it and made it non-violent.

*

Going along the way Maharaj Shri walked at his own pace, going further and further. He sees a Banyan tree some distance ahead of him, to the side of the tree is a deep dike, so deep in fact that it is impossible to go down into it without some assistance. Some way down is a spring of water, the place is surrounded by dense trees on all sides. Going closer he sees that the roots of the Banyan tree are hanging down below. *Seeing that here is a secluded and pleasing place, you take hold of the roots of the Banyan tree and descend below. Once down there a beautiful cave becomes apparent too.* Having seen this cool pleasing cave near a spring in the dense jungle, he decides to do *yogabhyasa* (to live and practice *yoga*) for some days there.

The trees are so dense in this place that the sunlight does not enter the place for six months of the year. Maharaj Shri dwelt here with pleasure. He survived on roots and fruit, and was always enjoined in thinking of Paramatma, day and night. If some rustic person came on account of cutting firewood then he would accept *kachcha* (boiled) food, and eating one or two handfuls his hunger would be satisfied. *In this way you stayed at that place for some time.*

This was at the time of the British Raj and Englishmen would sometimes come to the jungle for sport, to do *shikar* (hunting). On account of the spring in this secluded place an Englishmen thought this to be a good place for successful *shikar*. On receipt of his order, the local people brought a buffalo and after tethering it near the spring they all went away. The Englishman sat at a safe distance.

From evening time onwards the buffalo bellowed and for some hours Maharaj Shri heard the sound of the buffalo's bellowing. More of the night passed but the bellowing contiuned unabated. Maharaj Shri thought, that if there were an animal in distress nearby, that the suffering should be prevented. *So you came near the buffalo, placed a stone under the cord and with another stone you made efforts to cut the cord. The buffalo then became free and ran away. After having cut the cord you returned to your cave and again became immersed in meditation.*

All night the huntsmen sat waiting for a prey and at daybreak it became obvious to them, that during the night, the rope that tethered the buffalo had been cut. Then the Englishman became very angry indeed and in his wrath he jabbered excessively. But the local people said, 'You should not speak any disagreeable words here for there lives a *mahatma* hereabouts.'

With the *shikari* (huntsman) was his madam and on this occasion the white-skinned person was drunk. That European lady said, 'A *mahatma*! What can he do to us? We people are the bosses of this jungle, we are the owners, this is our kingdom!' - for at that time the government was English.

After the proud words tumbled forth, the secretions of the European lady became interrupted. This in turn affected her stomach, which was growing painful. The chances of getting treatment were slight so there was a good deal of concern.

The locals said, 'There is a *mahatma* who does *bhajan-tapa* (prayer and austerity) in the very dense jungle. Offence has been done to him, that is obvious. If not, then this kind of sudden suffering could not have happened.'

That Englishman said, 'That maybe or maybe not, but if this is really the cause, then go and find the whereabouts of that *mahatma.*'

When the people discovered the whereabouts of Maharaj Shri, they arrived there and saw that the *mahatma* was sitting meditating. They stood at a distance and having joined their hands (in greeting) explained him the situation and they prayed that the pain would go away. Maharaj Shri opened his eyes and saw in front of him an Englishman, his woman and some local people standing and praying. Having listened to their request, Shri Maharaj Ji said. 'This is a big jungle yet you people come here and prepare to commit murder in front of my eyes. In the middle of the night, at about twelve o'clock, I went to set the buffalo free.'

Then that English *sahab* (lord) said, 'I was not aware that there is such an influential a *mahatma* doing *tapa* (austerity) in this dense jungle. Please give your forgiveness, I will never come hunting in your direction again.'

Maharaj Shri said, '*Achchaa* (good), now you people should go.'

All the people went away from there and the English lady's suffering quickly went away. After this that Englishman never came hunting in this direction again.

*

About six months later Maharaj Shri emerged from the cave, and having roamed a while, arrived in the vicinity of a nearby village. The fame of the *siddha mahatma* had spread that way. People greatly revered him and surged about him for his *darshan* and for having his *satsang*. In this context Maharaj Shri sometimes mentioned the beauty of that *gupha* (cave) when giving a brief description of his life there. *You said this that,* 'Why think of enjoyment for oneself? That which one is seeking to enjoy comes quite automatically.'

*

[In his memoirs, Swami Rama recalls meeting Guru Dev. The following exerpts are taken from pages 257-260 of his autobiography *'Living With The Himalayan Masters'*, published by the Himalayan International Institute in 1978:-

Travelling toward the forests of Reva State, I went to the Satana forest and there met a swami who was very handsome and highly educated in the *Vedantic* and yoga tradition. He knew the scriptures and was a very brilliant *saadhaka* (spiritual practitioner). He was later nominated as Shankaracharya of Jyotirmayapitham, which is in the Himalayas on the way to Badrinath. His name was Brahmananda Saraswati.

He used to live only on germinated gram seeds mixed with a little bit of salt. He lived on a hillock in a small natural cave near a mountain pool. I was led by the villagers to that place, but I did not find anyone there and became disappointed. The next day I went again and found a few footprints on the edge of the pool made by his wooden sandals. I tried, but I could not track the footprints. Finally, on the fifth day of effort, early in the morning before sunrise, I went back to the pool and found him taking a bath. I greeted him saying, "Namo narayan," which is a commonly used salutation among swamis meaning, "I bow to the divinity in you." He was observing silence so he motioned for me to follow him to his small cave and I did so gladly. This was the eighth day of his silence and I gently spoke to him about the purpose of my visit. I wanted to know how he was living and the ways and methods of his spiritual practices. During our conversation, he started talking to me about Sri Vidya, the highest of paths followed only by accomplished Sanskrit scholars in India.

'Swami Brahmananda was one of the rare *Siddhas* who had the knowledge of Sri Vidya. His authoritive knowledge of the Upanishads, and especially of Shankara's commentaries, was superb. He was also a very good speaker. Swami Karpatri, a renowned scholar, was the disciple who requested him to accept the prestige and dignity of Shankaracharya in the North, a seat which had been vacant for 300 years. Whenever he travelled from one city to another, people flocked in the thousands to hear him, and after his nomination as Shankaracharya, his followers increased. One thing very attractive about his way of teaching was his combination of the bhakti and Advaita systems. During my brief stay with him, he also talked about Madhusudana's commentary on the Bhagavad Gita.

Swami Brahmananda had a *Sri Yantra* made out of rubies, and as he showed it to me, he explained the way he worshipped it. It is interesting to note how the great sages direct all their spiritual, mental and physical resources toward their ultimate goal. Among all the swamis of India, I only met a few who radiated such brilliance and yet lived in the public, remaining unaffected by worldly temptations and distractions. I stayed with him only a week and then left for Uttarkashi.']

*

One time Maharaj Shri stopped in a village near the Rewa jungle. Shri Kuberdatt Ojha who had infinite devotion, arrived there searching for his *darshan*. The time was dusk and Maharaj Shri lifted his *danda* (staff) and *kamandalu* (water pot) and left, going off in the direction of the jungle. Kuberdatt came walking after him, for about two miles they proceeded into the jungle. In Kuberdatt's mind this idea came, that we have come so far into the jungle there will not be returning tonight, so it seems that we will stay hungry all night. After a little while Maharaj Shri stopped under a tree. He spoke with Kuberdatt, 'You should sit here for a little while; I am going that way, to ablute.'

Kuberdatta sat alone in that very dense jungle. Meanwhile, whilst he was waiting, a man came near. He was carrying something in a container. He said to Kuberdatt, 'Take this pot for your own use.'

Kuberdatt said, 'Who are you? Where are you from and what

are you bringing?'

He gave this answer, 'You ought to take this and please inform Maharaj Shri, that is explanation enough.'

Having said this he went away and when Maharaj Shri came back he heard Kuberdatt's account of the whole occurrence.

Maharaj Shri said, '*Thik hai* - It is well! Look then! What is in that?'

Having looked it became clear to you that the pot was completely full of the cream of milk, whereupon Maharaj Shri said, 'In this work, accept. Eat. Drink. But when some stuff is brought in this way in seclusion sometimes, then you should not question further from him. You should not ask him who are you? and where are you bringing this from etc. etc.''

During the time he was wandering about at will, many such occurrences came to pass.

One time he arrived in a village in the area of New Ghat (in

Prayag - Allahabad). In the company of Maharaj Shri was a *brahmachari* in attendance. The place was isolated, there was not another village for many miles from there. Some of the night had already passed when a man came along bringing some foodstuffs for a meal. On that occasion Maharaj Shri was present there. The *brahmachari* gave this information to Maharaj Shri that a man has come bringing some goods to eat and drink.

Maharaj Shri said, 'Call that man near to us!'

When he had come, Maharaj Shri asked him, 'Who sent this stuff?'

He answered, 'Such and such man, who lives in such and such village.'

Maharaj Shri instructed the *brahmachari*, 'Look, make a *"note"* of whom he speaks of.'

Whilst that man put all of the stuff there on the spot, the *brahmachari* took a note of the sender's name, village etc.

Next day at daybreak Maharaj Shri ordered, 'Come. Fetch the address of the sender of the stuff and go enquire from him if yesterday he sent the stuff.'

The *brahmachari ji* searched out the location, then he found the person of that name at the address, but it transpired he had not sent anything to Maharaj Shri.

In this manner many such occurrences were always happening.

*

Your abode was mostly in caves and caverns of the Vindhya Mountains and the very dense forests of the Amarakantaka (source of the Narmada and Sone rivers). You were constantly detached from the association of people. For company were wild beasts, tigers, lions etc, carnivorous creatures, Kol and Bhilla men (wild mountainous tribal people) and cattle. But that brilliant *mahatma* could not always hide in his own caves from these living inhabitants of the jungle. Here and there, sometime or another he came in sight of the worldly existence. But he saw *samsara* (worldly existence) to be less. He understood and tested on a *kasauti* (touchstone), he was *vishuddha tatwa* (pure truth). Riding on that proof he went, and the very same he became. Whoever met with his company, they found this very same brilliance. He was perfect in all ways. There was nothing needed, There was nothing that he required. *From That everything is known, and your knowledge of this became complete. All people saw you from their own view.* In the view of ignorant worldly people they saw him as an ordinary *sadhu*, in the view of *sadhus* he was a *gyaani mahatma* (knowledgeable high soul) and in the view of *mahatmas*, he was one *siddha purusha* (perfected man).

*

[In *'The Way to Maharishi's Himalayas'* (Stockholm, 1972) on pages 255-256 of Elsa Dragemark presents some recollections of Guru Dev, from one of his devotees:-

'Doctor Varma continued his story: "It was when Guru Dev had come out from the jungle that I first met him. Then he was not yet Shankaracharya. Guru Dev was the pure and holy man with strict rules of life that he had been reputed to be. He was not interested in acquiring disciples and was therefore extremely restrained on the subject. In the 24 hours the public was allowed to meet him for half an hour. That was between six-thirty and seven o'clock at night. A *brahmachari* guarded his door.

I came to the house where Guru Dev lived and asked the *brahmachari* for permission to enter and to sit at Guru Dev's feet, but he said:

- No, no don't be in such a hurry to see Guru Dev.

I came evening after evening, but each time I was staved off in this way.

The *brahmachari* asked everyone who came to see Guru Dev:

- What is your name? Do you desire to see Guru Dev? He made a note of the name after which he went to Guru Dev and asked if such and such a person might have an audience.

Guru Dev closed his eyes for a moment and answered either "Let him come in" or "Ask him to leave", for by knowing the visitor's name he was able to tell what kind of person he was.

That was remarkable. I observed these incidents with wonder and excitement.

One day a rich, but dishonest and insincere jeweller came to seek an audience with Guru Dev. The *brahmachari* asked him: - What is your name? Do you desire to see Guru Dev?

- My name is Shuldrin Seraf and I desire an audience with Guru Dev, the man said in a superior manner.

The *brahmachari* went in to Guru Dev and said:- Shuldrin Seraf seeks an audience.

Guru Dev closed his eyes for a moment and then said: - No, tell him there will be no audience today.

The *brahmachari* came out and gave the message to Shulrin Seraf who then had to leave.

One day I decided that it would now have to be either a "yes" or a "no". I thought that I had waited long enough and couldn't wait any longer. I asked the *brahmachari* to place my name on the list and added:

- Tell Guru Dev that I can wait no longer.

The *brahmachari* answered:

- You will gain nothing by forcing the master. He again placed my name on the list, but it was no avail this time either and I had to wait still some time before I was allowed to enter and sit at Guru Dev's feet. It was in 1939 - and then I was also initiated.']

[Raj Varma wrote his own account of meeting Guru Dev in *'Strange Facts about a Great Saint'* (M/s, Varma & Sons, 1980). The following extracts appear on pages 61-70 of that book:-

'On 27th August 1940, in the morning I had gone to the market. While returning, on the way I saw two men, who were talking together that a *Siddha Yogi Mahatma* had come in our city.

The other man asked him, "What is his name?"

The former said, "I do not know his name."

The latter asked, "Where is he staying?"

The former replied, "Somewhere in Wright Town."

When I heard their talk, I got interested to know more about the *Siddha Yogi Mahatma*. I enquired from them the location of the house in Wright Town.

One of them said, "I have only heard this much."

This was a sort of message from Maharaj Shri of his coming to Jabalpur. Just then, I resolved to have his *darshan*, the same day. I thought so because such *Siddha Yogi Mahatmas* were very rare to be seen.

At 3 p.m.. I locked my Studio and started to find Maharaj Shri in Wright Town. The sun was shining brightly and there was no trace of any cloud on the sky, I was going at abnormal speed.

Then all of a sudden a call was heard from behind, "Varma ji Varma ji." I stopped, turned back and saw a man waving his hand for me. I went to him. He said, "Your friend Shankar Prasad a *tantrik* wants you."

I saw Shankar Prasad sitting in the room and asked him, "When did you arrive?"

He replied "Only two days back." He asked me, "Where are you going so swiftly?"

I said "I have heard that a *Siddha Yogi Mahatma* has come to our town and I was going to have his *darshan*."

Shankar Prasad said, "Yes, he is a great *Yogi Mahatma*."

I enquired from him, "How do you know him?"

He said "I know him from a long time and yesterday I had his *darshan*."

I asked his name and he said, "His name is Shri Brahmanand ji Saraswati Maharaj, a *Dandi Sanyasi Mahatma*. He is a *Siddha Yogi*."

I said, "I am eager to have his *darshan*, so please let me go now."

He said, "This is not the time to see him. At 6.30 p.m. daily his door is opened for men only. No woman is allowed in his premises to have his *darshan* and after 30 minutes at 7 p.m., the door is closed. It is 4 p.m. now, better wait, we both would go to have his *darshan*."

I thought to myself, "What a peculiar incident has happened. Instead of my own effort to find out the location where Maharaj Shri was staying, a suitable guide like Shankar Prasad has been arranged for me. The saying is true, Where there is a will, there is a way."

So I was waiting, talking with Shankar Prasad. In the meantime a gust of wind came and heavy clouds began gathering on the sky, wind was still blowing strongly and in no time the Sun hid behind the dense dark clouds. Darkness

spread with terrible thunderstorm and the rains started.

It was 6 p.m., I asked Shankar Prasad, "How could we go to Maharaj Shri in this stormy weather?"

He said, "This time it is not safe to go out."

We would go tomorrow surely. Our plan was upset due to bad weather and I had to go home disappointed.

Next evening at 5.30 p.m. I went to Shankar Prasad. We both purchased garlands and reached the building where Maharaj Shri was staying.

I had no idea how to meet or behave with a *Siddha Mahatma* till then. So I thought to follow Shankar Prasad's way of meeting him. I was very alert in this regard. There was a *brahmachari* standing at the main doorway, Shankar Prasad told him his name for permission. The *brahmachari* took the name to Maharaj Shri for his *darshan*. He consented and the *brahmachari* allowed us to enter.

In a hall, Maharaj Shri was seated on a comfortable chair. Shankar Prasad was the first to enter the hall. As he got the glimpse of Maharaj Shri he bowed down and went near him to garland him. On my turn, I too did the same and garlanded him. Beholding him, my alertness vanished and instead of moving aside to take my seat, I sat down near his sandals as if charmed by his Divine influence looking at him all the while, I had lost myself in his Grandeur. For a minute or two, I was in that position but all of a sudden I got a hint from within, "Where are you sitting?" I felt ashamed of my folly. I got up and sat down aside.

I again looked up to see if Maharaj Shri had taken ill of my unmannerly sitting at improper place but I noticed no change on his face as if nothing had happened. I was happy that no wrong was come on my part.

There were some 30 or 35 men in the hall sitting around Maharaj Shri but all were quiet. I wished to hear him but how? It was a tough problem. Nobody dared to speak. I moved to an aged gentleman and whispered into his ears requesting him to bring out a question to hear Maharaj Shri. He said to me "You put a question." I was helpless because I had no question. Then Maharaj Shri himself said "I am not in the habit of giving discourses but if any question comes, then adequate answer will be given to it."

Since I was inquisitive to hear him, I apparently thought it my concern to find out some question.

There were a few minutes to 7 p.m. and thinking whatever difficulty I had to face in my business, I should put before Maharaj Shri. With due respect I said, "Maharaj Shri, I am an Artist and a Photographer running a studio, here in Jabalpur. Customers come to my studio, I take their exposures and they deposit some money as advance. I note down their orders and give them dates to collect their works. I complete the works before the due dates but very often I observe that they do not turn up to collect their packets, in time. I cannot ask them to pay in full, in advance. This is my difficulty. How should I overcome it?"

Maharaj Shri paused a while and said, "You know family men, very often, have to face one problem or the other. If they have money and no time, they cannot come. If they are out of station then also they are helpless to collect their works. But as and when they are capable, they would surely come. It is a question of patience."

I said, "Maharaj Shri, there are many accumulated packets in the studio now."

It was 7 p.m. and he asked all the men present to leave. All of us, one by one left, bowing at his lotus feet. I resolved to come daily as it was very pleasant to have his *darshan*.

I marked that all the packets were cleared off within three days and I got good amount. The customers concerned gave the same explanations of their late coming to me, as Maharaj Shri had told me, three days back.

Daily I went to have his *darshan*.

On the fourth day, when I requested the *brahmachari* for permission, he said, "You need no permission now you may go."

I said "I do not want to violate any rule of Maharaj Shri. Please take trouble to go to him and get his permission."

He said "Last evening when I went to take permission for you, Maharaj Shri told me precisely that whenever Varma ji come let him come in. so you can go."

I was astonished, why this relaxation of his rule for Varma ji! I went in and bowed down at his feet and sat down. The *brahmachari* came naming a man, who was dishonest and of loose character, for permission. Maharaj Shri pausing for a while said, "Tell him, there is no *darbar* (meeting) today." The man was not allowed to come in.

Wonderful it was to mark that only the name of a man revealed the full character of the man.

Previously, I had decided not to make Guru in my life because I had been marking that the so-called Gurus make disciple for their monetary gain and couldn't do any good to enlighten the disciples. They themselves were not evolved spiritually nor they had *Vedic* knowledge. A blind cannot lead the blind.

But when I got Maharaj Shri, fortunately I became earnestly desirous to make him my Guru. So on the fifth day of his *darshan*, I requested him reverentially in loneliness, to make me his disciple. He said "To make a Guru, one should test him thoroughly."

I said, "Maharaj Shri, I have no knowledge to test a Guru but this much I know that your revered self is far beyond any test. The very moment I got a message of your arrival in Jabalpur, while I was going to the market on the road, my mind became restless to have your *darshan*, for I have heard that only by the *darshan* of a Yogi Mahatma the beholder is benefitted. Kindly, therefore make me your humble disciple."

Maharaj Shri said, "There shouldn't be hurry in choosing a Guru."

I said, "I am 41 years of age now and think that I am already very late to make a Guru. At what age should a man make a Guru Maharaj Shri?" At this he was silent. Then I asked him, "Should a man make a Guru, in his old age when his senses are weak enough to act to the wishes of Guru Dev?"

Maharaj Shri said, "No, not in old age." Then again I requested him kindly to make me his disciple. Maharaj Shri said, "The Guru also has to see whether a man is worthy of being a disciple."

I said, "When a name is enough to read the character of a man, I am here in person. Maharaj Shri, your revered self needs no time to know about me."

Maharaj Shri then said, "You are getting late to get home, so you may go now."

I said, "Maharaj Shri, kindly excuse me for taking so much of your valuable time." I bowed down and left saying that "My humble request is still at your lotus feet."

I was happy to have his *darshan* daily. After the meeting was over, every day, I talked to him with reverence about my request. He talked of this and that but there was no approval of my request so far.

In this way, 12 days passed in suspense. The twelfth day when I returned home and lay down to sleep, my mind was uneasy and I could not think what to do. Maharaj Shri had not given his consent to take me as his disciple even to that day. Instantly, it struck my mind. "Take a vow now to request Maharaj Shri to free me from this painful state of suspense by saying yes or no regarding my request. I took a vow.

Next day, after the meeting was over, I requested him, "Kindly free me from this painful suspense today. If I am considered worthy of being a disciple, kindly say "Yes" otherwise "No". If approved I shall feel very fortunate and happy and will be in the service of Shri Guru Dev for the whole of my life. If not, even then, I have already made Maharaj Shri my Guru Dev. Eklavya had done so when Guru Dronacharya refused to enrole him as his disciple. So please be kind to pass your worthy decision today, because I do not want any suspense of mind now. It is intolerable to me."

Hearing of my vow, Maharaj Shri laughed and said, "Why only today and not tomorrow?"

I said, "Maharaj Shri it matters little after tonight tomorrow comes and your will is supreme."

So next day, September 13, 1940 was fixed for my test, and I was asked to come at 9 a.m. I bowed down at his lotus feet and left.

Next morning, I got up early, gathered flowers, made a good garland, took my bath and got ready to start. I reached the *ashram* at 8.45 a.m. The *brahmachari* opened the door for me and asked me to sit down and went to inform Maharaj Shri. A few minutes later, I was asked to go to the room where Maharaj Shri was sitting. He allowed me to come in. I offered the garland and bowed down. He asked me to sit in front of him. He knew well about me, in fact, but for the sake of test he put a few ordinary questions which I replied. In the questions there was one particular and that was concerning diet. I said, "Maharaj Shri, I am from *Kayastha* Community, where non-vegetarian food and drink are allowed but I myself and my small family have no taste for that sort of diet and drink. We are happy to have vegetarian diet. If some times, such occasions come in the society where non-vegetarian diet is arranged I escape from that place any way by the grace of the Almighty."

Maharaj Shri said, "Non-vegetarian food and drink are a great obstacle in spiritual development. Therefore, it should never be thought of in life." He particularly warned me against it. I said, "That will be done by all means." Further he said, "When you come this way, be an ideal."

I said, "Maharaj Shri, I do not know what an ideal is but I with complete devotion assure your revered self that even a small hint would be strictly followed most dutifully by me and eventually, I hope to be an ideal of your wish."

Maharaj Shri then approved me to be his disciple and very kindly said to me, "Come this time tomorrow, (i.e. on September 14, 1940), with some *puja samagri* for initiation."

I bowed down at his lotus feet with great joy and took leave to go.

Next morning, *puja samagri* (things required for worship) such as camphor, incense sticks, sandal wood paste, rice, sacred thread, flowers, garland, coconut and some fruits etc., were gathered. I took bath and got ready to start. I reached the *ashram* at the fixed time. The *brahmachari* opened the door, allowed me to come in and asked me to sit for a couple of minutes.

I was called in the room where Maharaj Shri was sitting after *samadhi* (deep meditation). Devotedly I performed the *puja* of Maharaj Shri and he gave me a suitable *mantra* to repeat daily in a particular way. I was very grateful to him and bowed down at the lotus feet of Shri Guru Dev. Thus I got Maharaj Shri, the most illustrious *Siddha Yogi*, as my Guru Dev.

Two days after my initiation I requested Shri Guru Dev for permission to take his photograph. He said, "To take a photo of me is of no use. You must have seen pictures of deities in the rubbish. People do not take care of them."

I said, "Maharaj Shri I wish to keep one copy of your photo in the *puja* room for myself and nobody would get a copy without your permission."

He said, "You may take one later."

Next day, I loaded two cabinet size plates in the dark and took the camera to the *ashram* and told the *brahmachari*, "Look here, here is a camera loaded with two plates to take exposures of Maharaj Shri and unless they are exposed the camera would remain here." Saying so I came back home.

The *brahmachari* informed Maharaj Shri accordingly.

In the evening when I went to have *darshan*, Shri Guru Dev asked me, "Have you left your camera here?"

I said "Yes Maharaj Shri it will remain here till the plates, especially reserved for taking Shri Guru Dev's photo, are exposed."

Shri Guru Dev kindly said, "Then expose the plates tomorrow morning at 8 hours and take back the camera to do your business."

I bowed down and the next morning his photo was taken. In this way I got his photograph.

Shri Guru Dev stayed in Jabalpur for two months during the rainy season and by the middle of October, he left for Varanasi (Kashi or Benaras), City of Lord Shankar, Vishwanath. Benaras is an ancient seat of learning situated on the bank of the Holy Ganges.

In Varanasi, Maharaj Shri got an *ashram* built in Siddhagiri Bagh, Chhotigaivi. Moreover, a Sanskrit College was established in the memory of his Sad Guru Dev, where students receive free education up to Acharya. The *ashram* is a three storied building, where fifty families can be accomodated. These two buildings are under the management of Shri Krishnanand Saraswati Trust.

During the stay of Shri Guru Dev, we enjoyed very happy days in Jabalpur.']

'Procession of Ascetics at the great Hindu Fair at Allahabad'
[*'Religions and Hidden Cults of India'*, Sir G MacMunn, Sampson Low, 1931]

In 1930, on the occasion of a Kumbha Mela at Prayag (Allahabad) prior arrangements were made for Maharaj Shri to stay at Daraganj. A resident of Prayag at Gangaganj also had a place in Daraganj with about ten empty rooms. He was awaiting the arrival of Maharaj Shri, however, *mahatmas* are free-thinking and Maharaj Shri decided not to go to the Allahabad Kumbha Mela, where everyone else was going. Instead he decided to go ten or twelve miles to the west and stay on the shore of the Ganga at Kauraveshvar Mahadeva Mandir (temple) wherein was a small cell to rest in. However, as he also thought that this left an immense place to stay in the area of Prayag for any devotee then he wished that this should be used so that this service of devotion did not become useless. Therefore, he gave it to some of his *dandi sannyasi* disciples for them to stay for the entire *mela*. When it became known to the devotee that Maharaj Shri would not come to Prayag then he had been upset; but when he understood that Maharaj Shri had arranged for *dandi sannyasi* spiritual disciples to come and stay, he had been satisfied.

Then again in accordance with *"shreyaansi bahu vighnaani bhavanti mahataamapi"* ('hurdles appear for noble endeavours') an obstacle came!

A business associate of his, a wealthy resident of Calcutta, a beloved friend of the devotee made it clear that he wished for him to let him have the Daraganja house for the whole *mela* because his family wished to come to the *mela* in Prayag. Though the devotee knew that the house was not vacant he thought that as Maharaj Shri is not staying in the house, that it could be emptied so he did not put off the Seth Ji (respected merchant).

He entreated Maharaj Shri, 'You are not stopping in the house. So, provided that it is understood to be reasonable, after I ask the *sannyasi mahatmas* to vacate the house I will give it over for use of the family of Seth Ji who is a close friend.'

Kumbha Mela, Allahabad
[*'Religions and Hidden Cults of India'*, Sir G MacMunn, Sampson Low, 1931]

Maharaj Shri was extremely good at discerning the propriety of anything. The house was to be vacated by the *mahatma sadhu sannyasi* for the family of the Seth Ji. But this cannot be done because it will amount to disrespect of these *mahatmas*. This caused him to reply that, 'Now, it is agreed for those *dandi sannyasi* to go and stay in that house. So, if I agree for the house to be emptied for the children of the Seth Ji then it will be a big disrespect to the *sannyasi*. Therefore, the house cannot be emptied, for the whole *mela*. Make some other arrangement for them.'

The devotee figured that as the people who were stopping are just *sadhu mahatma* that, by applying a bit of pressure, the house could be emptied. This intention occurred to Maharaj Shri who sensed this intention and gave very firm instructions that the house of Tiwari Ji should not be vacated. It happened just like this and Tiwari Ji became quietly disappointed but the house was not vacated the entire *mela*. Maharaj Shri never stopped in that house again and it remained empty.

*

At this time Maharaj Shri happened to dwell in Kauraveshwar your principal devotee, Kuberdatt Ojha, heard that Maharaj Shri had come to Kauraveshwar so he went to that very place and obtained darshan. Every day he would go to work at his office in Prayag and at four o'clock in the evening he arrived by bicycle at Kauraveshwar for the service of Maharaj Shri. Kuberdatt actually lived in Daryaganj and when he came to know that Maharaj Shri's *guru deva* had arrived at Ganga Bhavan in Daraganj he went there to prostrate and do *pranaam*. In the evening, when he arrived at Kauraveshwar to take *darshan* of Maharaj Shri he informed him of the news of Guruji's arrival in Prayag. He took both Guruji's and Maharaj Shri's *darshan* regularly and conveyed messages from one to the other.

One day Guruji asked Kuberdatt, 'Won't Swami Ji come here on at the time of the Kumbha?'

This conversation reached Maharaj Shri via Kuberdatt. Maharaj Shri said, 'We are not thinking of going to the *mela*.'

When it became clear to Guruji that Maharaj Shri is not going to come Prayag then he said, 'Why? Is the *mela* a lion? Okay, some day we will go to meet him.'

Kuberdatt went and informed Maharaj Shri of these words of Guruji.

A thought occurred to Maharaj Shri and he said, 'That would be unfortunate, it will not happen that Guruji will come anywhere for me. Go, go right now! Come here early in the morning at four o'clock bringing a "motor". We desire that early morning tomorrow, really before sunrise, that we go and arrive in Prayag for *darshan* of Guru Ji.'

So it happened. The next day, Kuberdatt brought the motor, arriving in the early morning before four o'clock and so that they arrived at Maharaj Shri's *guru ji* about six-thirty. Maharaj Shri wanted to do *pranaam* by the proper code of conduct, by the lifting of the *danda* (staff). But Guru ji did not give him *pranaam* but having taken the *danda* from the hand he brought him flat with the chest (he hugged him) and sat him on a seat nearby.

He said, 'Maharaj, it is *maryaada* (proper code of conduct), please accept my doing *pranaam*.'

Guru Ji said, 'Go sit, the *maryaada* here is really our will.'

At that time many dozens gathered about Guru Ji. Having seen this behaviour all were astonished, that Guru Ji gives so much respect to Swami Ji.

One of them said, 'Why not? Having seen that he has arrived in his own position Guru Ji will also be acting accordingly. Then it is not improper. But look then at how impatient he is for bowing to Guru Ji. He is fostering an excellent standard of decorum.'

At this time Guru Ji commanded; 'You have stayed a long time in the jungles and mountains. Stay near the towns now, so that some of the people can benefit.'

After this, he too lived near to towns. *Guru Ji respected you and honoured you so much that sometimes he was given to say,* 'He then is much more fit than us, and is learned and is peerless in giving answers and in removing doubts.'

*

One time Maharaj Shri was spending the time of *chaaturmaasya vrat* (the 'four-month fast' of rainy season) near Shivakoti Mahadev (a temple at Prayag). A man wearing the clothes of a *sadhu* had come in that place and taken to abusing the name of Maharaj Shri. When the abusive person, the gossiping *sadhu*, would not stop his chatter then the inhabitants of the ashram were ready to beat him and drive him out. Then Maharaj Shri quickly called all of them near. 'By little conversations you have learned all about *yoga samadhi*, but the chapter on enduring insults has not been read. It is by the grace of Ishwar (God) that today this opportunity has become ready. You should practice the quality of endurance.'

One *brahmachari* spoke, 'Excuse me, the order of the first Manu was to expressly prevent hearing *ninda* (scorn) of the *guru*.'

Maharaj said, 'This is correct. But consider what is the loss or the gain? If by *ninda* (scorn, slander) damage is done in the world, then remember this, that prosperity, misfortune and all earthly activities are subject to destiny, fruitful or fruitless. Slanders cannot touch destiny. That which is dependant on previous destiny, the very same will be and *ninda* cannot make any little difference to you. Here is the doctrine of the *Shastra*, that a person who slanders accepts a share of the sin of *mahatmas*. Therefore, they are really assisting in one's advancement to the next world. In the spiritual community slanderers are put on a par with excellent devotees, because faithful devotees then, by means of worship *aarati* (ceremony), service and attendance, by way of grace, share the accumulated ultramundane energy of the *mahatmas*. But the people who censor do not want anything for themselves, but in doing this scorn they share their sin. Therefore the very same are excellent devotees and they are really a means of advantage. You shouldn't make any effort to stop the passage of *ninda* (scorn) but you should do your own work and allow them to do their work.' In this way, having understood him, the community of devotees were brought under restraint.

Here that rogue, dressed as a *sadhu,* having chattered his abuses for up to an hour went and sat beneath a nearby tree to rest. Then Shri Charan (blessed feet) called to him, 'You have spent a long time addressing these insults, you must have become weary. Please take some refreshment.'

The attendants of the ashram went to satisfy him with sweetmeats etc. and when it was time for him to go, at Maharaj Shri's order he was given two *rupees* for a carriage.

Later it transpired after he chatted with his associates, that he had gained a very good impression of the *mahatma* and that he very much regretted babbling the abuse. The next day, having come in front of the ashram, he declared, 'Swami Ji *ki jaya ho* (Victory be to Swami Ji). Swami Ji, please excuse me. A big offence has been by us,' etc etc., and for a long time he talked words of atonement and implored forgiveness.

So many examples of such happenings have come to light. We get instruction from them and Shri Charan's excellent example, getting a glimpse of a life of perfect surrender and a life abounding in austerity. *Therefore, some mention of brief occurences in your life are being made so that readers generally can get to know your holy biography.*

*

At one time Maharaj Shri was staying at the *kothi* (mansion) of Raja Dhingwas in Prayag. Very near there lived a *vakeel sahab* (lawyer) who was a devotee of his and when he heard that Maharaj Shri sat all night remaining in worship he wished to observe Maharaj Shri doing this. He prayed that he might see this scene and consequently he entreated, 'Maharaj Ji I heard that you sit in *asana* all night. I would like to see.'

Maharaj Shri laughingly said, 'Can you do an all night vigil?'

He answered, 'Certainly I will attempt to.'

Maharaj Shri said, 'Then do no interrupt me, don't utter a word in spite of the meditating,'

The *vakeel sahab* sat, and he completed the all-night sitting. When in a short while this news spread here and there, some became mean-hearted, envious and an enemy too, and they conspired amongst themselves.

Having given a prostitute a drug to lower her awareness, they made ready for her to go near to Maharaj Ji in the night. She was to attempt shaking his fixed position (of celibacy). Prostitutes are very greedy. She arrived there at 10 or 11 o'clock at night dressed in the clothes of a man along with the people who had devised the plot, and they flowed in to go for *darshan*, and to have *satsang*. After *satsang* all the people then left and went downstairs, but the *veshyaa* (prostitute) stayed seated there. Because she feared the energy of Maharaj Ji she did not speak but nevertheless she sat there for some time. Downstairs all the people who had been plotting this conspiracy were waiting below wondering what would happen. Upstairs, the *veshya* was suffering such great stomach pain that she screamed out loud and ran away.

Below, the people who were standing waiting became frightened. They asked, 'What happened?' and they all listened as she told them the news of her suffering. Then, having heard her story all the people were very sorrowful and remorseful. They expressed regret that they had given distress to Maharaj Ji.

When this news became public then extreme reverence flowed towards Maharaj Shri from all sides.

*

Maharaj Shri ordered that *sudras* - the fourth *varna* or caste of Hindus - and even women should not come for *darshan*, *pranaam* or *satsang* to his dwelling place in the ashram. If any *sudra* or woman wanted to do *pranaam* or have *darshan,* then when he was going outside for *yatra* (travelling, pilgrimage) or returning after staying somewhere outside, they could do *pranaam* at the gate.

The talk is that whilst you were staying in Prayag at a house on the shore of the Ganga, a widow woman requested darshan of Maharaj Shri. The woman was of the family of Mahaman Madan Mohan Malaviya [a prominent freedom fighter who is best remembered for establishing Banaras Hindu University]. The answer he gave was just the same as normal, that *sudra* and women classes cannot have *darshan satsang* at the place he stays. She was a learned woman and she also kept good company. She wrote a letter to Maharaj Shri that, 'Your birth has really been from one of our sisters. Why are you so disgusted by the gender of woman from whom you were born?' The letter was sent to Maharaj Shri via a servant and she said that she wanted him to come back with an answer to this.

Maharaj Shri gave it some indifference and told the servant that 'She will get this answer afterwards. Certainly not at this time.'

Again next day she insisted on a reply and impatiently issued forth, 'I certainly want to get this answer today.'

Having heard all she had to say, Maharaj Shri said, 'I am inclined to put an end to this question, I should give a special answer too.' He wrote of this controversy, 'I stayed in contact with you people for nine months. What was my condition at that time? I was hung upside down, I was fastened tight, the pain was without limit. I passed nine months in this utensil of faeces and urine. To this day those days are not forgotten. This is really the reason that I have no desire for the company of you people.' On this point he wrote further, 'The potter makes a pot. He gives birth to it. On completing that pot it then reaches the *yagya mandala* (the area of the *yagya*). But the one who made it, the potter, he remains standing outside the *yagya mandap* (the canopy of the *yagya*), he is not allowed in the *yagya mandala*.'

That letter reached the possession of the widow. Having read the letter her reverence for him increased and she watched for such an opportunity, looking to discover when Maharaj Shri went for a bath in the Ganga or when he went elsewhere. She got to realise that tomorrow he would go by boat to bathe at the *sangam*. She went to bathe at the same time and at the time of bathing in

Ganga she had *darshan* and did *pranaam* and became immersed
in bliss. She said, 'Here then, really all have the right to *darshan*.'

A prominent merchant of Calcutta, who was going through a
lawsuit in the high court, came to Prayag, Maharaj Shri was at that
time staying at Daraganja (in Prayag). Sometimes when the *seth ji*
(great merchant) was going to bathe in Ganga then he also had
darshan of Maharaj Shri. The *darshan* of Maharaj shri was
strangely attractive. He who had once taken *darshan*, would then
go again and again. After going once he came to be attached to
going again and again. It was agreed on by well thought of people
that he was the very highest *mahatma*. From his *darshan* and
ashirwaad (blessing) really every action became fruitful. Seth Ji
gave Maharaj Shri to know the news of his lawsuit and prayed for
favour in getting a successful lawsuit. On that occasion Maharaj
Shri did not give any answer then; but that petitioner certainly
received a wordless *ashirvaad* (blessing) for some days later Seth
Ji obtained success in the lawsuit. Then Seth Ji became very
happy and when he went to take *darshan* of Maharaj Shri, he took
a *dona* (leaf bowl) full of *asharphi* (gold coins, sovereigns), which

he covered with jasmine flowers and put it near the feet of Maharaj Shri, then he bowed and sat. He stayed for *satsang* and when night came he went home. Maharaj Shri also got up and went to his room to rest.

In the early morning, when Maharaj Shri's *brahmachari* assistant came to clean, at the place where Seth Ji had been sitting, he went to remove the *dona* and the flowers. But even with effort he could not sweep the flowers away and it became clear to him why. When he discovered the *dona* beneath the flowers he realised that whoever had placed them there had also left a *dona* of *asharphi* (gold coins). So he took them and placed them near Maharaj Shri. When Maharaj Shri realised Seth Ji had been the person who brought them, he gave orders, 'If Seth Ji comes for *darshan* this evening, then bar the gate and do not let him come up for our *darshan*.'

In this manner, that day, when Seth Ji came for *darshan,* then the *brahmachari ji* barred the entrance. Seth Ji was sitting two, two-and-a-half hours before the order was given to call Seth Ji. After Seth Ji did *pranaam,* Maharaj Shri said, 'Why did you cause these *asharphi* to be put here? Those who desire them, those who demand them from you, then to him you do not give. Why have you put them near us? Do I have to arrange a marriage for any son or daughter?...... Go! Go take these, give to those people who are wishing for these so eagerly.' Having spoken thus he returned the *arshaphi* and said, 'Our wealth is not here. Offer your defects. From that comes your welfare. Here wealth is not necessary.'

७

सातवाँ अध्याय
ज्योतिष्पीठोद्धारक आचार्य का अभिषेक

इस समय भारत-धर्म-महामंडल के बड़े-बड़े अधिवेशनों में जगद्गुरु भगवान् आदि शंकराचार्य द्वारा स्थापित उत्तर भारत के धर्मपीठ श्री ज्योतिर्मठ के पुनरुद्धार की चर्चा चलने लगी थी। सन् १९०८ ई० में कई नरेशों के अनुरोध हुये, जिन्होंने इस विषय के प्रस्ताव का पूर्ण रूप से समर्थन किया। फलतः विशिष्ट विद्वानों ने निश्चय किया कि ज्योतिर्मठ का पुनरुद्धार यथाशीघ्र होना चाहिये। प्रश्न उपस्थित हुआ कि ज्योतिर्मठ के पुनरुद्धार करने में समर्थ एवं पर्याप्त योग्यता सम्पन्न जगद्गुरु शंकराचार्य कौन हो? भारत-धर्म-महामंडल के विशिष्ट कार्यकर्तागण तथा उत्तर भारत के प्रसिद्ध विद्वान् शंकराचार्य पद के योग्य महात्मा की खोज में लग गये। इस पद के लिये वही व्यक्ति सबकी दृष्टि में उचित हो सकता था जिसने विशुद्ध एवं प्रतिष्ठत ब्राह्मण वंश में जन्म पाया हो तथा श्री जगद्गुरु शंकराचार्य के स्थापित चार मठों में से किसी मठ की शिष्य-परम्परा से सम्बन्धित हो। विधिवत् संन्यास दीक्षा प्राप्त दण्डी-स्वामी हो, विद्वान्, चरित्रवान्, विवेकशील तथा ज्ञानवृद्ध हो, वेदादि शास्त्र-प्रमाण को सर्वोपरि मान्यता देता हो, वर्णाश्रम मर्यादा की सदैव रक्षा करनेवाला हो, अद्वैत-सिद्धान्त का पोषक एवं अध्यात्म-विद्या का 'उत्तम प्रचारक हो, इष्ट पर निष्ठा रखनेवाला हो तथा योग आदि की सिद्धियों से सम्पन्न हो। ऐसे गुण-सम्पन्न महात्मा की खोज थी क्योंकि अधिक काल से उच्छिन्न धर्मपीठ का उद्धार करके जनता में धर्माचार्य पीठ को प्रतिष्ठत कर समाज को धर्मोन्मुख बनाना एक

महान् कार्य था, जो किसी विशिष्ट दैवीशक्ति-सम्पन्न व्यक्ति के द्वारा ही पूर्ण किया जा सकता था।

सौभाग्य से विद्वानों की दृष्टि उपर्युक्त गुण-सम्पन्न केवल आप पर ही पड़ी। किंतु आपके परम त्याग वैराग्यमय तेजपूर्ण निस्पृहता और एकान्तिक जीवन को देखकर किसी का साहस नहीं होता था कि जाकर पीठोद्धार का प्रस्ताव करें। जिसका सिद्धांत हो कि "जन सम्पर्क को सर्प के समान सदैव त्यागना चाहिये" जिसके ऐसे उद्गार हों कि "कोई शुकदेव के समान त्यागी हो, वृहस्पति के समान विद्वान् हो, और कुबेर के समान धनवान् हो तो भी हमें उसकी कोई आवश्यकता नहीं", तो इतने असंग व्यक्ति से पीठ-संचालन का प्रस्ताव करना कहाँ तक उचित अथवा न्यायसंगत हो सकता है? पाठक स्वयं अनुमान लगा सकते हैं। किन्तु धर्मपीठ का उद्धार होना था। महाराज श्री भी इधर नगरों में कभी-कभी आने लगे थे और चातुर्मास्य-व्रत करने लगे थे। धीरे-धीरे प्रभावशाली धार्मिक पुरुषों द्वारा पीठोद्धार का प्रस्ताव भी होने लगा। सब लोगों के प्रयत्न करते-करते, बुद्धिमानी से कहते-कहते महाराज श्री के अंतःकरण में पीठोद्धार के लिये कुछ स्थान बन ही गया। किन्तु फिर भी समय आने पर आपका विरक्त अन्तःकरण एक बार फिर चौंक उठा और अपने पूर्वरूप पर आ गया।

अभिषेक की पूर्ण तैयारी हो गयी थी। समय निश्चित् हो चुका था और इसीलिये काशी में सनातन-धर्म-सम्मेलन के नवम महाधिवेशन की पूरी-पूरी तैयारी कर ली गई थी। किन्तु अभिषेक की तिथि आने के दो दिन पहिले महाराज श्री जिनका अभिषेक होना था अंतध्यान हो गये और किसी अज्ञात स्थान को चले गये। यह सोचकर कि आपकी अनुपस्थिति में किसी दूसरे महात्मा का अभिषेक हो जायगा

और उसके अनन्तर फिर प्रकट हो जायँगे। महाराज श्री आश्रम से
न जाने कहाँ चले गये। वे कब गये और कैसे गये – यह कोई नहीं
जानता। वाता-वरण गम्भीर हो उठा, क्योंकि परसों ही अभिषेक होने
को है। वह दिन बहुत अधिक प्रयत्न व परिश्रम के बाद आया था।
इस घटना से धार्मिक जनता में क्षोभ व्याप्त हो गया। कार्यकर्ताओं के
मन में नाना प्रकार के तर्क-वितर्क उठने लगे। कुछ दूसरे दण्डी-
महात्माओं के लिये भी अन्तरंग रूप से प्रस्ताव उठने लगे। किन्तु
भारत-धर्म-महामण्डल के वयोवृद्ध महात्मा श्री स्वामी ज्ञानानंद जी
महाराज ने विद्वानों को धैर्य से कार्य करने का परामर्श दिया और
कहा कि "धर्म पीठोद्धार का यह महान् कार्य है; इस प्रकार के
निस्पृह, त्यागी और सुयोग्य महात्मा ही यह भार सम्भाल सकेंगे।
अन्य किसी का अभिषेक कर भी दिया जाय, तो उसमें उतनी
योग्यता न होने से पीठ की देवी-शक्ति का विकास नहीं हो सकेगा।
एक सौ पैंसठ वर्षों से सुप्त पीठ की शक्ति को जाग्रत करना है वह
सत्पात्र में ही विकास को प्राप्त होगी। इस सम्बन्ध में शीघ्रता करना
लोक-कल्याण की दृष्टि से उचित नहीं प्रतीत होगा। "सर्वत्र तार पत्र
आदि भेजकर अधिवेशन अनिश्चित समय के लिये स्थगित कर दिया
गया और महाराज श्री की खोज होने लगी। किसी को कहीं पता
नहीं लगा। किन्तु भावी बलवान होती है। महाराज श्री जहाँ थे, वहीं
उनके मन में यह भाव उठने लगा कि "अखिल भारतीय सम्मेलन
होना निश्चित् था, दूर–दूर के लोग आनेवाले थे, सब आ गये होंगे
और किसी न किसी को पीठ पर बैठा ही दिया गया होगा।" इस
प्रकार सोच-विचार कर निश्चित होकर लगभग २१ दिन पश्चात्
विचरते हुये रात्रि में काशी पहुँचे। काशी के विद्वान् सतर्क और
उत्सुक थे ही। तुरन्त कानोकान खबर फैल गई कि महाराज श्री आ
गये। एक घण्टा के अन्दर ही ११ बजे रात्रि में विशिष्ट विद्वानों का

दल आश्रम में पहुँचा। करबद्ध होकर सब ने प्रार्थना की, "भगवन्,
हम सब लोगों के परम श्रद्धेय प्रातः स्मरणीय भगवान् आदि
शंकराचार्य द्वारा स्थापित उत्तर भारत का धर्मपीठ ज्योतिर्मठ बहुत
समय से उच्छिन्न एवं आचार्यहीन है। हम लोग धर्मगुरु के बिना
अनाथ से हो रहे हैं। इसका पुनरुद्धार आपके द्वारा ही हो सकता है।
साधारण व्यक्ति से इस गुरुतम कार्य का होना असम्भव है। आप
जन्म और कर्म, त्याग और तप के द्वारा बाल्यावस्था से ही विशिष्ट
साधुसमाज में एवं समस्त राजा तथा प्रजा में शंकराचार्यवत् ही
सम्मानित हैं। आदि गुरु शंकराचार्य के प्रति आप की श्रद्धा भी है
ही, क्योंकि आप उसी आचार्य-पम्परा के दण्डी-स्वामी हैं। इसलिये
अब हमारी प्रार्थना अवश्य स्वीकार हो।" पंडितों की इस प्रार्थना पर
श्रीचरण मौन रह गये। "मौनं सम्मति लक्षणम्" मानकर यथाशीघ्र
अखिल-भारतीय-सनातन धर्म-महा-सम्मेलन अधिवेशन का
आयोजन हुआ। अभिषेक की पूर्ण तैयारियाँ तो पहिले से थीं ही;
"शुभस्य शीघ्रम्" सब को इष्ट था।

श्री भारत-धर्म-महामण्डल के यज्ञमण्डप में सहस्र चण्डी महायज्ञ
हो रहा था। कुछ मनीषियों की सम्मति हुई कि भगवती की अराधना
के बीच महायज्ञ मण्डप में आचार्य का अभिषेक किया जाय। किंतु
सुयोग्य विद्वानों ने कहा, "उनका तो हमलोग एक प्रकार से बलात्
अभिषेक कर रहे हैं। उन्हें यह पद स्वीकार करने की तनिक भी
इच्छा नहीं है। अभिषेक कराने के लिये वे कहीं जायँगे, ऐसी आशा
नहीं है। यदि वे इसके लिये लालायित होते तब तो जहाँ हम लोग
चाहते, चले आते। किन्तु अभिषेक के नाम से एक बार भाग ही
चुके हैं, यह सब को विदित ही है। इसलिये अभिषेक के विधान की
पूर्ति तो जहाँ वे हैं, वहीं चलकर कर देनी चाहिये। फिर अभिषेक के

बाद उन्हें आचार्योचित गौरव के साथ सार्वजनिक सभा में (अखिल-
भारतीय-सनातन-धर्म-सम्मेलन के पण्डाल में) आदर पूर्वक लाया
जाय और वहीं आचार्यत्वेन पूजन किया जाय और पीठोद्धार की
घोषणा की जाय "दूर-दर्शी विद्वानों के इस विचार को सबने स्वीकार
किया और तदनुसार कार्यक्रम बना।

अखिल-भारतीय-सनातन-धर्म-सम्मेलन में आये हुये विभिन्न
प्रान्तों के विद्वान् तथा विभिन्न धार्मिक संस्थाओं के गण्यमान्य
प्रतिनिधिजन काशी-निवासी विद्वन्मण्डली के सहित अभिषेकोपयोगी
समस्त सामग्री लिये हुये प्रातःकाल ही श्री चरण के आश्रम
"ब्रह्मनिवास, सिद्धिगिरिबाग" में आ गये। स्मरण रहे कि शंकराचार्य
के पद पर आसीन होने के पहिले ही सन् १९३६ ई० में महाराज श्री ने
अपने पूज्य श्री गुरुदेव की पुण्य स्मृति में "श्री ब्रह्मविद्या-निकेतन"
तथा "श्री ब्रह्मानन्देश्वर महादेव जी" का मंदिर छोटी गैबी, वाराणसी
में निर्मित करवाया था। इस आश्रम और मन्दिर आदि के सुचारु
रूप से संचालन के निमित्त "श्री ब्रह्म निवास" के नाम से एक बड़ा
आश्रम "सिद्धि गिरि बाग," वाराणसी में बनवाया था और
बहादुरगंज, प्रयाग के दो अन्य भवन भी इससे संबद्ध कर दिये गए थे
और इस सम्पत्ति की रक्षा व देखरेख के लिये आपने एक ट्रस्ट "श्री
१००८ स्वामी कृष्णानन्द सरस्वती ट्रस्ट" भी स्थापित किया था,
जिसका उल्लेख महाराज श्री ने अपनी अन्तिम वसीयत में किया है।

भारत-धर्म-महामण्डल के संस्थापक वयोवृद्ध पूज्य स्वामी
ज्ञानानन्द जी महाराज भी अपने चिर-अभिलषित पीठोद्धार कार्य को
अपने समक्ष सुसम्पन्न कराने की इच्छा से सिद्धिगिरिबाग में पधारे।
उत्तराम्नाय धर्म पीठोद्धार के महा संकल्प से श्रीचरण का षोडशोपचार
पूजा होकर लगभग १० बजे अभिषेक-कृत्य पूर्ण हुआ। अपराह्न में

महाराज श्री की सवारी बड़े समारोह के साथ ठीक समय पर अधिवेशन के पाण्डाल में लाई। जगद्गुरु भगवान् शंकराचार्य की गम्भीर जयध्वनि से दशों दिशायें गूँज उठीं। वैदिक विद्वानों के चारों वेदों की मन्त्रध्वनि से गगनमण्डल प्रतिध्वनित हो उठा। काशी के विशिष्ट वैदिक कर्मकांडी विद्वानों द्वारा अभिषेचन कृत्य सम्पादित होते ही, महाराजाधिराज श्री दरभंगा नरेश ने उत्तर भारत के धर्माचार्य श्री ज्योतिष्पीठाधीश्वर जगद्गुरु भगवान् शंकराचार्य के महाभिषेचन एवं धर्मपीठाधिरोहण की घोषणा की। भगवान् शंकराचार्य की बारम्बार जयध्वनि करती हुई सम्पूर्ण जनता ने श्री जगद्गुरु शंकराचार्य महाराज का अभिवादन किया। इस प्रकार १६५ वर्षों से रिक्त उत्तराम्नाय के धर्म सिंहासन पर चैत्र शुक्ल ४, विक्रम सम्वत् १९९८, तदनुसार १ अप्रैल १९४१ ई० को महाराज श्री का अति सुयोग्य धर्माचार्य भगवत्पूज्यपाद अनन्त श्री विभुषित जगद्गुरु भगवान् शंकराचार्य जी महाराज का पदार्पण हुआ।

देश-विदेश में सर्वत्र पत्र-पत्रिकाओं द्वारा ज्योतिष्पीठोद्धार का समाचार फैल गया। चारों ओर सनातन धर्म-संस्थाओं ने पीठोद्धार के उपलक्ष में उत्सव मनाये और आचार्य-चरणों में अभिनन्दन आदि भेजते हुये अपने कर्तव्यपालन तथा आचार्याज्ञापालन का वचन दिया। उत्तर भारत में स्वभावतः धर्मिक जाग्रति की अपूर्व लहर दिखाई पड़ने लगी और चारों ओर से आचार्य-चरण का आह्वान होने लगा।

इस समय, आचार्य श्री के सम्मुख पीठोद्धार के नाते मुख्य दो कार्य थे :-

(१) पीठस्थान में मठ, मन्दिर का नव निर्माण करना,

(२) उत्तर भारत में धर्म-प्रचार करके जनता को वैदिक पथ पर लाते हुये पीठ की मर्यादा व आदर्शपूर्ण गौरव को पुनः स्थापित करना ।

इन दोनो कारों को आपको एक साथ प्रारम्भ करना था । काशी के विद्वन्मण्डल के कुछ लोगों ने महाराज श्री से प्रार्थना की कि पीठोद्धार होने के लिये समस्त कार्य सुचारु रूप से करने हैं और उसके लिये द्रव्य की नितान्त आवश्यकता है । अतएव बम्बई, कलकत्ता आदि सम्पन्न नगरों में धर्म-प्रचार के लिए कुछ ऐसे कार्यक्रम बनाये जायँ, जिससे धार्मिक जाग्रति हो और पीठोद्धार के लिये द्रव्य भी संचय हो । महाराज श्री ने उन विद्वानों को इस प्रकार उत्तर दिया –

"धर्म-सिंहासन पर अब तो आप लोगों ने हमें बैठा ही दिया है और तत्सम्बन्धी सभी कार्यभार भी सौंप दिया है । इसलिये अब आप लोग निश्चिन्त बैठें । ज्योतिष्पीठोद्धार का उत्तर-दायित्व अब हमारे ऊपर है और वह हो जायगा ।"

उसके बाद सर्व प्रथम आपने दक्षिण की यात्रा की । दो-चार दिन कटनी में रहकर जबलपुर पधारे । बलदेव बाग में आपने निवास किया । श्रद्धालु भक्तों का ताँता लग गया । अधिकाधिक लोग सम्पर्क में आने लगे । अपार जन-समूह दर्शन के लिये दौड़ पड़ा । नित्य प्रति उपदेश होने लगे । इस समय मध्य प्रदेश प्रान्त, जिला खंडवा, बुढ़ानपुर में महारुद्र याग हुआ । आपका आवाहन हुआ । वहाँ गये । उस प्रान्त में यह एक ऐतिहासिक अनुष्ठान एवं धार्मिक समारोह था । लाखों की संख्या में जनता एकत्र हुई । बहुत बड़ा आयोजन हुआ । महाराज श्री ने इस समारोह की अध्यक्षता की । दर्शनार्थी इतनी अधिक संख्या में एकत्र हुये कि आपका दर्शन लोगों को दुर्लभ होने

लगा। दर्शन सुलभ बनाने के लिये तीन तख्त एक दूसरे के ऊपर रखे गए। उस पर आपका आसन लगाया गया। इस मच पर से आपके सदुपदेश हुये और जनता कृत-कृत्य हुई।

Chapter 7

Installing an Acharya to Restore Jyotish Peeth

At this time at a very big meeting of Bharat Dharma Mahamandal (All-India Dharma Organisation), there was a discussion that the Dharma Peeth situated in Northern India at Jyotirmath by Jagadguru Bhagwan Aadi Shankaracharya, be restored again. Many years before, in 1908, several Indian kings had advocated a full preliminary discussion of this subject. In consequence, prominent scholars believed that Jyotirmath should be quickly renovated in whatever way possible. The question at hand was; who is capable and eligible enough to be an accomplished Jagadguru Shankaracharya and to revive Jyotir Math? A specific group of officials from the Bharat Dharma Mahamandal went in search of a suitably celebrated scholar of Northern India with the qualities of Shankaracharya. He should have these qualities; (i) that in everyone's opinion he is suitable, (ii) that he is pure, respected, born in the Brahman lineage and (iii) is a disciple of the *parampara* (lineage) of the four maths (monasteries) instituted by Shri Jagadguru Shankaracharya.

Therefore, in accordance with law, having gained *sannyas diksha* (initiation as a *sannyasi*) and be a *dandi swami*, he should be learned, of good moral character and conduct. He should also have the virtue of reasoning, and be knowledgeable, and above all to give respect to the *Shastras*, *Vedas* etc, always protecting the decorum of *varna ashram* (caste and stage system). He should support the theory of advaita (non-dualism) and be the greatest herald of spiritual knowledge, of putting faith on the *ishta* (the Beloved) and be accomplished with *yoga siddhis* etc.

*

[With regard to *yoga siddhis*, perhaps it would be useful to get Guru Dev's perspective on them, as outlined in an *upadesha*, later published in the ashram newsletter, Shri Shankaracharya Upadesha on 24th August 1953:-

स्वाध्यान्मा प्रमद: उत्तिष्ठत जाग्रत प्राप्य वरान्निबोधत ।

श्री शंकराचार्य उपदेश
साप्ताहिक पत्र

यदा यदा हि धर्मस्य ग्लानिर्भवति भारत । अभ्युत्थानमधर्मस्य तदात्मानं सृजाम्यहम् ॥

वर्ष ४ अंक ७-८	लखनऊ चन्द्रवार २४ अगस्त १९५३ श्रावण शुक्ल १५ सं० २०१० वि० श्री शंकराचार्य संवत्सर २४२२	सामान्य वार्षिक १५) साधारण वार्षिक ६)

अनन्त श्री विभूषित धर्म सम्राट जगद्गुरु शंकराचार्य भगवत्पूज्यपाद
स्वामी ब्रह्मानन्द सरस्वती जी महाराज का उपदेश
अपने आश्रम 'श्री ब्रह्मनिवास' प्रयाग में उपदेश करते हुये महाराज श्री ने कहा—

परमात्मा निष्काम पर प्रसन्न होते हैं ।

इस समय अधिकांश लोग सिद्धियाँ ढूँढते हैं । सिद्धि का समागम चाहते हैं । सिद्धियाँ मिलने के क्या लच्चण हैं ।

योग शास्त्र जन्मौषधमन्त्र तप समाधि ।

कोई तो जन्म से सिद्ध होते हैं । पूर्व जन्म की तपस्या रही परन्तु कोई वासना शेष थी अथवा प्रारब्ध रहा तो इस जन्म में प्रारम्भ से ही सिद्ध होते हैं जब भरत का उदाहरण सामने है । आज भी कुछ महात्मा जन्म सिद्ध होंगे ।

औषधि से भी सिद्ध होते हैं, हम लोग जंगलों में रहे हैं जानते हैं । "कण्टकारि द्वयम्" किसी वैद्य ने भटकटैया (छोटी बड़ी) के स्थान पर कण्टकारी (जूता) का काढ़ा तैयार किया । औषधियाँ ऐसी हैं कि आप उनके बल से कल्पपर्यन्त जीवित रह सकते हैं । औषधि से कल्प करते आत्रो । जीव तो अजर-अमर है । जब श्रीऔषधियों से कल्पपर्यन्त रह सकते हो तब छुद्र व्याधियों का क्या कहना ।

गंगाजी के किनारे श्रृंगवेरपुर के निकट कौरवेश्वर में रीवाँ राज्य के एक बाबा थे उन्हें पादुका सिद्धि थी । गंगा जल पर चल कर दूसरी ओर से घी ले आये । दूसरे को गुटका सिद्धि थी । वे "खबेरी के बाबा" नाम से प्रसिद्ध थे । औषधि के बल से उसे सिद्धि थी । यह सब लौकिक वासना की पूर्ति कर सकती हैं कल्याण नहीं होता ।

मंत्र से भी सिद्धि होती है यदि मंत्र से देवता प्रसन्न हो गया तो जितनी उसकी शक्ति है उतना कार्य यह कर देगा । सर्वशक्तिमान तो परमात्मा है । रामनाम के बल पर सब कुछ किया जा सकता है पर लौकिक बातों की याचना भगवान से मत करो । तैंतीस कोटि देवता इसी लिए हैं । हल बैल का होता है हस्ती का नहीं ।

परमात्मा निष्काम पर प्रसन्न होते हैं । भगवान राम ने बाल्मीकि से पूछा कि हम कहाँ रहें बाल्मीकि ने कहा कि कौन सा ऐसा स्थान है जहाँ आप न हों । वहाँ हम बता दें रहने के लिये । परन्तु आप पूछते हैं तो बतातें हैं'—जो निष्काम प्रेमी है । जिसे कभी कोई वासना

अनन्त श्री विभूषित धर्म सम्राट जगद्गुरु शंकराचार्य भगवत्पुज्यपाद

स्वामी ब्रह्मानन्द सरस्वती जी महाराज का उपदेश

अपने आश्रम 'ब्रह्मनिवास' प्रयाग में उपदेश करते हुये महाराज श्री ने कहा –

परमात्मा निष्काम पर प्रसन्न होते हैं।

इस समय अधिकांश लोग सिद्धियाँ ढूँढ़ते हैं। सिद्धि का समागम चाहते हैं। सिद्धियाँ मिलने के क्या लक्षण हैं।

योग शास्त्र जन्मौबधमन्त्र तप समाधि।

कोई तो जन्म से सिद्ध होते हैं। पूर्व जन्म की तपस्या रही परन्तु कोई वासना शेष थी। अथवा प्रारब्ध रहा तो इस जन्म में प्रारम्भ से ही सिद्ध होते हैं जड़ भरत का उदाहरण सामने है। आज भी कुछ महात्मा जन्म सिद्ध होंगे।

औषधि से भी सिद्ध होते हैं। हम लोग जंगलों में रहे हैं जानते हैं। "कण्टकारि द्वयम्" किसी वैद्य ने भटकटैया (छोटी बड़ी) के स्थान पर कण्टकारी (जूता) का काढ़ा तैयार किया। औषधियां ऐसी हैं कि आप उनके बल से कल्पपर्यन्त जीवित रह सकते हैं। औषधि से कल्प करते जाओ। जीव तो अजर – अमर है। जब औषधियों से कल्पपर्यन्त रह सकते हो तब छुद्र व्याधियों का क्या कहना।

गंगाजी के किनारे श्रृंगवेरपुर के निकट कौरवेश्वर में रीवाण् राज्य के एक बाबा थे उन्हें पादुका सिद्धि थी। गंगा जल पर चल कर दूसरी ओर से घी ले आये। दूसरे को गुटका सिद्धि थी। वे "अबेरी के बाबा" नाम से प्रसिद्ध थे। औषधि के बल से उसे सिद्धि थी। यह

सब लोकवासना की पूर्ति कर सकती हैं कल्याण नहीं होता ।

मंत्र से भी सिद्धि होती है यदि मंत्र से देवता प्रसन्न हो गया तो जितनी उसकी शक्ति है उतना कार्य वह कर देगा । सर्वशक्तिमान तो परमात्मा है । रामनाम के बल पर सब कुछ किया जा सकता है पर लौकिक बातों की याचना भगवान से मत करो । तैंतीस कोटि देवता इसीलिए हैं । हल बैल का होता है हस्ती का नहीं ।

परमात्मा निष्काम पर प्रसन्न होते हैं । भगवान राम ने बाल्मीकि से पूछा कि हम कहाण् रहें बाल्मीकि ने कहा कि कौन सा ऐसा स्थान है जहाण् आप न हों । वहीं हम बता दें रहने के लिये । परन्तु आप पूछते हैं तो बताते हैं । - जो निष्काम प्रेमी है । जिसे कभी कोई वासना नहीं, कामना नहीं, सहज ही आप से प्रेम करता है वहीं आपका घर है । भगवान उसी से प्रेम करते हैं । जो कामनाशून्य है । अतः छोटे-छोटे काम की चाहना भगवान से न करो । इन कामों के लिये देवता हैं ।

हमने जंगलों में देखा है कि शाबर मंत्रों वाले अधिक लोग रहते हैं । एक मंत्र सिद्ध हो जाय तो लौकिक कार्यों में सहायता मिल सकती है ।

तप द्वारा सिद्धि हो सकती है । तप कहते हैं "क्लेश उठाते हुए भी साधन करते जाना "तप कहते जाना" तप तीन प्रकार के हैं । - सात्विक, राजस, तामस, मारण, मोहन, उच्चाटन यह तामस भाव के तप हैं । सात्विक तप यह है कि किसी कामना को लेकर तप न किया जाय । सात्विक तप से ज्ञान होता है । राजस से लोभ ।

समाधि से भी सिद्धि होती है । समाधि के सम्बन्ध में आजकल

लोग बड़े चिन्तित रहते हैं। योगी बनने की बड़ी आतुरता देखी जाती है। परन्तु इन्द्रियों के भोग तो छूटते नहीं, योग करने की इच्छा करते हैं। स्त्री, पुत्र परिवार छूटे नहीं। मन का संयम कर लेने पर स्त्री, पुत्र के मध्य में भी योगाभ्यास हो सकता है।

जिसने वायु को जीता ऐसे गुरु की शरण में रहो तो उसके वाक्यों से तुम्हें सफलता प्राप्त हो सकती है। साधक को लवण, सरसों की वस्तु, अम्ल पदार्थ, तिक्त, रुक्ष, अति उष्ण वस्तुओं को त्यागना चाहिये। गोंद (वृक्ष निर्यास, होंग आदिक) नहीं खाना चाहिये। अग्नि के निकट तथा स्त्री सेवन, पथ सेवन, नहीं रहना चाहिये। प्रातः स्नान तथा उपवास भी निषेध है। वस्त्र इत्यादि बदल कर बैठ जाता है। धूप निकलने पर स्नान करेगा। कायक्लेश नहीं होना चाहिये। प्रारम्भ में दुग्ध और घृत अधिक मिलना चाहिये। सिद्ध होने पर इसकी आवश्यकता नहीं परन्तु साधन में अवश्य चाहिये। परन्तु दुग्ध घृत शुद्ध होना चाहिये, अर्थात उसके अर्जन का प्रकार ठीक हो। संसारी लोग कामना करके सेवा करते हैं। दुग्ध घृत देंगे तो पचास कामनायें बता देंगे तो साधक की बुद्धि एकाग्र नहीं हो सकती। दुर्योधन का अन्न खाकर भीष्म जैसे महात्मा की भी बुद्धि भ्रष्ट हो गई।

यदि ऐसा सिद्ध गुरु मिल जाय कि वही सब प्रबन्ध

-

करदे तो हमारा योग चल सकता है। आजकल आहार की अशुद्धि के कारण योग सिद्ध नहीं हो रहा है। योगाभ्यास तो दूर की बात, साधारण माला लेकर बैठते हो तो मन भागा भागा फिरता है क्योंकि आहार बिगड़ा है। खाना ऐसा भी खा सकते हो जैसा किसी गण्वार ने जामुन के साथ गुबरोड़ा भी न छोड़ा। यदि आहार – शुद्धि

के साथ जप करोगे तो देवता आपके वश होकर रहेगा। "देवो भूत्वा देव यजेत" अर्थात आचार विचार, आहार विहार ठीक करके जप करो। हमारे यहाण् प्राचीन काल में स्त्रियाण् भी योग मार्ग में सिद्ध हुई हैं।

निष्काम भक्ति करो। हनुमान ने राम को अपना ऋणी बना लिया। ईश्वर से कुछ न माण्गों। हम लोगों का यह अनुभूत नुस्खा है।

x x x

पुरानों इतिहासों में जो घटाएण् लिखी हैं कि अमुक महर्षि को तप करते - करते इतना बल प्राप्त हुआ अथवा अमुक का पतन हुआ तो इस पर विचार करना चाहिये।

किसी के पतन की बात उसके परोक्ष में भी नहीं कहनी चाहिये। "सत्यं ब्रूयात प्रियं ब्रूयात न ब्रूयात सत्यमप्रियं"। किसी अन्धे को अन्धा कहो तो बुरा मानेगा परन्तु उससे सूरदास कहो तो बुरा नहीं मानेगा।

चापलूसी करने की आवश्यकता नहीं है पर अपने शब्दों को ऐसा रक्खो जो सुनने में प्रिय हों।

विचार यह करना है कि ऋषियों का स्त्रियों को देखकर पतित हो जाना मुख से कहना दोष है।

तब फिर लेखनी में लाना तो और भी बुरा है। परन्तु वह इसलिये लिखा गया है कि भविष्य में लोग उन दृष्टान्तों को देखकर सर्तक

रहें । वह प्रसंग ही न आने दे जो पतन हो ।

शास्त्र कहत है कि माता । पुत्री । और भगिनी के साथ भी एकान्त में न बैठें । क्योंकि इन्द्रिय ग्राम बड़ा बलवान है, जब अपनी माता और पुत्री के साथ भी अकेले नहीं बैठना चाहिये तब फिर अन्य स्त्रियों अथवा पुत्रियों के साथ शिमला, मंसूरी में सैर सपाटे करना कहाण् तक उचित होगा ।

सत्य और प्रिय बोलेन्गे, तो किसी से व्यर्थ विरोध भी नहीं होगा और सत्य बोलते-बोलते बाणी में बल - आयेगा "सत्यं प्रतिष्ठायां वाक सिद्धि" पर जिसे दिनभर बोलना ही बोलना है उसे सत्य और प्रिय वचन कहाण् से मिलेंगे । क्योंकि ऐसे मनोहर बचन जो सत्य भी हो बहुत कम होते हैं । अतः वाणी पर संयम होना चाहिये ।

आज कल योग मार्ग की ओर लोगों की रुचि बढ़ रही है । परन्तु योगाभ्यास के पूर्व इन्द्रिय और वाणी पर संयम प्राप्त कर लेना आवश्यक है । सब कुछ प्राप्त किया जा सकता है, पर् जब ठीक उपाय किया जाय । आजकल डाक्टर लोग किसी रोगी को असाध्य बताकर उसे निराश कर देते हैं । परन्तु उसके लिये असाध्य है तो यह नहीं कहा जा सकता कि सबके लिये असाध्य है ।

ईश्वर और जीव इस प्रकार हैं जैसे बाग़ और पेड़ यदि बाग़ से पेड़ अलग कर लें तो बाग़ ही न रह जाय । भगवान सनातन धर्म की रक्षा के लिये अवतार लेते हैं । सनातन धर्म समुद्र है और भिन्न २ मतान्तर तरङ्ग । समुद्र से तरंग उठकर बाहर जाती है और वहाण् से गन्दगी समेट लाती है । ईश्वर और जीव में भी समुद्र और तरंग का सम्बन्ध है ।

जीव ही सीव है। सीव ही जीव है। सीव परमात्मा को कहते हैं। श्रुति कहती है कि ईश्वर ने सृष्टि को रचा और जीव रूप से उसमें प्रवेश कर गया। "ईश्वरो जीव कलया प्रविष्टो" यह पुराण वाक्य है। जब तक भूसी लगी रहती है तब तक धान है और भूसी अलग होने पर तन्दुल (चावल) हो जाता है। यध्यपि धान में तन्दुल पहले ही था जब तक कर्म लगा है तब तक जीव है कर्म नष्ट होने पर् यही सीव है। कर्मपाश में बण्धे हो तब तक जीव है। अन्तर करने वाला यही पाश है। धान में अंकुर होता है जल मृत्तिका का योग देने से परन्तु चावल में मनों जल और मृत्तिका का योग दो अंकुर नहीं हो सकता। अंकुर होना है गर्भवास में आना। जब जीव ही सीव है तब यह कर्मपाश क्यों न हटाये जो उसे परमात्मा से दूर रखता है।

परन्तु कर्मपाश दूर होगा सत्संग और भक्ति से। सत्संग के अभाव में द्रौपदी यह न सोच सकी कि कृष्ण

भगवान व्यापक हैं। इसीलिये उसने उन्हें द्वारिका से पुकारा। तात्पर्य यह कि अपने इष्टदेव को दूर न मानो। निकट से निकट देखो। यह कर्म पाश दूर किये बिना ही कोई अपने को ब्रह्म समझने लगे तो यह ठीक नहीं। भूसी लगी रहने पर धान को चावल नहीं कहा जा सकता। आजतक किसी को धान उबाल कर खाते नहीं देखा गया। हम तभी तक अंश हैं जब तक यह कर्म रूपी भूसी लगी है।

हनुमान ने यही उत्तर दिया था कि शरीर से आपका दास हूँ, जीव रूप में आपका शिष्य हूँ तथा वस्तु-तत्व तो जो आप् हैं वही मैं। भक्ति मार्ग द्वारा भी यद्द्त्वा न निवर्तन्ते कहा गया है। भला भूसी एक बार चावल से अलग हुई तो क्या दुबारा फिर उसमें लगाई जा

सकती है। यदि किसी प्रकार उसमें चिपका भी दी जाय तो क्या उसमें अंकुर आयेगा।

बस एक बार ज्ञानाग्नि में कर्म राशि दग्ध की फिर दुबारा कर्म बाधक नहीं हो सक्का। प्रारब्ध, संचित, क्रियमाण तीन प्रकार के कर्म हैं। प्रारब्ध कर्म को भोगकर संचित कर्म ज्ञान के द्वारा और क्रियमाण भगवान को अर्पितकर, कर्म बन्धन मुक्त हो जाना चाहिये। क्रियमाण कर्म भगवान को इसलिये अर्पण करना चाहिये कि आप बिना कर्म किये रह नहीं सकते। कहीं उसके फल की इच्छा कर बैठे तो नया बन्धन तैयार हो जायगा।

आजकल वेदान्त पढ़ पढ़कर शुद्धोऽहं, विशुद्धोऽहं करने लगते हैं पर दिवाला निकल गया तो रोते दिखाई देते हैं। ऐसे शुष्क वेदान्ती मत बनो। अपने अधिकार के अनुसार साधन अपनाओ तो निश्चय ही सफलता मिलेगी। वेदान्त निष्ठा की वस्तु है। बकने की वस्तु नहीं। उसकी निष्ठा पुष्ट करने का अभ्यास करो तब ठीक है नहीं तो निर्मली निर्मली जपो तो जल शुद्ध नहीं होगा। दीपक की चर्चा करने से अँधेरा नहीं हटेगा।

आप लोग ऋषियों की सन्तान हो उनका मार्ग अपनाओ तो कल्याण होगा। परानुकरण से पतन ही हुअ है और उससे आगे भी उन्नति की आशा नहीं करनी चाहिये।

'This time the majority of people search for *siddhis*, desire the arrival of *siddhi*. What are the methods of getting *siddhis*?

Yoga *Shastra* (Patanjali's Yoga Sutras) says:-

"जन्मौषधिमन्त्रतपः समाधिजाः सिद्धयः ।"

"janmaushhadhimantratapah samaadhijaah siddhayah."

'*siddhis* are attained by birth, drug, *mantra, tapa* & *samadhi*.'
[*yogadarshanam* (*Patanjalis Yoga Sutras*) 4:1]

Some then become a *siddha* by birth. Doing *tapasyaa* in the previous life but with some remaining desire. Or even *praarabdha* (already commenced action from previous birth) remains, then from the beginning of this life he becomes a *siddha*, Jad Bharata is an instance before us [the tale is told of Jadbharat, who was naturally realised.

Today too some *mahatma* will be born a *siddha*. From a *aushadhi* (herbal drug) *siddha* occurs too. We people who are living in the jungles know *kantakaari dvayam*. Any *vaidhya* can make ready a decoction of *kantakaarii* at the place of a *bhatakataiyaa* (gorse - a small prickly shrub which is used in medicine).

Kantakari (Solanum xanthocarpum)

[Kantakaarii (Solanum xanthocarpum), Yellow-Berried Nightshade - Choti Katheri - Kantkari - Solanaceae; Kantkari (Solanum Xantho-carpum) is one of the members of the *dasamula* (ten root) of the Ayurveda].

The herbs are such that you can exist by their strength for a very long time. Go do treatment with *aushadhi*! Life then is not liable to decay, immortal. When from *aushadhiyon* you can be living up to aeons, then what to say of trifling diseases?

On the shore of Ganga ji, near Shrangaverpur at Kauraveshvara, Rewa territory, there was one *baba*, their sandals were perfection. Having moved Ganga from one side, he would take *ghee* with the other.

Another was a *gutakaa siddhi*, (*gutakaa* is said to be a magic ball the putting of which in the mouth makes the man invisible), renowned by the name of "Aberi-ke-Baba". The *siddhi* was to him from the strength of *aushadhi*. This could fulfil all worldly desires, but not in becoming happy.

Also *siddhi* exist from *mantras*. If the *devata* becomes pleased with the *mantra*, then however much *shakti* (energy) it has, that much it will give. Paramatma then is Almighty. On the strength of the name of Rama everything can be done, but don't be making entreaties with earthly words to Bhagwan. There are three hundred and thirty million *devatas* (semi-divines). The ox is put to the plow, not the elephant. Paramatma is pleased with *nishkaama* (desirelessness).

Bhagwan Rama asked of Valmiki, 'Where do We exist?' Valmiki answered, 'There is not a place where you are not. We are talking exactly on this. But you ask so to tell.' - He who is disinterested is a *premi* (lover of Paramatma), from that there will never be any desire, no wish. Naturally, there is love from you. At that very place your house is. With the love of Bhagwan is he who is desireless. Therefore you shouldn't desire little matters from Bhagwan. For these desires are the *devata*.

We have seen living in the jungles a good many practitioners of *shaabara mantra* (*sharbar mantra* is a *mantra* for a specific occasion). If one became a *mantra siddhi*, then he can help in worldly matters.

Siddhi can be had by *tapa,*. We say that *tapas* are, 'If *kleshas* are arising then go and do *saadhana* too.' (A *klesha* is literally an 'affliction' - the five *kleshas* are *avidyaa* (ignorance), *asmitaa* (egotism) *raaga* (attraction), *dvesha* (aversion) and *abhinivesha* (fear).)

We say *tapas* are; 'There are three kinds of *tapa*, *saatvika*, *raajasa*, *taamasa*' - killing, enchantment, and distraction by incantations, are *taamasa* ideas of *tapa*.

Saatvika tapa, this is, that having taken to *tapa,* any *kaamana* (wish, lust, desire is not done. *Gyaana* (knowledge, realisation) comes from *saatvika tapa*.

From *rajas* comes greed.

Siddhi also comes from *samadhi*. People are greatly concerned in connection of *samadhi*. To be made a *yogi* is seen as a great perplexity. But the senses of enjoyment are not abandoned to do *yoga*, the desires for wife, son or family are not abandoned. Having taken self-restraint of the mind, even in the midst of the wife and son too, can be *yoga bhaashya* (the manner of living and practice of Hindu ascetics according to the rules of *yoga* philosophy).

Whosoever is in the care of such a *guru* who lives on air then from the expressions thereof you can gain success. A *sadhaka* should forego ingredients such as salt and mustard, *amla* (sour/acidic) things, *tikta* (bitter), *ruksha* (harsh, dried up), substances that are excessively *ushna* (hot, pungent, caustic). Should not eat gum. Not be in the proximity of fire and female service, should not stay in the custom of service. Dawn bath is prohibited and fasting also. Having changed clothing etc., go be seated, and on turning out the light you will bathe.

You should not have body problems. At the beginning you should get more milk and clarified butter. On becoming *siddha* this is not necessary, but in *saadhana* certainly you must. But milk, clarified butter should be pure, that is to say, it should be acquired by the correct method. Worldly people having wishes are doing service. They will give milk and clarified butter, then it is said fifty desires will have been given, then the mind of the *sadhaka* cannot be disturbed.

Having eaten Duryodhana's food, Bhishma who was of the manner of a *mahatma* became fallen [because it was impure].

If a *siddha guru* is encountered, the very same is assisting arrangements, then our *yoga* can move on. But nowadays, because of impurity of food none are being *yoga siddhi*. Talk of *yogaabhyaasa* (the manner of living and practice of Hindu ascetics according to the rules of *yoga*) is far away, generally having taken the food he becomes seated, the mind runs, runs away and he becomes dejected, because the food is spoiled. The experience can also be similar to some uncivilised person with a black plum and a dung beetle that is not spared [being eaten by mistake]. If alongwith pure food you will do *japa*, then the *devata* will remain with the wish you are having.

"देवो भूत्वा देव यजेत"

"devo bhuutvaa deva yajeta"
'Having become the god, one should worship the god'

That is to say, 'think about your conduct', consider your food well, do *japa*. We were here in former times, the women too, on the path of yoga, and have been *siddha*. Do *bhakti* free from any wishes. Hanuman made Rama indebted to him. Don't make any requests from God. This is the prescription of us folk.

* * *

In the stories of the Puranas, occurences are written of such and such a *maharshi* doing *tapa* and gaining so much strength or there has been the downfall of so and so, you should consider this. In the absence of any word of downfall, you also should not [assume it].

"सत्यं ब्रूयात प्रियं ब्रूयात न ब्रूयात सत्यमप्रियं"

"satyam bruuyaata priyam bruuyaata na bruuyaata
satyamapriyam"
'One should speak the truth, one should say that which is pleasing,
one should not say the truth that is not pleasing.'
[*Manu Smriti* 4:138]

"किसी अन्धे को अन्धा कहो तो बुरा मानेगा"

"kisii andhe ko andhaa kaho to buraa maanegaa"

'Tell anyone that is blind that they are blind, then expect badness'
(15th Century blind Hindi poet Surdas)

From that which Surdas says, don't get badness.

It is not necessary to flatter, but put your words so they are
lovely to hear. Consider this, having seen the women of *rishis*
become degenerate, to speak with the mouth, this is harmful. Then
again fetching a pen, that too is bad. In future people having seen
the examples of that which has already been written about, and
will be cautious. Really that subject of who is fallen is not to come
about.

It is said in the *Shastra* not to sit alone with mother, daughter
and sister, because the habitation of the senses is very strong.
When you should not sit alone with mother and daughter, then
again, where will it be reasonable to be merrymaking and running
with other women or daughters, in Simla, in Mussoorie?

If you will speak that which is true and pleasing, then you will
not be met with resistance to no purpose. Then speaking truth,
power will come in the speech. On the *siddhi* of truthful respectful
speech, from that is to be able to talk, and talk all day. From
where is met with that truthful and respectful speech? Because
such a beautiful voice which is also truthful is very rare,
consequently, you should apply self-restraint to the voice.

Nowadays there is a growing liking by people for the way of

yoga. But prior to *yogaabhyaasa* (the manner of living and practice of Hindu ascetics according to the rules of *yoga* philosophy) it is necessary to take self-restraint of the senses and voice. When everything is obtained you can go, when good preparation is done. Nowadays, a *"doctor"* person informs a patient he is incurable, this gives hopelessness to him that he is incurable, but nothing can be said to be incurable.

Ishwar (God) and *jiiva* (life) are of this kind, in the manner of the garden and the tree, if the tree is separated from the garden, in that case it no longer occupies the garden. The Avataar comes to protect the Sanatana Dharma (eternal religion) of Bhagwan. Sanatana Dharma is an ocean and other opinions are waves. The wave of the sea rises beyond and ebbing from there brings dirtiness. In Ishwar (God) and the *jiiva* (life) is the relationship of ocean and wave.

Jiiva (life) is really Shiva, Shiva is really *jiiva.* Shiva is said for Parmatma. *shruti* says that Ishwar (God) brought forth creation and then entered the form of life.

"ईश्वरो जीवकलया प्रविष्टो"

"iishvaro jiivakalayaa pravishto"
'The Almighty has entered the form of individual life'
[*Shrimad Bhagavat* 11:29:16 & *Yajnavalkya Upanishad* 4]

This is the ancient expression.

Whilst the husk remains it is paddy and when the chaff is removed it becomes rice. Though the rice was in the paddy up until when action is applied it is *jiiva,* and on the action of destruction here really is Shiva.

Whilst he has become bound in *karma paasha* (binding action) then he is *jiiva.* The inner being is trapped. In paddy it sprouts by being given water in the soil, but in giving water to rice and giving it contact with soil it does not become an offshoot.

An offshoot (scion) comes into the womb. When *jiiva* is really Shiva, then this is *karma paasha* (binding action), why should you not drive away that which places him far from Paramatma? But the *karma paasha* (binding action) will become distant by *satsang* and *bhakti*.

By lack of *satsang*, Draupadi could not think of Bhagwan Krishna as being everywhere, therefore she called him from Dwarka. The gist of this is not to regard one's *ishta deva* (desired one, god) as being far away. From near see near. Without the *karma paasha* (binding action) being distanced, no one will understand Brahman himself. This is not good. When the husk is attached to the paddy then it cannot be said to be rice. Up to today it has not been seen that boiled paddy is to be eaten. For this reason, whilst we still have a fraction, then this form of *karma* is attached as a husk.

Hanuman gave this answer, 'With the body I am your servant, in the form of *jiiva* I am your disciple, and of the essential stuff I am you.'

Also, by way of *bhakti* it has been said;-

"यद्गत्वा न निवर्तन्ते"

"yadgatvaa na nivartante"
'Having gone thither, they do not return'
[*Bhagavad Gita* 15:6]

Good, once the husk is separated from the rice then can it be attached again? Provided there is also a way of sticking to you then a sprout will come in you.

Once is enough, the *karma raashi* (heap of past *karma*) is burnt in the fire of knowledge then the *karma* cannot be troubling one again.

Praarabdha (already commenced, fate), *sanchita* (amassed), *kriyamaana* (present) are three types of *karma*. Having endured the *praarabdha karma, sanchita karma,* by means of *gyaana* and *kriyamaana* (present performance of work, what is being done) and having presented *kriyamaana* to Bhagwan, you should become liberated. *kriyamaana karma,* you should give to Bhagwan as you cannot be without *karma,* anywhere the fruit of desire is seated, then new bondage will become ready.

Nowadays, studying *Vedanta,* on doing *"shuddho aham, vishuddho aham"* - 'I am perfect, I am pure', but if bankruptcy appears then there is a display of tears. In this way *Vedantic* teaching is made withered. If according to your own right have your own *saadhana* you will certainly meet with success. Belief in *Vedanta* is not a thing to prattle about. Practise with strong faith, then afterwards if it is not good, then *nirmalii, nirmalii japa* (*nirmalii* is a water purifier - *strychnos potatorum*), then the water will not be impure. By investigation of the light the darkness will not recede. You folk bring the ancient teaching of the rishis, make their way your own, then there will be *kalyaana* (happiness, welfare). By running away you have fallen and from that you should not hope to progress in the future either.']

[**Strychnos Potatorum** L. *Chilbinj. Cleaning Nuts. Indian Gum Nuts.* (Fam. *Loganiaceae.*)—The nuts of this species of *Strychnos* are very largely used in some parts of India for clearing muddy water, and are stated to have found their way into American commerce. (*A. J. P.*, 1871.) The fruit is also employed by the native practitioners of Hindostan, under the name of *nirmali*, as an *emetic* and in *dysentery*. They do not contain strychnine. In clearing water, one of the dried nuts is rubbed hard for a short time around the inside of the earthen water pot; on settling, the water is left pure and tasteless. *The Dispensatory of the United States of America, 1918*]

So the search was on for a *mahatma* possessing these qualities; viz. (i) that in everyone's opinion he is suitable, (ii) that he is pure, respected, born in the Brahman lineage and (iii) is a disciple of the *parampara* (lineage) of the four maths (monasteries) instituted by Shri Jagadguru Shankaracharya. The principal duty of the committee was to reinstate that seat of religious conduct in the community as for a long time the seat of *dharma* had been destroyed. It was a great task and only one possessed of divine energy could accomplish it.]

[Prior to 1833 Jyotirmath appears to have had an unbroken succession of Shankaracharyas going back to at least 1500. In more recent years the names of the Shankaracharyas are recorded to have been:-

Acharya Shivanand Swami	1639-1646
Acharya Balkrishna Swami	1646-1660
Acharya Narain Updendra Swami	1660-1693
Acharya Harishchandar Swami	1693-1706
Acharya Sadanand Swami	1706-1716
Acharya Keshav Swami	1716-1724
Acharya Narain Tirtha Swami	1724-1766
Acharya Ram Krishna Swami	1766-1776
- vacant -	1776 onwards

– quoted from *'Jyotirmathasya Guruparampara'*,
Shree Jyotishpeetha Shankaracharya Sevak Sangh,
Allahabad, c1995]

By good fortune, looking amongst the learned men it was found that you alone possessed the aforementioned qualities. Therefore, having seen your ideal surrender, your freedom from worldly desires, your full energy, contentment and singular life, none had the nerve to suggest anyone else to go and restore the peeth (seat of Jyotirpeeth). Whereof the rule is, 'To be a *tyaaga* (a renunciate) you should always be like the snake when in the company of mankind.' Similar sentiments are that; 'Someone who is a hermit is similar to Shukadeva (the son of Veda Vyasa), someone who is a scholar is similar to Vrihaspati (a *guru* of Mahabharata era) and he who is wealthy is similar to Kubera (god of wealth), so nobody is indispensable.' So, how could it be reasonable or a proper method to suggest that someone who was so detached should be running of the *peeth*? The reader can judge for himself. But the *dharma peeth* was to be restored.

Maharaj Shri sometimes came to stay in towns when doing *chaturmasya-vrat* (the fast observed by Hindus which lasts for the four months of the rainy season). Slowly, slowly the influential upright people suggested that everyone make an effort to speak to him intelligently and to make a place in the inner conscience of Maharaj Shri for the restoration of the *peeth*. *But, when the time came (for the inauguration) your stoical inner self reasserted itself and you reverted to your former appearance (of non-attachment and uninvolvement).*

Preparations for the *abhisheka* (inauguration) were completely ready and the time had been announced, therefore, at the ninth convention of the Sanatan Dharma Sammelan in Kashi (Varanasi) they were in a state of complete readiness. But two days before the day of Maharaj Shri's inauguration, he thought deeply and disappeared off to an unknown place! *You had wondered whether in your absence some other mahatma might be installed, and therefore afterwards this would become obvious.*

No one knew when he had left the ashram or where he had gone, or how he had travelled. Since the *abhisheka* (inauguration) was to be the day after next the atmosphere became tense. So that day they put in a great amount of effort and there was painful discussion. Agitation pervaded amongst the religious folk and various sorts of arguments were raised in the minds of the officials. Confidentally, suggestions arose suggesting that some other *dandi mahatma* be appointed. But an aged *mahatma* of Bharat Dharma Mahamandal, Shri Swami Gyananand Ji Maharaj, advised the scholars to work patiently. He said, 'It is a great task to restore the *dharma peeth*; and this kind of load can only be undertaken by one who is free from desire, one who is a recluse and a worthy *mahatma*. By installing anyone else, they will lack the capacity to develop the divine energy of the *peeth*. To reawaken the energy that has been dormant for a hundred and sixty-five years, only such a worthy person will achieve this. For the happiness of the world I don't believe it is sensible for there to be any hurry in this connection.'

Having sent telegrams, letters etc. to everyone, postponing for an indeterminate time, they searched for Maharaj Shri, but nobody knew where he was. However, destiny is powerful! A feeling arose in the mind of Maharaj Shri was, 'The Akhil Bharatiya Sammelan was announced and people were going to come from far away. All were coming but none will have been given to occupy the *peeth*.' Having thought this way, it was another three weeks before he returned to Kashi, at night. But immediately gossip spread of Maharaj Shri's return and the scholars of Kashi were very eager and alert. Inside of an hour, by eleven o'clock at night, a group of scholars had arrived at the ashram. They gathered together requesting him that, 'Bhagwan, all of us have the greatest respect for Bhagwan Aadi Shankaracharya who erected a *dharma peeth* in north India which has for a long time been destroyed and now we are without an *acharya* (religious instructor). We people who are without a *dharma guru* have become without a master. This can again be resolved, but only by you. This work of *gurudom* is impossible for an ordinary person. By your birth, *karma* and *tyaaga,* and also you are really special in the community of *sadhus* by means of *tapa* from childhood. You are revered like Shankaracharya by all the kings and subjects. You are the equal of *guru* Shankaracharya, you are also really revered because you are really a *dandi swami* of the lineage of that *acharya*. Therefore, our prayer is that certainly you now accept.'

To this entreaty of the pandits, Shri Charan remained silent. Quickly appreciating 'Silence is an indication of agreement', a meeting was arranged of the Akhil Bharatiya Sanatan Dharma Mahasammelan. Preparations for the *abhisheka* had been ready from before, now all wished 'to do good things quickly' [to quote an old Indian proverb]

The Sahasra Chandi Mahayagya was being performed in the *yagya mandap* (canopy of *yagya*) of Shri Bharat Dharma Mahamandal. Some advice had been to do the *abhisheka* of the *acharya* in the *maha yagya* pavilion at the middle of worship of *bhagavati* (goddess). But the able scholars said, 'Us folk are sort of inaugurating him forcefully. He has not wished to give even a small sign of consent so there is no chance he will go anywhere to be installed. If he wished this then he would have gone anywhere we people wished, but at the mention of *abhisheka* (inauguration) he has already run away once. All this is understood, therefore to complete the arrangements we need to conduct the *abhisheka* at that very place. After completion of the *abhisheka* with honour he can be brought to the public committee (in the marquee of the Akhila Bharatiya Sanatana Dharma Sammelan) as the proper *aachaarya*. And at that very place the *acharyatvena pujana* (*puja* of the 'reality of *acharya*') made and announcing the restoration of the *peeth*.'

All the far-sighted scholars accepted this and accordingly made a programme. At daybreak scholars of diverse orders of respectable religious organisations together with the assembly of learned men residing in Kashi all came to the Akhil Bharatiya Sanatana Dharma Samellan (All-India Eternal Dharma Conference). They went with all the materials needed for the *abhisheka* and proceeded to the ashram of Maharaj Shri's *ashram* at Brahma Nivaas in Siddhigiri Baag.

It is to be remembered that back in 1936, before being offered the post of Shankaracharya, Maharaj Shri had had built the Shri Brahmavidya Niketan and the Shri Brahmanandeshwar Mahadev Ji Mandir (a temple) in Choti Gaibi, Varanasi, in rememberance of his own venerable Shri Gurudeva. The beautiful appearance of the *ashram* and *mandir* (temple) etc, was made on account of the management and another major *ashram* in Siddhi Giri Baag, Varanasi, was built by the name of Shri Brahma Niwas. This, the two other buildings and one at Bahadur Ganj, Prayag (Allahabad) were all connected, and these properties were placed under the protection of the Shri 1008 Swami Krishnanand Saraswati Trust, whereof mention is made in Maharaj Shri's final will.

Swami Gyananand Ji Maharaj, the senior founder of Bharat Dharma Mahamandala, Pujya had long wished for the restoration of the *peeth* so he proceeded to Sidhhigiri Baaga hoping for the fulfilment of this desire. With a great declaration from Shri Charan to restore the northern seat of Dharma the *shodashopachara puja* (of sixteen offerings) was done and the *abhisheka* was accomplished by about ten o'clock.

In the afternoon there was a magnificent great procession of the
Shankaracharya and at the proper time Maharaj Shri was brought
in the *pandal* (marquee) for a meeting.

Profuse applause of *"Jagadguru* Bhagwan *Shankaracharya"*

echoed in all directions. The sounds of mantras from Vedic scholars of the four *Vedas* resonated up to the canopy of the sky. The annointing was performed by a special Vedic Karma Kandi (ones who perform religious ceremonies) of Kashi, and the king, Maharaaj Dhiraaj Shri Darbhanga, announced the great annointment and the ascension to the *dharmapeeth* of Dharmacharya Shri Jyotishpeethadhishwara Jagadguru Bhagwan Shankaracharya. After having cheered "Bhagwan *Shankaracharya*" again and again they did *abhivadana* (deferential salutation) to Shri Jagadguru Shankaracharya Maharaj.

In this way, on fourth *shukla* day of Chaitra in the Vikram year of 1998, on 1st April 1941, Maharaj Shri was throned as the extremely worthy Dharmaachaarya (religious preceptor) Ananta Shri Vibhushit Bhagwan Ji Maharaaj, on the Sinhaasana (lion throne) of *dharma* at Uttaraamnaaya Peeth, Badrinath. The seat had been empty for one hundred and sixty-five years. Accordingly, news of the saviour of Jyotishpeeth spread by newspapers and periodicals everywhere in the country and abroad.

Realising that the the *peeth* was being saved all four organisations of *sanatan dharma* had cause to rejoice and necessarily sent congratulations in praise of Acharya Charanon (the teachers feet), and voiced their obedience to the *acharya*. In north India an unprecedented huge wave of religious awakening occurred, and invitations came from all directions.

*

At this time the chief two tasks before Acharya Shri in relation to the restoring the *peeth* were:-

(1) Creation of a new *math* (monastery) and *mandir* (temple) at the place of the *peeth*.

(2) Returning the people of north India to the Vedic path, back to the conduct of *dharma*, and to revive the standing and perfectly glorious ideal of the *peeth*.

These two tasks you were to start simultaneously. Some people of the community of wise men of Kashi suggested to Maharaj Shri that since all the tasks for restoring the *peeth* should be done in a very beautiful form then a lot of wealth would be necessary. Therefore, they suggested that some programmes should be made for the prevalence of *dharma* in well-off cities such as Bombay (Mumbai) and Calcutta, and from that there will be a spiritual awakening and also funds for the restoration of the *peeth*. Now Maharaj Shri answered these learned men like this:- 'You people gave me to sit on the Dharma Sinhaasana (the Lion Throne of *dharma*), and I am sitting on it, and all the tasks relating to that are given to us too. Therefore, you people should now sit free from anxiety. Subsequently, responsibility for the regeneration of Jyotishpeeth is now ours, and that restoration will indeed happen.'

After all that you travelled southwards. For a few days you stayed in Katni before gracing Jabalpur and making your abode in Baldev Baag. A retinue of faithful devotees was attached to him, and more and more people came joined his company. An immense crowd rushed for *darshan,* coming constantly for *upadesha* (counsel). *At this time, near the border of Madhya Pradesh at Khandwa in Burhanpur, a Maharudra Yagya was being held, and you were invited there.* This was a traditional religious ceremony and to that end it was magnificently spiritual. It took a lot of arranging, with hundreds of thousands of people gathering together in the same place. *In one place, so many more were getting the wealth of darshan of Maharaj Shri's magnificent authority, whereas it had been difficult for people to get your darshan. For to make darshan easy, three benches made of planks were put one upon the other, and on these was placed your seat. This was done on your advice and accomplished by the folk.*

८

आठवाँ अध्याय

धर्म-प्रचार

इस प्रकार धार्मिक यात्रा में भ्रमण करते हुये आप फिर जबलपुर आये और कुछ दिनों तक वहाँ निवास किया। जबलपुर प्रवास के पश्चात् शीघ्र ही जनवरी १९४२, सम्वत् १९९८ का लोक-प्रसिद्ध प्रयाग का महान् कुम्भ पर्व आ गया। सम्पूर्ण भारतवर्ष के योगी, यती, सन्त, महन्त, राजा, महाराजा, मण्डलेश्वर एवं समस्त धर्मपरायण विद्वान् और प्रजावर्ग तथा उनके विभिन्न सम्प्रदाय और संस्थायें दशनाम संन्यासियों के अखाड़े आदि वहाँ उपस्थित थे। कुम्भ के ऐतिहासिक एवं धार्मिक महान् पर्व के अवसर पर सम्पूर्ण भारतवर्ष के साधु-समाज तथा धार्मिक जनता का नेतृत्व करने के लिये आप भी प्रयाग पधारे। आचार्य-चरणों के दर्शन करने तथा अभिनन्दन आदि करने के लिये उपस्थित साधु समाज के अग्रगण्य तथा दशनामी संन्यासियों के अखाड़ों के महंत आपके स्थान पर आये और उन्होंने प्रार्थना की, "प्रभो, हम आपकी सेना हैं। योग्य आज्ञा प्रदान की जाय, हमारी सेवा स्वीकार की जाय।" उत्तर में श्री भगवान् शंकराचार्य जी ने आदेश दिया, "आप लोग अपने अपने गुरुपदिष्ट विधानों के अनुसार योगसाधन तथा इष्ट की सिद्धि में लगे रहें, त्याग और तप के द्वारा शक्ति को बढ़ावें, अनुशासन एवं संगठन का दृढ़तापूर्वक ध्यान रखें, समय पर उचित आदेश दिया जायगा। इसमें सन्देह नहीं कि आप लोग जगद्गुरु शंकराचार्य की धर्मपीठ की अध्यात्मशक्ति सम्पन्न विजयिनी सेना हैं। अपने उत्तराम्नाय के ज्योतिर्मठ की मान-मर्यादा का ध्यान आप लोगों को सदैव रखना

चाहिये।" तदन्तर आये हुये सभी मंडलेश्वर व साधु समाज द्वारा आयोजित आपकी अभूतपूर्व शोभायात्रा निकाली गई। सम्पूर्ण भारत के महंत, मण्डलेश्वरों तथा धार्मिक राजा-प्रजा द्वारा आपका यहाँ सर्वात्मना स्वागत किया गया और त्रिवेणी तीर्थ पर पर्व का महास्नान सर्वप्रथम आपका ही हुआ।

महाराज श्री ने ज्योतिर्मठ के पुनरुद्धार के लिये ही इस कार्यभार को सम्भाला था। इसलिये जगद्गुरु शंकराचार्य पद पर होते हुए भी आपके अतीतकालीन त्याग और वैराग्य-वृत्ती में कोई अन्तर नहीं आया। आपकी कठोर आज्ञा थी, "इस धर्म-सिंहासन के आगे धन का चढ़ावा नहीं, मन का चढ़ावा होना चाहिये और अपने प्रिय दोषों को, जिन्हें आप छिपाये रखते हैं और कभी छोड़ना नहीं चाहते, उन्हीं को, यहाँ चढ़ाइये। इसी से आप लोगों का कल्याण होगा। मन को जब आप धर्म के लिये अर्पण कर देंगे, फिर आप लोगों का पवित्र जीवन परम शान्ति की ओर अग्रसर होता जायगा।"

महाराज श्री के दर्शन अब जन साधारण को सुलभता से प्राप्त होने लगे। ऐसा देखकर एक विरक्त महात्मा ने कहा, "भगवन्, यदि हम लोग जानते कि ये दर्शन इतने सस्ते हो जायँगे तो कुछ दिन और रुक जाते, जंगलों में इनकी खोज में अनुष्ठान करते हुये मारे-मारे न भटकते।" कितना रहस्य है विरक्त के इन शब्दों में। उसी से स्पष्ट होता है कि कितना दुर्गम, दुष्प्राप्य और पूर्ण जीवन रहा है घनघोर जंगलों में आपका। अपने त्यागमय एकाकी जीवन की झाँकी कभी-कभी महाराज श्री स्वयं ही भक्तों के सामने बताने लगते – वे कहा करते, "कौन जानता था कि एक दिन धर्म सिंहासनारूढ़ होने की आवश्यकता पड़ेगी और अपना स्वच्छंद जीवन बन्धन में बँध जायगा?" उस समय एक गेरुआ अचला होता, उसी की कभी

सिर पर पगड़ी बँधी होती और वही कभी कटि में लिपटा हुआ
होता। एक छोटे से चौरस पत्थर को तवा बनाकर आटा गूँथ कर
जब उस पर रोटी की सेंकाई करते और वह पत्थर आग की गर्मी से
चटाचट की आवाज़ें करने लगता तो हृदय अपने स्वच्छंद जीवन की
हिलकोरों में आनन्द मनाने लगता। इस प्रकार की दशा देख कर
कोई कहता कि परमहंस है और कोई अवधूत समझता। परन्तु नहीं,
वह तो जीवन्मुक्ति के साक्षात् स्वरूप थे और अंतरतम में जीवन्मुक्ति
का अपार आनन्द ले रहे थे।

प्रयाग कुम्भ के बाद महाराज श्री काशी पधारे। कुछ दिनों तक
विश्राम किया। धर्म-प्रचार-यात्रा के निमित्त फिर प्रस्थान किया।
दूसरी बार जबलपुर की यात्रा हुई और उसी पुराने स्थान, बलदेव
बाग में निवास किया। भक्तों ने जबलपुर ही चातुर्मास्य-व्रत करने
की प्रार्थना की। आपने जबलपुर में दो चातुर्मास्य-व्रत लगातार
किये एक रैन बसेरा ''गोल बाजार में और दूसरा ''सेठ राधाकृष्ण की
कोठी'' गंजीपुरा में। इसी कालावधि में शंकर दिग्विजय के अनुसार
आचार्योंचित् पीठ की सामग्री स्वर्ण-रजत सिंहासन, पालकी, चमर,
छत्र, दण्ड आदि निर्मित हुये। ज्योतिष्पीठ-भवन-निर्माण-कार्य भी
इसी समय हुआ।

पीठ को उच्छिन्न हुये अधिक समय व्यतीत हो जाने के कारण
उत्तराखंड-स्थित भगवान् आदि शंकराचार्य की लीला-भूमि जो
लगभग ४ बीघा थी, कुछ तो गवर्नमेण्ट के अधिकार में चली गई थी
और कुछ वहाँ के कृषक लोग अपने अधिकार में कर लिये थे। इस
प्रकार से छिन्न-भिन्न हुई ज्योतिष्पीठ भूमि को भारत-धर्म-महामंडल ने
अपने अथक प्रयास से और के डिप्टीकमिश्नर सरजेम्सक्रे की
सहायता से प्राप्त कर वहाँ ली थी और अभिषेक हो जाने के बाद

उसके उद्धार के निमित्त महाराज श्री को अर्पण कर दिया था।
महाराज श्री ने इसी समय में अपने सुयोग्य शिष्यों द्वारा उक्त भूमि
में पहले स्थानीय विधेष चिह्नों द्वारा पीठस्थान निश्चित् कराया तब
ज्योतिष्पीठ-भवन-निर्माण-कार्य प्रारम्भ किया। उन दिनों सुगमता
एवं शीघ्रता से सामग्री अथवा धन भेजने की सुविधा डाक के
अतिरिक्त अन्य नहीं थी। अतएव सभी आवश्यक सामग्री जो
पर्वतीय प्रदेश में उपलब्ध नहीं हो सकती थी जैसे रंग, कीले,
चटखनी आदि-आदि, पोस्ट पारसल द्वारा और हजारों रुपये पोस्टल
बीमा द्वारा साप्ताहिक ज्योतिर्मठ को भेजवाये और निश्चित स्थान पर
सुन्दर दो – मंजिला पीठभवन निर्माण कराया। इसके सामने ही कुछ
दूरी पर श्री पूर्णागिरि देवी का मन्दिर, जिसका निर्माण स्वर्गीय
दरभंगा – नरेश, हिजहाईनेस, महाराजा रामेश्वर सिंह ने आरम्भ
कराया था, किन्तु अधूरा ही रह गया था, उसे पूर्ण कराया और देवी
जी की प्रतिमा की प्रतिष्ठा की। यह भवन ज्योतिष्पीठ-भवन के नाम
से प्रसिद्ध हुआ। यह अत्यंत रमणीक और विशाल है। श्री
बदरीनारायण जानेवाले मार्ग पर स्थित है। इसमें ३० कमरे हैं और
सैकड़ों व्यक्ति एक साथ निवास कर सकते हैं।

धर्म प्रचारार्थ भ्रमण हो रहा था। विभिन्न प्रान्तों में जा-जाकर
जनता को अपने दर्शन व उपदेशों से आकृष्ट कर रहे थे। इतनी
शीघ्रता से ज्योतिष्पीठ की सर्वोपरि प्रतिष्ठा बढ़ी कि दो तीन वर्ष में
ही समस्त उत्तर भारत की धार्मिक जनता को अपने धर्मपीठ पर
अभिमान होने लगा और अपने धर्माचार्य श्री ज्योतिष्पीठाधीश्वर
महाराज की आदर्श व्यवस्था से धार्मिक समाज गौरवान्वित हो
उठा। सर्वोपरि प्रतिष्ठा में शीघ्रता से प्रचार होने में कुछ विधेष कारण
निम्नलिखित थे –

(१) श्री चरण के व्यक्तित्व में, जो विलक्षण शांति पूर्ण तेजोमयी आभा थी, उसे जो एक बार दर्शन कर लेता था वह बार-बार दर्शन करना चाहता और प्रत्येक दर्शनार्थी दर्शन हो जाने के उपरान्त ऐसा प्रभावित होता और ऐसा अनुभव करता कि महाराज श्री उससे अधिक किसी से प्रेम नहीं करते ।

(२) महाराज श्री के मुख से निकले हुये शब्दों में एक विशेष आकर्षण था । आपके उपदेशों में सरलता, सरसता, और विषय मार्मिकता थी, जो अन्यत्र नहीं पाई जाती । इसके अतिरिक्त आपके अन्तर्यामित्व की कुछ ऐसी विचित्र व्यवस्था थी कि आपके उपदेशों में समीप में बैठे हुये श्रोताओं की शंकाओं का समाधान बिना पूछे ही हो जाता था । आपके उपदेश अपने अनुभवों की अचल आधार-शिला पर प्रतिष्ठत होने के कारण अत्यन्त प्रभावशाली होते थे ।

(३) आपके व्यक्तित्व में जो प्रत्यक्ष महानता थी वह तो थी ही, आपकी अनुपस्थिति में भी आपकी विलक्षण सिद्धियों का परिचय जनता को मिलता रहता था । आपके जिस भक्त ने जब भी अपने आपत्तिकाल में आपका स्मरण किया, उसी समय उसकी आपत्ति हट गई । सैकड़ों श्रद्धालु भक्त नित्य ही अपनी-अपनी आपत्तियों का निराकरण करने के पश्चात् उसी की कथा कहा करते थे । बड़े-बड़े नास्तिक आस्तिक बन गये । जो कभी किसी देवी-देवता को प्रणाम तक नहीं करते थे और ईश्वर की मान्यता को ढोंग समझते थे, वे भी अपने अपने घरों में नित्य सायं-प्रातः श्री चरण के चित्र की आरती उतरने लगे ।

(४) आपके पूर्णतया त्यागमय व्यवहार की नीति से जनता पर बड़ा प्रभाव पड़ा । आपकी नीति थी कि कभी किसी से भेंट-पूजा,

विदाई आदि स्वीकार न की जाय। इस नीति का स्वष्टीकरण करनेवाली विज्ञप्ति का साइनबोर्ड आपके शिविर में तथा पीठभवन में लगा रहता था, जिसमें लिखा था –

"भगवत्पूज्यपाद् अनन्तश्री विभूषित, जगद्गुरु, शंकराचार्य ज्योतिष्पीठाधीश्वर, स्वामी ब्रह्मानन्द सरस्वती जी महाराज के दर्शन, पूजन, दीक्षा, आदि में द्रव्य चढ़ाने का निषेध है।"

इस नीति से जनता आश्चर्यचकित थी, क्योंकि सबने देखा कि इनके साथ पचासों सैकड़ों गृहस्थ, विरक्त-महात्मा रहते हैं। सबके साथ धर्म-प्रचार यात्राएँ भी करते रहते हैं और कभी किसी से द्रव्य स्वीकार नहीं करते। इसकी व्यवस्था किस प्रकार होती है। इस विचार से लोगों की बुद्धि किंकर्तव्यविमूढ़ हो जाती और उन्हें महाराज श्री की योगजन्य एवं तपोजन्य सिद्धियों पर विश्वास करना पढ़ता था। इसी से प्रभावित होकर विद्वानों ने महाराज श्री के नाम के आगे "अनन्त श्रीविभूषित" लिखना प्रारम्भ कर दिया। आचार्य-परम्परा की विरुदावली में यह "अनन्तश्री विभूषित" पद सर्व प्रथम पूज्यपाद महाराज श्री के लिये ही प्रयोग में लाया गया।

मध्यभारत के विभिन्न नगरों में भ्रमण करके शताब्दियों से शंकराचार्य जी की सुषुप्त भावना को पुनः जाग्रत किया। फलतः शंकराचार्य के जयघोष से सम्पूर्ण मध्यभारत गूँज उठा। कुछ समय जबलपुर में निवास करके आप पुनः प्रयाग पधारे। प्रयाग की जनता ने अत्यंत हर्ष एवं उत्साह के साथ आपका अभूतपूर्व स्वागत किया। एक वृहत् शोभायात्रा निकाली गई, जिसमें प्रयाग के प्रमुख धनी-मानी सेठ साहूकार, पंडित, विद्वन्मन्डल तथा राज्य कर्मचारी, पदाधिकारी वर्ग सम्मिलित हुआ। स्थान स्थान पर फाटक सजाये

गये। मुहल्ले मुहल्ले के प्रमुख धनी-मानी भक्तों ने शोभायात्रा रोक रोक पर आरती उतारी और पूजन किया। अपूर्व दृश्य उपस्थित हो गया। आपकी यह शोभायात्रा प्रयाग के मुख्य मुख्य सड़कों से होती हुई चौक एवं घंटाघर पार करती हुई पुरुषोत्तमदास पार्क में सभा के रूप में परिणत हो गई। यहाँ महाराज श्री ने अपने उपदेशामृत से लोगों को कृतार्थ किया और चाँद प्रेस के विशाल भवन में, जहां कुछ दिन प्रयाग में विश्राम लेना था, आ गये।

उत्तर भारत के धर्मगुरु का कार्य-भार ग्रहण करने के अनन्तर आप धर्म पीठ की मर्यादा-वृद्धि में संलग्न हुए। अपने गुरुदेव को इस प्रकार कार्य परायण देख कर, आपका सभी शिष्यवर्ग, त्यागी-महात्माओं, विद्वानों से भी न रहा गया और धर्म-प्रचार ही अपना ध्येय बनाकर श्री महाराज जी के कार्य में पूर्ण सहयोग किया। बंगाल, विहार, उत्तर प्रदेश, राजपूताना, पंजाब एवं काश्मीर में सनातन-धर्म की ध्वजा फहराने लगी। महाराज श्री के धर्म प्रचार की इच्छा मात्र से सम्पूर्ण उत्तर भारत में विशिष्ट पंडितगण, महात्मागण एवं समस्त सन्त, महन्त कार्यक्रम बनाने लगे। हिन्दू समाज का एक स्थायी धर्म-संघ बन गया।

इधर संसार के लोग अनुभव कर रहे थे कि यह समय राजा-प्रजा, चर-अचर आदि सभी के लिये महान् संकट का है। भूमि के किसी भाग में शान्ति व सुख नहीं है। भूकम्प, अकाल, तरह तरह की महामारी व्याधियाँ तथा विश्व-ब्यापी प्रलयकारी महायुद्ध, राष्ट्र-विप्लव आदि से सभी चिन्तित और व्यग्र हैं। ऐसे अवसर पर भौतिक बल पर विश्वास रखने वाले राष्ट्र युद्ध द्वारा शान्ति स्थापन का उपाय कर रहे हैं। विश्व की यह दयनीय दशा देख कर धर्म पीठ की देवी-शक्ति जाग्रत हुई, प्रेरणा हुई और फलस्वरूप संसार की रक्षा के लिये

आशुतोष भगवान् शंकर और पुत्र-वत्सला करुणामयी परराम्बा दुर्गा की सामूहिक रूप से आराधनाओं के वृहत आयोजन स्थान पर होने लगे।

दिल्ली के पुण्य-सलिला-यमुना-तट पर भगवान् शंकर की सब से बड़ी देवी अराधना "शतमुख कोटि होमात्मक महायज्ञ" का आयोजन हुआ। महाराज श्री की संरक्षता के के लिये प्रार्थना हुई। आचार्य श्री तथा धर्म पीठ का सहयोग था ही। पूज्यपाद ज्योतिष्पीठाधीश्वर आचार्य श्री ने संरक्षता प्रदान की। महाराज श्री दिल्ली पधारे। आपके दिल्ली पहुँचते ही महान् उत्साह और आनन्द फैल गया। स्वागत में आये हुये लोगों द्वारा दिल्ली स्टेशन का प्लेटफार्म इतना भर गया कि तिल धरने को भी स्थान नहीं रहा। भीड़ के कारण महाराज श्री को गाड़ी से उतर कर प्लेटफार्म से हो कर वाहर जाने में इतनी अधिक कठिनाई हुई कि बाहर तक पहुँचने मात्र में डेढ़ घण्टे लग गये। स्टेशन से ही शोभायात्रा प्रारम्भ हुई। उसके भव्य दृश्य एवं विशालता के विषय में केवल इतना ही कहा जा सकता है कि समाचार पत्रों को यही लिखना पड़ा कि ऐसी शोभायात्रा दिल्ली में और कभी नहीं निकली। चारों ओर जन-समुद्र ही दीख पड़ता था। इस प्रकार आप दिल्ली के यज्ञशिविर में पहुंचे।

महायज्ञ के साथ साथ अखिल भारतीय-धर्म-संघ का महाधिवेशन, गोरक्षा-सम्मेलन, वर्णाश्रम स्वराज्य संघ का विशेषाधिवेशन आदि विराट् समारोह महाराज श्री की ही अध्यक्षता में हुये, जिनसे समस्त भारत में धार्मिक जागृति की एक लहर फैल गई। इस समय जो वैदिक सर्वशाखा सम्मेलन हुआ वह भारत के धार्मिक इतिहास में अभूतपूर्व था। भारत की राजधानी दिल्ली में इस प्रकार महान् धार्मिक समारोह का नेतृत्व करके महाराज श्री ने ज्योतिष्पीठ की देवी प्रभा

से समस्त भारत में धर्म प्रकाश फैलाया।

जिस समय यमुना तट पर उपर्युक्त सम्मेलन हो रहे थे, चारों और जन समुद्र उमड़ रहा था, इन्द्र आदि देवता भी सम्मिलित होने के लिये उत्सुक हो उठे। अपने दल-बादल सहित पहुँच गये। जाड़े के दिन थे ही। कड़ी ठण्ढ पड़ने लगी। ठंढी हवा के झोकों ने सारे तम्बू कनातों और खेमों को उड़ाना ही प्रारम्भ कर दिया। काले काले बादल घिर आये। छोटी-छोटी बूंदें पड़ने लगीं। ऐसा मालूम होने लगा कि घोर वृष्टि तथा ओले पत्थर पड़ने ही वाले हैं। बादलों की गरज भयानक होती गई। प्रातःकाल लगभग ७ बजे का समय था। महाराज श्री अपने शिविर के एक खेमे से निकल कर दूसरे में गये। देखा – इस समय इन्द्र को कुछ बौखलाहट? सी हो गई है। थोड़ी देर में अपने खेमे में लौट आये। बोल उठे, "इस समय यदि पानी पत्थर पड़ेगा, तो लोगों को बड़ा कष्ट होगा" फिर चुप हो गये और अपने किसी दूसरे कार्य में लग गये।

यमुना-तट पर इस महान् यज्ञ का जो वृहत् आयोजन हो रहा है, जिसमें जाड़े की ठंढ में यमुना जी की बालू पर लाखों की संख्या में छोटे-बड़े, धनी-मानी सेठ-साहूकार ब्रह्मचारी साधु-महात्मा तथा स्त्री-बच्चे धर्मयज्ञ में सम्मिलित होकर कष्ट उठा रहे हैं, उन सब की संरक्षता का भार महाराज श्री ही के ऊपर तो था। ऐसे कठिन समय में वह क्यों न रक्षा करते? उन्होंने जिन उपर्युक्त शब्दों का उच्चारण किया था, वे इसीलिये कि इन सभी भक्तों की रक्षा हो जाय। महाराज श्री ने इन शब्दों का उच्चारण ७ बजे प्रातःकाल किया था। उसके एक घण्टे बाद आकाश का दृश्य बदल गया। आकाश निर्मल हो गया। बादल जाने कहां चले गये। वायु साधारण रूप से बहने लगी। धूप निकल आई। अधिवेशन का कार्य सुचारु रूप से, जिस प्रकार

प्रतिदिन चलता था, उसी प्रकार चलता रहा । सभी बाधायें अकस्मात् शान्त हो गईं और दिल्ली का 'शतमुख कोटि होमात्मक महायज्ञ' निर्विघ्न समाप्त हुआ ।

दिल्ली के इस महान् धार्मिक समारोह के पश्चात् तीन महीने के भीतर ही भगवती भागीरथी के तट पर कानपुर के केवल ब्राह्मण-मंडल ने द्वितीय 'शतमुख कोटि होमात्मक महायज्ञ' का आयोजन किया । इसमें भी महाराज श्री ने पधार कर अपनी दैवी संरक्षता प्रदान की । बड़े ही सात्विक ढंग से यह द्वितीय 'शतमुख कोटि होमात्मक महायज्ञ' सम्पन्न हुआ । विश्व शांति के उद्देश्य से इन दो 'शतमुख कोटि होमात्मक महायज्ञ, के द्वारा उत्तर भारत में यज्ञयुग की नींव सुदृढ़ हुई । आप कानपुर से प्रस्थान करके कुछ दिन विश्राम करने के लिये प्रयाग आ गये ।

ता। २७ मई, १९४४ ई० को महाराज श्री ने प्रथम बार पीठयात्रा के लिये प्रस्थान किया । समाचार मिलते ही हरिद्वार से बदरीनाथ धाम तक जनता में अपूर्व उत्साह छा गया और गढ़वाल में धार्मिक जनता ने स्थान स्थान पर स्वागत-समितियों का निर्माण कर लिया । त। २८ मई, १९४४ ई० को हरिद्वार में पधारते ही, वहाँ की दण्डी-संन्यासी मण्डली, निरंजनी अखाड़ा, निर्वाणी अखाड़ा; जूना अखाड़ा, सन्त आश्रम के साधु सन्त महात्मा, कर्म वीर महन्त श्री शान्तानन्द नाथ जी, स्वामी शिवदयालु गिरि जी आदि संन्यासियों के समुदाय ने तथा विद्वत् समिति, गंगा सभा, महावीर-दल, अग्निदल, वर्णाश्रम-स्वराज्य-संघ आदि संस्थाओं, ऋषिकुल आदि पाठशालाओं एवं म्युनिसिपल तथा सरकारी अधिकारी-वर्ग और कर्मचारियों ने जिस समारोह के साथ भगवान् शंकराचार्य महाराज का स्वागत और शोभायात्रा का आयोजन किया वह हरिद्वार के इतिहास में अपूर्व दृश्य था । सभी

वर्ग ने महाराज श्री का श्रद्धापूर्वक अभिवादन और अभिनन्दन
किया। श्रवणनाथ-ज्ञान-मन्दिर में तथा कुशावर्त में आपके उपदेश
हुये। जिस समय महाराज श्री ब्रह्मकुण्ड पर पधारे और अपने
ब्रह्मदण्ड से उत्तराखण्ड के प्रधान तीर्थ का स्पर्श किया उस समय
भगवती भागीरथी का हृदय मानो उछल उठा, जिन्होंने देखा उन्होंने
उसका अनुभव किया। वह दृश्य वर्णनातीत था। धर्म के जयघोष से
आकाशमंडल गूंज उठा। लाखों नर-नारियों ने जगद्गुरु का दर्शन्
प्राप्त कर अपना जीवन सफल किया।

ता। १ जून, १९४४ ई० को आचार्य श्री ऋषीकेश पधारे। ऋषीकेश
महात्माओं की नगरी है। वहां की शोभा-यात्रा और स्वागत में देवी
चमत्कार प्रत्यक्ष हुआ। मध्याह्न की कड़ी दोपहरी में जैसे जैसे
जुलूस बढ़ता था, आगे आगे मेघ छाया करते चल रहे थे।
शताब्दियों के बाद इस प्रदेश में शंकराचार्य का दर्शन हुआ। सभी
सन्त-महात्मा इस प्रकार धर्म की जागृति देखकर प्रसन्न हुये। इसी
प्रकार देवप्रयाग और श्रीनगर में महान् समारोह के साथ आपका
स्वागत हुआ। श्रीनगर में पौड़ी के भी गण्यमान्य पुरुष पधारे थे।
वहाँ की जनता का उत्साह देखकर और ज्योतिर्मठ के प्रति इस
उद्देश्य की श्रद्धा भक्ति – देखकर महाराज श्री को भी सन्तोष हुआ।
तदनन्तर रुद्रप्रयाग, कर्णप्रयाग तथा नन्द प्रयाग का स्वागत ग्रहण
करते हुये आप चमोली (लालसांगा) में पहुंचे। वहां की जनता ने भी
आपका हार्दिक स्वागत सत्कार किया। इस प्रकार महाराज श्री ता।
९ जून, १९४४ ई० को ज्योतिर्मठ पहुंच गये। वहां की जनता आपके
स्वागत के लिये अत्यन्त उत्सुक थी ही, अतः जोशीमठ से लगभग
१ मील प्रथम से यहाँ की जनता श्री आचार्य चरण का स्वागत कर
एक शोभायात्रा के रूप में श्री महाराज जी को ज्योतिर्मठ तक ले

गई। पीठ भवन में पहुँचते ही आपने उपस्थित जनता तथा उत्तर भारत की समस्त हिन्दू राजा प्रजा को शुभाशीर्वाद देते हुये पीठभवन में पदार्पण किया।

इस वर्ष १९४४ ई० में आपने यहीं चातुर्मास्य व्रत किया। आषाढ़ी पूर्णिमा को जगद्गुरु शंकराचार्य महाराज श्री का महान् समारोह के साथ पूजन हुआ। इस काल में सम्पूर्ण पर्वतीय प्रदेश में विशेष धार्मिक जागृति हुई। आश्विन शुक्लाष्टमी (शारदीय नवरात्र) को नव-निर्मित भव्य मन्दिर में जिसे महाराज श्री ने ही पीठभवन निर्माण के साथ साथ बनवाया था, श्री पूर्णगिरि देवी की विशाल मूर्ति की प्रतिष्ठा कर वहां एक संस्कृत-विद्यालय की स्थापना की। इसके पश्चात् महाराज श्री ने धर्म-प्रचारार्थ पर्वतीय प्रदेश ज्योतिर्मठ से प्रस्थान किया।

ज्योतिर्मठ से आचार्य श्री भारत के विद्याकेन्द्र भगवान् विश्वनाथ की पुरी काशी जी पधारे। इस समय काशी के अस्सी घाट गंगा तट पर सात अतिरुद्र और पाँच महारुद्र महायज्ञों का एक साथ ही एक विशाल मण्डप में आयोजन किया गया था। उसी अवसर पर अखिल-भारतीय-धर्म-संघ का चतुर्थ वार्षिक महाधिवेशन भी हुआ। दिल्ली के वृहत समारोह के समान काशी के इस धार्मिक समारोह का नेतृत्व महाराज श्री ने ही किया। आप की संरक्षता में वृहत आयोजन पूर्ण हुआ, जिसका धार्मिक प्रभाव समस्त देश पर पड़ा।

विश्वनाथपुरी में भगवान् शंकर की वृहत् उपासना के बाद अब विश्व-कल्याणार्थ भगवती दुर्गा की आराधना प्रारम्भ हुई। भगवती की सब से बड़ी आराधना लक्षचण्डी महायज्ञ का आयोजन प्रथम वार लखनऊ में हुआ। देवी की उपासना में विघ्न स्वाभाविक हैं। किन्तु

आचार्य श्री के पदार्पण से समस्त परिस्थिति अनुकूल हो गई। द्वितीय लक्षचण्डी यज्ञ उदयपुर राज्य में और तृतीय बम्बई नगर में सम्पन्न हुए। आचार्य श्री बम्बई के लक्षचण्डी महायज्ञ मे पधारे। वहां अखिल-भारतीय धर्मसंघ के वार्षिक महाधिवेशान का नेतृत्व किया और अपने तेजोमय आभापूर्ण व्यक्तित्व एवं त्यागपूर्ण व्यवहारों और मार्मिक उपदेशों द्वारा दक्षिण पश्चिम भारत मे उत्तराम्नाय के धर्माचर्य के स्वरूप का सर्वोपरि आदर्श स्थापित किया।

प्रयाग के सन १९४२ ई० के कुम्भ से १९४८ ई० अर्द्ध कुम्भ तक भारत में सर्वत्र बड़े-बड़े महायज्ञ सम्पन्न हुए। महाराज श्री के पीठाधीश्वर होने के पश्चात् समस्त भारत में एक अपूर्व धर्म जाग्रति हो गई और जहाँ तहाँ सभी ओर सनातन धर्म का डंका बजने लगा। यह सब महाराज श्री के व्यक्ति त्व की महानता थी।

बम्बई के लक्षचण्डी महायज्ञ का नेतृत्व करने के पश्चात् आप मध्यप्रांत मे जबलपुर के पास बंधा ग्राम में कुछ समय विश्राम करने के लिये आगए। यहाँ भी आपका एक चातुर्मास्य व्रत हुआ और चारों ओर अपने उदेशामृत से सब लोगों को कृतार्थ किया। यही से अर्द्धकुम्भ के अवसर पर प्रयाग पधारे। इस समय पूज्यपाद् शारदा-पीठाधीश्वर स्वामी अभिनव सच्चिदानन्द तीर्थ जी महाराज भी प्रयाग पधारे। पर्वस्नान के लिए दोनों धर्मचार्यों की सम्मिलित शोभायात्रा का हृरप परम मनोहर था। महाराज श्री की सवारी एक चान्दी सोने की शिविका पर आगे थी। उसके बाद दूसरी चान्दी-सोने की शिविका पर शारदापीठ धीश्वर जी की सवारी थी। इसके बाद निर्वाणी, निरंजनी, जूना अखाड़ों के महन्त मंडले श्वरो की पंक्ति थी। दोनो धर्माचार्यों का साथ साथ स्नान हुआ और संसार ने देखा की

धर्मपीठो के आचार्यगण कितनी अभिन्न हृदयता के साथ परस्पर व्यवहार रखते हैं ।

अर्द्धकुम्भ के पश्चात् भी कुछ दिन महाराज श्री प्रयाग मे ही रहे और उस वर्ष का चातुर्मास्य व्रत, चाँद प्रेस एडमान्सटन रोड में सम्पन्न हुआ । तत्पश्चात् पुनः धर्म प्रचार यात्रा प्रारम्भ की । भक्तों की प्रर्थना पर सर्व प्रथम इटावा पधारे । वहाँ डा । विश्वम्भरनाथ मेहरोत्रा के स्थान "श्री ज्योतिर्धम में निवास किया । दैनिक प्रातःदर्शन दीक्षा आदि एवं सायं काल उपदेश का कार्यक्रम चलता रहा ।

कुछ दिन इटावा में निवास करके श्री चरण कछलाघाट एक यज्ञ में पधारे । यहाँ पर श्री शंकराचार्य महाराज के स्वागत में एक वृहत् शोभायात्र निकाली गई और जनता ने अपने धर्माचार्य का भव्य स्वागत किया । प्रतिदिन सायंकाल महाराज श्री का उपदेशामृत पान करने के लिये जनता की अपार भीड़ होती रही । सरल सुबोध भाषा में धर्म के गूढ़ रहस्यों का प्रतिपादन सुन कर जनता अत्यंत लाभान्वित होती रही ।

कछलाघात का यज्ञ सम्पन्न करके महाराज श्री शूकरक्षेत्र (सोरों) पधारे । यहाँ के तीर्थ-पुरोहितो एवं धार्मिक जनता ने अपने धर्माचार्य के स्वागत मे एक भव्प शोभायात्रा निकाली । अंत में सभा हुई, जिसमें जनता तथा विशिष्ट संस्थाओं द्वारा अभिनन्दन आदि भेंट किये गये ।

कासगंज (एटा) से कुछ विशिष्ट व्यक्तियों ने आकर महाराज जी से कासगंज पधारने की प्रार्थना की । भक्तों की विशेष आतुरता देख कर श्री चरण कासगंज पधारे । यहा भीं भव्य शोभायात्रा निकाली गई और स्थान स्थान पर भक्तों द्वारा आरती-पूजन द्वारा स्वागत हुआ ।

यहाँ आपका शिविर एक बगीचा में रहा, जहाँ प्रातःकाल से रात्रि
११-१२ बजे तक दर्शनार्थियों एवं जिज्ञासुओं का ताता बँधा रहता।

आगरा के विशिष्ट व्यक्तियों द्वारा कई बार की गई प्रार्थना पर
महाराज श्री कासगंज से आगरा पधारे। यहाँ पर कुछ दिन आपका
निवास 'भदावर हाउस' और कुछ दिन 'हरि पर्वत' पर रहा। सदा
की भाति नित्य दर्शन-दीक्षा, उपदेश आदि का कार्यक्रम चलता रहा।

मुरादाबाद के विद्वानों एवं जनता द्वारा प्रार्थना पर आप आगरा से
मुरादाबाद पधारे। स्वागत में विशाल शोभायात्रा निकाली गई।
स्थान स्थान पर जनता ने अपने धर्माचार्य का पूजन आरती द्वारा
स्वागत किया। दशनार्हियों की अपार भीड़ बढ़ती गई। सभी
मंत्रमुग्ध की भाँति श्री शंकराचार्य का दर्शन् पाकर उपदेश सुनकर
तृप्त होते रहे।

इस प्रकार क्रमशः धर्म प्रचार करते हुये महाराज श्री ने इस वर्ष
ग्रीष्मारम्भ में ज्योतिष्पीठ की दूसरी यात्रा की। पर्वतीय जनता इस
समय विकट परिस्थिति में दिन व्यतीत कर रही थी। पर्वत में बहुत
काल से वर्षा नहीं हुई थी और और जनता अत्यंत दुखी थी। खेतों
की सारी फसल सूखकर समाप्त हो रही थी। वर्षा होने की सम्भावना
हो सकने का कोई आभास भी नहीं होता था। परंतु जिस दिन
महाराज श्री ने पीठभवन में प्रवेश किया पर्वत की चोटियों पर बादल
दिखने लगे। दूसरे दिन बादलों से सारा आकाश आच्छादित हो गया
और वर्षा भी होने लगी। चार दिन तक लगातार वर्षा होती रही।
पर्वत की सारी जनता अत्यन्त प्रसन्न हो गई और सभी के मुख से
यही शब्द निकल पड़े कि महाराज श्री के प्रसाद से ही वर्षा हुई है।
दूर-दूर से महाराज श्री के दर्शन के लिए लोग दौड़ पड़े। दर्शन करते

हुये भावुक और सरल भक्तों ने कहा "महाराज, हमने सुना है कि आपके पधारने से ही वर्षा हुई है। यह प्रत्यक्ष भी है, क्योंकि आपके आने के पूर्व तीन माह से यहाँ वर्षा नहीं हुई थी। सारी जनता में हाहाकार मच गया था। वर्षा होने से हम सब प्रसन्न हैं और यह सब आपके पदार्पण का ही प्रभाव है।,'

महाराज श्री ने इस वर्ष १९४९ ई० का चातुर्मास्य व्रत यहीं किया और अपने धर्मोपदेश से पर्वतीय जनता को आनन्दित करते हुए वैदिक धर्म की ओर अग्रसर किया। अपना चातुर्मास्य-व्रत समाप्त करके फिर धर्म-प्रचार-यात्रा के लिये प्रस्थान किया। प्रयाग, काशी, कलकत्ता, हरिद्वार, देहरादून, मंसूरी आदि स्थानों में भ्रमण करके स्थान स्थान पर सनातन धर्म की विजय-पताका फहराई। सभी स्थानों में धार्मिक जागृति हुई। जनता में अपूर्व उत्साह और भगत्परायणता में अनूठी निष्ठा का विशिष्ट बीजारोपण हुआ।

१९५० ई० में महाराज श्री का निवास लखनऊ में हो रहा था। राजा दिलीपपुर, श्री पशुपति प्रताप सिंह उस समय श्रीचरण के दर्शनार्थ वहाँ गये हुये थे। एक दिन उन्होंने महाराज श्री से प्रार्थना की, "इस विचार से कि प्रयाग में एक आश्रम बन जाय, मैं अलोपीबाग-स्थित अपनी कोठी ज्योतिर्मठ गद्दी को अर्पण करना चाहता हूँ।" महाराज श्री ने उनकी यह प्रार्थना अस्वीकार कर दी। कारण यह था कि आपकी यह नीति थी कि कभी किसी से कोई भेंट पूजा, बिदाई न लेना और जहाँ जाते थे अपने शिविर के सामने के यह सूचनापट टँगवा देते थे कि इस शिविर में कोई भेंट, पूजा-द्रव्य आदि नहीं चढ़ेगा। किन्तु राजा साहब के बार-बार आग्रह करने पर महाराज श्री ने कहा, "यदि कोठी का बयनामा हमारे नाम कर दो, तो हम ले लेंगे।" इस पर वह राजी हो गये। इसके बाद महाराज श्री ने

राजा दिलीपपुर के सेक्रेटरी को बुलाया और कोठी की कीमत पूछी। सेक्रैटरी ने कहा, "पिछले वर्ष यह कोठी बिकाऊ थी। उस समय राजा साहब ने उसकी कीमत एक लाख रुपये माँगी थी, किन्तु खरीदार ने ६५०००) पैंसठ हजार रुपये लगाये थे। इससे यह कोठी नहीं बिकी "। इसके बाद महाराज श्री ने विचार किया कि हमारा तो जिस खदान से ६५,०००) आयेगा उसी से एक लाख भी आ जावेगा। इसलिये उसकी कीमत एक लाख ही क्यों न दे दी जाय।

एक दिन महाराज श्री ने राजा दिलीपपुर को बुलाया और उनको एक लाख रुपया कोठी की कीमत और रजिस्ट्री आदि के खर्च के लिये रुपये दिये और कहा कि कोठी का बयनामा इलाहाबाद में जाकर हमारे नाम कर दो। उन्होंने महाराज श्री से एक आदमी माँगा। महाराज श्री ने उनके साथ अपना एक अन्तरंग सेवक कर दिया। बयनामा हो गया और कोठी महाराज श्री के नाम से बय हो गई।

बयनामा हो जाने के बाद इलाहाबाद में चर्चा चली कि महाराज श्री के पास एक लाख रुपया कहाँ से आया। वे किसी से द्रव्य लेते नहीं और कहीं से कोई आमदनी भी नहीं है। पहिले तो रजिस्ट्रार ने कहा मेरे सामने रुपया दिया गया। उनसे पूछा-नोट कैसे थे। उन्होंने कहा जैसे साधारण-तय होते हैं, वैसे ही थे। लोग बड़े आश्चर्य में हो गये। इसके दो महीने बाद महाराज श्री स्वयं इलाहाबाद आये। लोगों ने महाराज से पूछा, "महाराज श्री किसी से कुछ लेते तो हैं नहीं और एकटठा एक लाख रुपये महाराज जी ने दे दिया। इससे लोगों को बड़ा आश्चर्य है कि यह एक लाख रुपये कहां से आया।" महाराज श्री ने कहा कि इस रुपये के आने में किसी मनुष्य का हाथ नहीं है। जब बहुत पूछा गया तो महाराज श्री ने कहा "महाभारत् के

समय जब द्रौपदी की चीर बढ़ी थी तो हजारों गज बढ़े हुये वस्त्र कहाँ से आये? दूसरी बात यह है कि द्रौपदी जैसी साड़ी पहने पहने थी, वैसा ही कपड़ा आया । कुछ लाल, कुछ हरा, कुछ पीला, ऐसा नहीं हुआ । भगवान् जब देते हैं, तो पूरा देते हैं और सच्ची वस्तु देते हैं । जो काम महाभारत के समय में हो सकता था, वह अब भी हो सकता है । भगवान् सदा एक रस रहते हैं, उनमें कोई अंतर नहीं आता ।"

जिस समय यह कोठी खरीदी गई थी, उसकी स्थिति जर्जर थी । महाराज श्री ने प्रयाग में इसे ज्योतिर्मठ का एक विशिष्ट स्थान बनाने के लिये उसमें पूर्णतया सुधार तथा नवनिर्माण कराया । वह एक विशाल आश्रम बन गया, जो आज दिन "ब्रह्म-निवास" के नाम से विख्यात है । उसमें पचासों कमरे हैं और ऊपर नीचे सैकड़ों की संख्या में साधक, ब्रह्मचारी, संन्यासी आदि निवास कर सकते हैं ।

Chapter 8
Promotion of Righteousness

After travelling about on your spiritual travels you again came back to Jabalpur and for some days made your abode there. After sojourning in Jabalpur a while, in January 1942 (the year of 1998 in the Indian Vikrami calendar), he moved on and soon came to the world-renowned Maha Kumbha festival. All the *yogis*, ascetics, saints, *mahants* (heads of monasteries), *rajas*, *maharajas*, the heads of the circles of *swamis* and all the scholars dedicated to *dharma* etc, and the diverse *sampradaya* (sects), and the *akharas* of the *dashnaama* organisations of *sannyasis* were present there. *On the occasion of the great festival of the traditional and devout Kumbha you came for to Prayag for the leadership of the community of sadhu and virtuous mankind. The foremost of the sadhu samaaj and all the heads of the akhaaras of the dashnaami sannassi were present in your prescence for darshan of the feet of the acharya and to give their greetings. And they entreated you,* 'Prabho (Lord), we are your *sena* (army). Given us your able command. We promise you our service.'

In reply Shri Bhagwan Shankaracharya ji gave this instruction, 'You people should do *yoga sadhana* according to the spiritual instruction you receive from your own *guru,* and remain applied in success of *ishta* (desired, beloved, god). By *tyaaga* (surrender) and *tapa* (austerity) you will raise the *shakti* (spiritual power). Advice and strong organisation will be considered and at the proper time instructions will be given, in this matter there is no uncertainty. You people are the victorious *sena* (army), possessed of the spiritual energy of the *dharmapeeth* of Jagadguru Shankaracharya. You people should always put your thoughts on the reputation and decorum of the northern *peeth* of Jyotirmath.'

Afterwards, all the mandaleshwars (the heads of mandalas of swamis) and the sadhu samaaj turned out and arranged a wonderful procession. All India's mahants (heads of monasteries), the mandaleshwars (heads of the orders of swamis), and the upright kings and subjects welcomed you fully here. And on the occasion of the mahasnaan (the great bathing) at Triveni Tirth (the sacred place of the confluence of the three rivers of Ganga, Yamuna and Saraswati) yours had been the first dip before everyone else. This was their support for Maharaj Shri and his task of restoration of Jyotirmath. But having gained the title of Jagadguru Shankaracharya made no difference to him, for as before he lived in *tyaaga* (surrender) and *vairaagya* (freedom from desires).

Your relentless command was, 'Don't offer wealth to this Dharma Sinhaasana (Lion Throne of Dharma), you should offer of the mind's beloved vices - those you are hiding and do not want to let go. Those you should offer here. Really by doing this you people will be happy. When you have made an offering of *dharma* to the mind, then the pure life of you people will be going ahead, in the direction of greatest peace.'

*

Nowadays it was possible even for the common person to obtain the *darshan* of Maharaj. Having seen this, one recluse, a *mahatma* said, 'Bhagwan, if we people had known that these *darshans* were going to become so cheap then for this reason we would have stayed more days in the jungles undertaking austerities in search of these *darshans*, we were not deceived.'

How much mystery is there in these words of a recluse? From them it becomes very clear how inaccessible he was, how rare and perfect a life he was living in the jungles.

Sometimes, of his own accord, Maharaj Shri spoke in front of devotees providing a glimpse at his own solitary life abounding in surrender. He once said. 'Who was to know that one day it would be necessary to ascend the Sinhaasana (Lion Throne) and that in this act of attachment my own life of freewill would be chained? Back at that time we had been constantly always wore a loin-cloth. Sometimes that was bound as a *pagari* (turban) on the head and sometimes it was been hung on the waist. Making one smallish flat stone to be a *tava* (a pan to cook flat bread), and kneading the *aataa* flour. When the *roti* (a flat round unleavened bread) was baking and the sounds of cracking came from that stone, then the heart spontaneously was caused to invoke *ananda* (bliss), in waves. Having seen this sort of circumstance anybody would have said: 'This is a *paramahansa*' and someone else would be thinking that 'This is an *avadhoota* (an ascetic of a certain class)'. But no, it was similar to possessing *jeevanmukti* (freedom of human life) and was giving boundless *ananda* (happiness) of *jeevanmukti* to the inner soul.'

*

After the Kumbha at Prayag Maharaj Shri proceeded to Kashi, to relax for some days. But he set out again, on account of the need to travel to promulgate *dharma*. *So a second time he travelled to Jabalpur staying again at his old place in Baldev Baag and devotees requested you stay in Jabalpur for chatrumasya vrata (fasting in the four months rainy season). You stayed and did a continuous chatrumasya vrata at Raina Besaraa, in the Gol Bazaar, and another at the kothi – mansion - of Seth Radhakrishna in Ganjipur.* During this period, the silver and gold articles of the worthy *achaarya* of the *peeth* were made. The Sinhaasana (Lion Throne), the *palaki* (sedan chair), the *chamara* (whisk), the *chatra* (parasol), the *danda* (staff) etc., all in conformity with the wishes of the victorious Shankara.

At this time too the building of Jyotish Peeth was being organised since the *peeth* had been laid to waste for a long time past. Situated in Uttarkhand (the 'northern region') Bhagwan Aadi Shankaracharya's place of *'leela bhoomi'* was an area of about two-and-a-half acres. Some of it had gone into the possession of the government and some of it peasant folk had appropriated for themselves, and because the land of Jyotish Peeth had been cut about in this way, Bharat Dharma Mahamandal itself had made renewed efforts to restore the land. Gaining the assistance of Deputy Commisioner Sir James Clay, the land was taken back. After the inauguration it was presented to Maharaj Shri, given to him for him to restore. After his able disciples told him of the distinctive features of the location then Maharaj Shri himself decided the position of the *peeth*. Then the work commenced of building the Jyotishpeeth Bhavan. In those days there was no practicable or speedy way to send materials other than by suitable post. For the reason that none of the requisite materials such as paint, nails, latches etc etc can be obtained such a mountainous area, these were obtained by parcel post. It was arranged for thousands of *rupees* to be sent by insured post to Jyotirmath every week in order that a two-storey *peeth* building be constructed at that tranquil place. In front of this, at some little distance, arrangements were made for the completion of the building of a temple to Shri Purnagiri Devi which had been started but only half-finished by Maharajah Rameshwar Singh, the late king of Darbhanga (Bihar), then the image of Devi Ji was installed. [Maharaja Rameshwar Singh Bahadur, 1860-1929, ruled from 1898 to 1929 and was known as the "Siddha Tantik" & "Rajarsi", 'the Sage King'.] The *bhavan* became famous by the name of Jyotishpeeth Bhavan. This is an extremely pleasing and roomy building situated on the way to Shri Badrinarayana (at Badrinath). In this there are thirty rooms and several hundred people can stay at once.

*

Maharaj Shri was travelling about for the purpose of promulgating *dharma* (religion). *You went to diverse places and the masses were attracted to your darshan and upadesha (instruction).* So much did the reputation of Jyotirmath grow that within two to three years all of north India's devout folk had become proud of their own *dharmapeeth* and the religious community were proud the ideal management of their own *dharmacharya*, Shri Jyotishpeethadhishvara Maharaaj ("Jyotishpeethadhishvara" meaning 'Restorer of Jyotish Peeth'). On the whole his reputation spread quickly and the main reasons were as follows:

(1) In the personality of Shri Charan was an extraordinary peaceful complete enlightenment. Having once had his *darshan* one wished for repeated *darshan.* Each person who had sought *darshan* afterwards became so influenced by the *darshan* that he got the feeling that none could love him more than Maharaj Shri.

(2) There was a special attraction in the words that appeared from the mouth of Maharaj Shri, simplicity in the *upadeshas* (teachings), which had a freshness and a touching quality, which could not be got elsewhere. *Additionally, your inner being was in such an amazing state that anyone sitting near, hearing your upadeshas had their doubts removed without even asking the questions. Your upadesha (advice) was highly influential because*

they it was solidly supported by the rock of your own experience

(3) In your personality something great was evident. Even in your absence folk became acquainted with uncommon siddhis (successes, powers). Whilst in a predicament, if a devotee of yours remembered you, at that time the predicament would shift. Numerous trusting regular devotees have afterwards told the story of the removal of their own predicaments. Very great atheists have become religious. Those who never did *pranaam* to a *devi* or *devata*, they too have become involved in doing *aarati* to a picture of Shri Charan regularly morning and evening in their own homes

(4) *By virtue of your complete unattachment to vyavahaara (daily business) you had a great influence on folk. Your guidance was that you did not accept puja donations, he did not accept money etc. left at someone's departure, on any occasion.* A signboard was placed in your tent and attached at the peeth bhavan informing svashtikarana karanevaali (ones who chant benedictory mantras), whereupon was written;

भगवत्पूज्यपाद अनन्तश्री विभूषित,

जगद्गुरु शंकराचार्य ज्योतिष्पीठाधीश्वर

स्वामी ब्रह्मानन्द सरस्वती जी महाराज

के दर्शन पूजन दीक्षा आदि में द्रव्य चढ़ाने का निषेध है।

"Bhagavatpuujyapaada Anantashrii Vibhuushhita,
Jagadguru, Shankaraachaarya Jyotishhpiithaadhiishvara,
Swaamii Brahmaananda Sarasvatii jii Mahaaraaja
ke darshana, puujana, diikshaa, aadi men dravya chadhaane kaa
nishhedha hai."

IT IS PROHIBITIED TO MAKE OFFERINGS OF WEALTH
IN THE *DARSHAN, PUJA, DIKSHA* etc.
OF
BHAGWATPUJYAPAD ANANTASHRI VIBHUSHIT JAGADGURU SHANKARACHARYA JYOTISHPEETHADHISHWAR SWAMI BRAHMANAND SARASWATI JI MAHARAAJ

The people were astonished at this guidance, because all saw that several hundred householders stayed with the recluse *mahatma*, also travelling together to promote spirituality, but no wealth was accepted from anyone. What sort of arrangement existed then? Knowing this perplexed people's minds and so they credited this to *siddhis* (spiritual powers) of their Maharaj Shri's life of *yoga* and penance. It was because of this that the learned men wrote before his name "Ananta Shri Vibhushit" 'Limitlessly Adorned with Wealth'. In the history of the *parampara* (lineage) of *acharya* this was the first time this title had been used, for Pujyapaad Maharaaj Shri.

Roaming amongst the various towns of Central India you reawakened dormant feelings for Shankaracharya Ji from centuries before. Consequently, the cheering for Shankaracharya echoed throughout Central India. Again you stayed some time in Jabalpur and again departed for Prayag. The people of Prayag were very happy and enthusiastic, and together they gave you an unprecedented reception. A huge procession turned out, united wherein were the leaders, the wealthy, significant merchants and moneylenders, the *pandits*, the learned community, government workers and officials. The doors of the houses had been decorated. Devotees who were wealthy significant leaders of the neighbourhoods, interrupted the procession to offer *aarati* and to do *puja*. *It was a wonderful pleasure as this procession of yours made its way by the main roads of Prayag, going to the limits of*

the Chauk (the market place) and the Ghantaghar (Clock Tower)
it then turned into a meeting in Purushotam Das Park. There
Maharaj Shri gave his own *"upadeshaamrita"* (nectar teachings)
which gratified the people. Then he came to relax for some days
in the roomy building of Chand Press in Prayag (Allahabad).

After accepting the burden of tasks of the dharmaguru of
Northern India you then engaged in advancing the status of the
dharmapeeth. Having seen their own Gurudeva devote himself in
this way to the work, all your devotees, recluse mahatmas,
scholars too, those who were not remaining to make their own
thoughtful promotion of dharma, all helped Shri Maharaj Ji in
accomplishing the task. In Bengal, Bihar, Uttar Pradesh, Rajputna,
Punjab and Kashmir the flag of Sanatana Dharma was caused to
flutter in the air. Because Maharaj Shri wished to spread *dharma*
in Northern India, all the individual communities of *pandits*, the
communities of *mahatmas* and all the ascetics and *mahants* (heads
of monasteries) made programmes to promulgate *dharma*. One
permanent Dharma Sandha (Righteous Union) was made in the
Hindu community.

At this time all the people of the world, *rajas* and subjects, the animate and the inanimate, etc. all were experiencing a great crisis. There was not peace or pleasure in any part of the earth. All were concerned and bewildered, whether by the untimely earthquake, all kinds of pestilence and plague, civic disorder etc, and the annihilating great worldwide war. Putting their trust in material strength, people were now planning to establish peace by means of warfare.

Having seen the pitiful state of the world, the dharma peeth instigated the awakening of divine energy and for the protection of the world at certain places a great effort was made to worship the Ashutosh ('easily pleased') Bhagwan Shankar (Shiva) and the Paramba Durga, the Ultimate Mother, child-loving and compassioniate

On the shore of the holy water of Yamuna at Delhi preparations were made for Shatmukh Koti Homatmak Mahayagya, the great sacred worship of Bhagwan Shankar by all. Maharaj Shri's support was requested. Acharya Shri and the *dharma peeth* co-operated. Pujyapad Acharya Shri gave his support and set out for Delhi.

Actually, there was such great enthusiam for your arrival in Delhi, and that delight spread. The reception on the platform at Delhi Station was so full that there was no place that could be brought into use. Because of the crowd Maharaj Shri had great difficulty moving, once he had alighted from the train it took him about an hour and half to reach the waiting vehicle. Then from the station a procession commenced that was such a beautiful sight and so much could be said about this great subject. It was written about in the newspapers, that such a procession had never been seen in Delhi. *A sea of humanity appeared on all four sides and this continued all the way until you arrived at the tent in the yagya.*

Along with the Mahayagya were also conventions of the Akhil Bharatiya Dharma Sangha (All India Dharma Association), the Goraksha Sammelan (Cow Protection Society) and a special meeting of the Varnashram Swarajya Sangha (The Varnashram

Home-Rule Association), etc.. Really, by having the governership of the great magnificence of Maharaj Shri, a huge wave of spiritual awakening was spreading throughout all India. This event was unprecedented in the history of the Indian religion in having all the Vedic sections assembled together at one time. By this kind of great religious leadership at Delhi, the capital of India, the divine light of Jyotishpeeth spread the light of *dharma* to the whole of India.

At the time of this gathering on the aforesaid shore of the Yamuna, the sea of humanity surging was on all four sides, and Indra etc. and the *devata* too, as they were keen not to be excluded, all got up and arrived together with their own heavy clouds. It was a winter's day and the cold became a difficulty. Blasts of cold wind caused all the tents and marquees to begin to fly away. Very black clouds gathered. Little drops of water were falling. So it became obvious that there would soon be a dense shower and hailstones too. The view of the clouds became dreadful.

At about seven o'clock in the early morning Maharaj Shri went around the camp looking from one tent to another. After some while, having seen that Indra appears to have gone a little mad, he returned to his own tent. He spoke up, 'If at this time a sleet falls, then it will be a great hardship for the people.' Again he became silent and got on with other work of his.

On the shore of Yamuna in the cold weather was this great *yagya* which had taken so much work to prepare. On the sand of Yamuna Ji, in their hundreds of thousands, little and large, rich and well-thought of, merchants, money-lenders, *brahmachari, sadhu mahatma,* and women and children, suffering arising but all united in the *dharma yagya*, the burden of protecting them all was on Maharaj Shri.

Why does he not protect at this difficult time? But he who had uttered the aforementioned words, he therefore became protector of every devotee. Maharaj Shri had uttered those words in the early morning at seven o'clock and one hour later the outlook of the sky had changed. The sky had become clear. Where had the clouds gone? The wind blew them out of view of the public and the sun came out. The meetings that day appeared to go very well, and it was the same on the following days. All the interruptions had become unexpectedly quietened and Delhi's Shatmukh Koti Homatmak Mahayagya was accomplished without obstruction.

'Pontoon bridge across the holy Jumna carries the faithful toward Brahmans' pandal (rear). Where clear blue Jumna joins yellow Ganges is a famous place of pilgrimage. About 150,000 pilgrims a day passed the stone platform of the holy fires.'
[*'Life Magazine'*, March 13, 1944]

[With an headline proclaiming; 'HINDUS SAY 10.000.000 PRAYERS FOR PEACE' *'Life Magazine'* covered this event in a photospread article over several pages, 37-40, of its March 13, 1944 issue:-

'Last month in Delhi, India, the end of World War II was prayed for on a mass scale unmatched in modern history. Over 10,000,000 verses of praise to the sun god were recited by 1,000

Brahmans (Hindu priests) around a 100 sacred fires for 10 days, six hours a day. This meant 60,000 priestly man-hours, an easy rate of three verses a minute per Brahman. The occasion was the first mahayajna (great sacrifice) under British rule since the time when the Brahmans prayed for the end of slaughters and Moslem baptisms of the tyrant Aurangzeb, one of the last and greatest Mogul emperors. This time the Hindus had decided the time had come to put a stop to the war and distress of the world. Above is the great thatch and bamboo pandal, with the smoke from the sacred fires issuing from the roof and the faithful gathered around among the living tents of the notables.

'The smoke of 100 sacred fires and the murmur of 1,000 praying Brahmans issue from great Pandal outside Delhi beside sacred River Jumna (rear) Feb, 12'
[*'Life Magazine'*, March 13, 1944]

The master verse or Mantra from the 3,000-year-old Veda was: "The sun is the centre of the entire universe; all intelligence, all energy and health are derived from the sun." The fires were made of *peepal*, banyan, *goolhar* and dhak, and fed with ghee (clarified butter), wheat, copra, rice, barley, til and *sarson*. The cost of the mahayajna: $500,000. Headman: His Holiness Shri Jagadguru, Shri Shankaracharya Swami, Shri Yogeshwaranand Teerthaji Meharej, Shri Govardhan of the math (monastery) of Puri.

'Brahmans pray around one of 100 fires, starteed by rubbing sticks together. Devotees of Vishnu wear vertical white and red stripes on the forehead (right). Devotees of the more popular Shiva wear horizontal stripes of gray or yellow earth (center).'
[*'Life Magazine'*, March 13, 1944]

The essence of the tolerant, hold-all religion of Hinduism is that what a man does in life determines how he will be reborn and what will happen to him in his next life. The great sacrifice, therefore, was to atone for the past evil behavior of mankind. To die, the Hindus believe, is merely to begin living again; to be born is a disaster; both are small expressions of the One Absolute, Infinite, Impersonal, Self-Existent, Inexpressible "It" that can be worshipped as one red, four-headed God, Brahma, or as many gods. There are thousands of varieties of Hinduism, but Hindus worship at the shrine nearest to them, whatever it is.']

*

Within three months of this magnificent *dharmik* event in Delhi, the Brahman Mandal made preparations for a second Shatmukha Koti Homatmak Mahayagya, only this one was on the shore of Bhagavati Bhagirathi [an alternate name for the River Ganga] at Kanpur. Maharaj Shri graced this event too, giving his divine support. And this second Shatamukh Koti Homatmak Mahayagya was accomplished in a very sincere way. By way of these two Shatmukh Koti Homatmak Mahayagyas a strong foundation was laid during this period of *yagyas* in Northern India towards creating the goal of world peace,.

After your departure from Kanpur you went to Prayag to rest for a few days. On the 27th May 1944 Maharaj Shri departed for his first journey to the peeth, and on receipt of news of your coming, unprecedented enthusiasm spread amongst the populace to as far away as Badrinath Dham. Reception committees were organised at the houses of devout people in Garhwal.

On 28th May 1944 you arrived in Hardwar. There the Dandi-Sannyaasi Mandali, the Niranjani Akhaara, the Nirvaani Akhaara; the Juuna Akhaara, the Sant Ashram of *sadhus*, the Karma Vir Mahant Shri Shantanand Nath Ji, Swami Shivadayaalu Giri Ji etc., the community of *sannyaasis* and Vidwat Samiti, Ganga Sabha, Mahavir Dal, Agni Dal, Varnashram Swaraajya etc organisations, Rishikula etc, schools, and municipal and government officer sections, all came together in order to welcome Bhagwan

Shankaracharya Maharaj, and arrange a procession. That scene was unprecedented in the history of Hardwar.

[note: *"Akhaara"* means literally the 'place for practice'. In the beginning Adi Shankaracharya established seven Akharas namely Mahanirvani, Niranjani, Juna, Atal, Avahan, Agni and Anand Akhara. The Akhaaras were established by Shree Adi Shankaracharya who divided Sannyasa into two categories: Astradharis (weapon holders) and *Shastradharis* (scripture holders)]

Every class greeted and praised Maharaj Shri. *You lectured in Shravananath Gyaan Mandir and at Kushavarta Ghat.* At this time Maharaj Shri then proceeded to Brahmakund (Har ki Pauri Ghat, the place of the 'Footprint of Vishnu') and he touched the most sacred place in Uttarkhand with his *brahma danda* (staff). At that moment the heart of Bhagavati Bhagirathi (Ganga River) leapt, and that was also the perception of those who watched. That sight was beyond description. The sphere of the sky roared with the cheering of *dharma*. Having obtained *darshan* of Jagadguru hundreds of thousands of lives became fruitful.

On the 1st June 1944 Acharya Shri then proceeded on to Rishikesh. Rishikesh is a town of *mahatmas*. A beautiful journey there and a divine spectacle became apparent, for in the difficulty of midday (which is generally very bright and hot in this season] the calvacade of cars moved forwards in the shadow of clouds. It had been a century since the region had received *darshan* of a Shankaracharya and all the saints and *mahatmas* were delighted to see this kind of awakening of *dharma*. *In Devaprayag and Shrinagar you were received in like fashion too, with great grandeur.* In Shrinagar, those men of Pauri who were considered respectable, arrived there. Having seen the enthusiasm of the folk there' and having seen the reverence towards Jyotirmath and their faith in this goal, Maharaj Shri was gratified too. *Afterwards you accepted welcomes at Rudraprayag, Karnaprayag and Nandaprayag before arriving in Chamoli (Lal Sanga). There the people gave you a hearty respectful welcome.* In this way Maharaj Shri eventually arrived in Jyotirmath on 9th June 1944. *The people there were very keen to welcome you.* Therefore people came out to welcome Shri Acharya Charan, and from about one mile before Joshimath they formed a procession to take Shri Maharaj Ji to Jyotirmath. *When you reached the peeth bhavana (building) you gave your auspicious blessing to the people present and to all the kings and subjects of North India.*

In this year of 1944 you did the chaaturmaasya vrata (rainy season fast - from July to October) right there. On the full moon day of Ashada (Guru Purnima, July 6th 1944) Jagadguru Shankaracharya Shri was worshipped with great grandeur. In this time there was an abundant spiritual awakening in the entire mountainous province. For the Autumnal Navaratra (the nine-day worship of Durga during September 1944), in the newly constructed beautiful *mandir,* which Maharaj Shri had built together with the creation of the *peeth* building. Having installed a large *murti* (statue) of Shri Purnagiri Devi he arranged a Sanskrit school there. After this, Maharaj Shri set out from the mountainous region of Jyotirmath in order to promote *dharma.*

From Jyotirmath Acharya Shri arrived at India's centre of learning, Kashi (Varanasi), the city of Bhagwan Vishwanath (Lord Shiva). At this time at Kashi on the Ganga shore at Assi Ghat seven Atirudra (a ritual to Lord Shiva) and five Maharudra Mahaayagyas (great rituals to Lord Shiva) were together being arranged in a big *mandap* (pavilion). At this time was also the fourth annual congress of the Akhil Bharatiya Dharma Sangha (All India Dharma Assembly). Under the leadership of Maharaj Shri this spiritual magnificence was equal in magnificence to the Delhi *mahayagya. With your support a great effort was made and a religious influence descended upon the whole country.*

After Lord Shankar's great worship in the city of Vishwanath, now was the worship of Durga the goddess of all happiness and wealth. The greatest worship of Bhagavati (Durga) was the Lakshachandi Mahayagya (a great sacrifice for the benefit of the entire humanity), first performed in Lucknow. Hindrances in the worship of Devi (Durga) are natural, but by Acharya Shri going to the place, all things became propitious. A second Lakshachandi

Mahayagya was accomplished in Udaipur State (Rajastan), and a third in Bombay (Mumbai) city. Acharya Shri arrived at the Lakshachandi Mahayagya in Bombay where he took leadership of the Akhil Bharatiya Dharma Sangha (All-India Dharma Association). With his brilliant fully illuminated personality and by way of his moving *upadeshas* (teachings) he established a lofty example of their religious conduct of the northern *math* (Badrinath -Jyotirmath) to those in south-west India.

En Guru ved Offerfest i Bombay.

Guru. I Hind. = rel. Vejleder, Rabbi. Bruges 1) Om Stifteren af et rel. Parti, se f.Eks. Sikherne. 2) Om den enkeltes personlige G. — En G. gør Disciplen til et med sig ved en Indvielse, G u r u-D i k s h a, og lærer ham en hemmelig Mantra, Sentens, Kraftord, der indeholder hans Lære. Disc. tjener sin G. med kritikløs Lydighed og tilbeder ham oftest som en Inkarnation af Guddommen. Det hævdes alm., at man aldrig naar den endelige Forløsning uden en G.   P. H. L.

[Contained in the Danish *'Illustrated Religion Dictionary'* of 1946 Volume 2, page 62, is a photograph of Guru Dev attending the *mahayaagya* with the caption 'A Guru at an Offering Feast in

Bombay'. The entry offers a definition of the word 'Guru':-

"Guru" – I Hindi = Religious supervisor.

(1) The founder of a religious group (e.g. Sikhs)

(2) The individual's personal Guru. A Guru makes the disciple merge with himself through initiation, Guru-deeksha, and teaches him a secret mantra, a powerword, containing his teaching. The disciple serves his Guru through uncritical service and worships him, often as an incarnation of that God. It is said that "You never get final liberation without a Guru"]

*

[Guru Dev's teachings were not restricted to the spiritual progress of his devotees. In 1946 the Gita Press in Gorakpur produced a special issue of their magazine *'Kalyana'* in which Guru Dev gave support raising awareness concerning the sacred cow;

गोधन

भगवत्पूज्यपाद अनन्तश्रीविभूषित जगद्गुरु श्रीशङ्कराचार्य ज्योतिष्पीठाधीश्वर श्री ब्रह्मानन्द सरस्वती जी महाराज क उपदेश:-

धमशास्त्र में गोधन का विशेष माहात्म्य बतलाया गया है । लिखा है -

सर्वेषामेव भूतानां गावः शरणमुत्तमम् ।

हिन्दू - संस्कृति इस भावना से परिपूर्ण है कि -

यद्गृहे दुःखिता गावः स याति नरके नरः ।

किन्तु जब से पाश्चात्त्यों की सभ्यता - संस्कृति का हमारी सभ्यता - संस्कृति के साथ सम्मिश्रण हुआ है, तब से भारतीय शिक्षा - विधान के लोप होने से अधिकांशतः शास्त्र-पुराणादि की अनभिज्ञता के कारण गो-ब्राह्मण आदि के प्रति शास्त्रीय धार्मिक बुद्धि का लोप-सा हो गया है ।

गोवंश आज व्यावहारिक उपयोगिता की दृष्टि से भौतिक तुला पर तौला जा रहा है । किन्तु स्मरण रहे कि आज का भौतिक विज्ञान गोवंश की उस सूक्ष्मातिसूक्ष्म धरमोत्कृष्ट उपयोगिता का पता ही नहीं लगा सकता, जिसे भारतीय शास्त्रकारों ने अपनी दिव्यद्रिष्टि से प्रत्यक्ष कर लिया था । गोवंश की धार्मिक महानता उसमें जिन सूक्ष्मातिसूक्ष्म कारण-रूप तत्त्वों की प्रखरता के कारण है, उनकी खोज और जानकारी के लिये आधुनिक वैज्ञानिकों के भौतिक यन्त्र सदैव स्थूल ही रहेंगे । यही कारण है कि बीसवीं सदी का प्रौढ़ विज्ञानवेत्त भी गोमाता के लोम-लोम में देवताओं के निवास का

रहस्य और प्रातः गोदर्शन, गोपूजन, गोदेवा आदि का वास्तविक तथ्य समझने में असफल रहता है। गोधन का धार्मिक महत्त्व भाव - जगत से सम्बन्ध रखता है और वह या तो ऋतम्भरा प्रज्ञाद्वारा अनुभवगम्य है अथवा शास्त्रप्रमाणद्वारा जाना जा सकता है, भौतिक यन्त्रोंद्वारा नहीं।

धमशास्त्र तो गोधन की महानता और पवित्रता का वर्णन करता ही है, किन्तु भारतीय अर्थशास्त्र में गोपालन का विशेष महत्त्व है। कौटिलीय अर्थशास्त्र में गो-पालन और गो-रक्षण का विस्तृत विवरण मिलता है। जिस भूमि में खेती न होती हो, उसे गोचर बनाने का आदेश अर्थशास्त्र का ही है। इस प्रकार गोधन 'अर्थ' और 'धर्म' दोनों का प्रबल पोष क है। अर्थ से ही काम कामनाओं की सिद्धि होती है और धर्म से ही मोक्ष की। अतएव गोधन से अर्थ, धर्म, काम, मोक्ष - चारों की प्राप्ति होती है। इसीलिये भारतीय जीवन में गोधन का इतना ऊँचा माहात्म्य है। जो हिंदू धर्मशास्त्र पर विश्वास रखते हैं, उन्हें चाहिये कि चतुर्वर्ग-फल-सिद्ध्यर्थ शास्त्रविधान के अनुसार गो सेवा करते हुए गोधन की वृद्धि करें और जो धर्मशास्त्र पर आस्था नहीं रखते, उन्हें चाहिये कि 'अर्थ' और 'काम' की सिद्धि के लिये अर्थशास्त्र के नियमों के अनुसार गोपालन करते हुए गोवंश की वृद्धि करने का प्रयत्न करें।

प्रत्यक्षवादियों के लिये इससे अधिक गोमाता की दयालुता हो ही क्या सकती है कि वह सूखे तृण भक्षण करके जन्म भर उन्हें दुग्ध-घृत - जैसे पौष्टिक द्रव्य प्रदान करे। इतने पर भी यदि वे गोमाता के कृतघ्न हुए, तब तो उन में मानवता का लेश भी नहीं माना जा सकता। गोमाता के द्वारा मानवसमाज को जो लाभ है, उसे पूर्णतय व्यक्त करने के लिये सहस्रों पृष्ठों की कई पुस्तकें लिखनी होंगी।

संक्षेप में यही कहा जा सकता है कि गोमाता से मानवसमाज को जो लाभ है, उससे मानवजाति गोमाता की सदा ऋणी रहेगी ।

वध आदि हिंसक उपायोंद्वारा गोवंश का ह्रास करना धार्मिक और आर्थिक दोनों दृष्टियों से राजा-प्रजा दोनों के लिये हानिकर है । अतएव ऐसी भयंकर प्रथाओं को सर्वथा रोकने का प्रयत्न सभी को करना चाहिये । कई देशी रजवाड़ों ने इस सम्बन्ध में प्रशंसनीय कार्य किया है किन्तु जबतक केन्द्रीय सरकार को इसके लिये बाध्य नहीं किया जायगा, तबतक सन्तोष - जनक परिणाम असम्भव-सा प्रतीत होता है । इसके लिये देशव्यापी यथेष्ट प्रयत्न होना चाहिये ।

साथ-ही-साथ प्रत्येक गृह में गोपालन की प्राचीन प्रथा को बढ़ाने का प्रयत्न भी सभी सद्‌गुरुहस्थों को करना चाहिये । तालुकेदारों, जर्मींदारों, सेठ-साहूकारों आदि को चाहिये कि गोशालाओं की वृद्धि करें, जहाण् से आदर्श हृष्ट-पुष्ट गौओं और बैलों की प्राप्ति हो सके । गोचर भूमि के सम्बन्ध में आज कल की व्यवस्था अत्यन्त शोचनीय है । इस सम्बन्ध में मनुजी ने लिखा है - 'प्रत्येक गाण्व और शहर के चारों ओर काफी गोचर भूमि छोड़नी चाहिये ।' सभी समर्थ किसानों, जर्मींदारों और सेठ-साहूकारों को अपने-अपने केन्द्रों में गोचर भूमियों का यथोचित्र प्रबन्ध करना चाहिये । और गोधन की वृद्धि का सदैव ध्यान रखना चाहिये । इसी में भारत और भारतीय सभ्यता का गौरव तथा सच्चा स्वार्थ निहित है ।

'The special greatness of the treasure of cows is pointed out in the *Dharma Shastra*;

"सर्वेषामेव भूतानां गावः शरणमुत्तमम् ।"

" *sarveshhaameva bhuutaanaan gaavah sharanamuttamam.* "
'Of all living beings give cows the most excellent protection'

Hindu culture is filled to the brim with this sentiment:-

"यद्गृहे दुःखिता गावः स याति नरके नरः ।"

"*yadgrihe duhkhitaa gaavah sa yaati narake narah.*"
'The man who gives suffering to a cow goes to hell.'

But our civilisation and culture have been become intermixed with the culture of Westerners, and from that time, the extensive disappearance of the Indian method of teaching has caused ignorance of the *Shastra*, *Purana* etc - that the cow, the *brahmana* etc are the same, this devout scriptural knowledge is disappearing.

Today it is usual to be pleased at measuring the material weight of the cow stock; but remember now of the subtler-than-the-subtlest of material knowledge of cow stock, of the excellent *dharma* and usefulness. The very whereabouts may not now be connected with, that was evident through supernatural powers to that Indian lawgiver. The greatness and holiness of cow stock, in you is one which is subtler-than-the-subtlest, the cause and form, the reason of keenness of the elements. For their investigation and knowledge the instrument of modern material scientists will always remain too crude. Right here is also the cause of the clever twentieth century knowledge remaining unsuccessful in the understanding of the real truth. The secret is that in the hairs on the body of the mother cow the gods are dwelling, and the dawn sighting of a cow, the worship of the cow, the cow-god etc., the universal feeling is held of the holiness of the cowherds. One bears the truth oneself by way of intellect, attainable experience, or else by confidence in the way of the *Shastra*, but not by physical instruments.

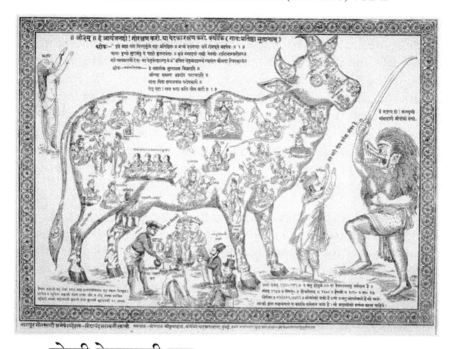

चोरसी देवतावाली गाय - *chorasii devataaovaalii gaaya*

The Cow with 84 Deities
[Nagpur Cow Protection League - Vidyananda Saraswati Swami, 1890]

[According to Skanda Purana every part of the cow houses a
deity, Referring to the illustration above, Brahma is in her back,
Vishnu in her throat, Rudra (i.e. Shiva) is established on her face,
Sun and Moon are in her eyes, Yama and Indra on the tips of the
horns, the Ashvins in her nostrils, Lakshmi and Ganga behind her
tail, etc, etc.]

Dharmashastra then is indeed a description of the greatness and
sanctity of *godhana* (cow wealth), but in the Indian Arthashastra
is the special importance of *gopalana* (cow protection). In the
Arthashastra (science of wealth) of Kautilya we meet with a
comprehensive explanation of cow custody and cow protection.
The Arthashastra commands that earth that is not being cultivated
is to be made into grazing ground for cattle. This manner of
ownership of cattle strongly cherishes both wealth and *dharma*.
Indeed from wealth desires are fulfilled and from *dharma* comes

moksha (salvation). Thence from *godhana* (cow wealth) wealth, *dharma*, desire and *moksha* - the four are gained. Therefore in Indian life the property of cattle is highly valued. He who puts faith in the Hindu Dharmashastra ought to have the reward of wealth and success for his service to the cow and progressing the cow herd according to the regulations of *Shastra*. And those who do not put their faith in the Dharmashastra, they still want wealth and fulfilment of desires and so will make an effort to progress the cow stock and protect cows according to the regulations of Arthashastra.

For those who believe only in tangible proof, think of the abundant kindness of the mother cow! What might be the pleasure of eating grass the whole life and donating milk and ghee which contains nutritive matter? If they have been so grateful to *gomata* (mother cow), then afterwards might they not weigh up a small portion of humaneness. The mother cow is by way of an advantage to human society, to him whom this is completely apparent, several thousand pages of books will be written. In brief it can be said that the mother cow is an advantage to the society of man, and from this the human race is always indebted to the mother cow.

Schemes to slaughter and kill are the downfall of the cow and its progeny, and injure the holy and financial delights of both *raja* and subject. So for this reason everyone should make an effort to put a stop to these gristly practices. Several states have done laudable work in this connection, but unless central government will be compelled, it is impossible to satisfactorily speak of the effects. For the sake of this, effort should be made countrywide.

Together everyone should make an effort to promote the old custom of houses of cow protection. All householders, landlords, land owners, merchants, money-lenders etc should progress cow houses from where can be gained ideal able-bodied cows and bulls. Nowadays the lack of establishment of grazing ground is lamentable. In this connection Manu wrote:-

'On the four sides of every village and city there should be sufficient ground for pasture of cows.'

All capable farmers, landlords, merchants and moneylenders should make arrangement for centres to provide proper pasture for cattle. Also you should always consider advancing the cows. In this the honour of India and of Indian civilisation kept true.']

Between the 1942 Kumbha Mela in Prayag (Allahabad) and the 1948 Arddha Kumbha (half-Kumbha), very great *mahaayagyas* (great ritual sacrifices) were accomplished everywhere in India. After Maharaj Shri became master of the *peeth* (Jyotir Math) there was an unprecedented religious awakening in all India, and at whatever place, in whichever direction, the drum of *dharma* was sounded. This was all a manifestation of Maharaj Shri's greatness.

After you had performed the leadership of the Lakshachandi Mahaayagya of Bombay (Mumbai) you spent some time coming to relax in a village attached to Jabalpur in the Central Province (Madhya Pradesh). You also observed chaturmasya vrata (the rainy season fast) here and your upadesha amrita (nectar lectures) to all four directions gratified all the people. After this you graced the occasion of the Arddha Kumba at Prayag and at this time Pujyapad Sharada Pith Adhiswar Swami Abhinava Sachidananda Tirth Ji Maharaj (the head of the Shankaracharya Sharada Pith*) also arrived at Prayag (Allahabad). For Pravasnaana (the occasion of ritual bathing at the Adha Kumbh) both religious leaders were united in a procession, which was a beautiful sight. Maharaj Shri came on a silver and gold palanquin in the procession. After that came another silver and gold palanquin in which the leader of Sharada Pith Adishwar Ji (the master of Sharada monastery) rode. After this came a line of the heads of the *mandal* (circle) of Nirvani, Niranjani, & Juna Akhaaras (*sadhu* organisations). Both of the *dharmacharyas* (Shankaracharyas) bathed together and the world saw how much the heads of the *dharmapeeths* spiritual communities, the Shankaracharyas, behaved in the same hearty way to one another.

[*note: Identifying the Shankaracharya of Shringeri Sharada as

Swami Abhinava Sachidananda appears incorrect as the heads of Sharada Pith over the last century are recorded as having been:

Sri Sacchidananda Shivabhinava Nrisimha Bharati	1879 - 1912
Sri Chandrasekhara Bharati III	1912 - 1954
Sri Abhinava Vidyatirtha	1954 - 1989
Sri Bharati Tirtha	1989 –Present

Ref: http://www.sringeri.net/history/guru_parampara.php]

After the Ardha-Kumbha festival Maharaj Shri stayed for some days in Prayag (Allahabad) and finished that rainy season fast at Chand Press at Edmonston Road. *After that, again you began travelling, promulgating dharma (religion).* At the request of devotees, first of all he graced Etawa, a town about 300kms north-east of Allahabad). There, he dwelt in the house of Dr. Vishwambharanath Meharotra's, a house called "Shri Jyotirdham" and proceeded with a programme of early morning *darshan*, *dikshaa* (initiation) etc and evening lectures.

After dwelling for some time in Etawa Shri Charan then proceeded onwards, for a *yagya* at Kachala Ghat. Whilst here a large procession turned out to welcome Shri Shankaracharya Maharaj and the fold received their own religious leader. Every evening an immense crowd of people gathered in order to drink the nectar of Maharaj Shri's discourses. In direct intelligible language, thorough knowledge of the obscure mysteries of *dharma* were heard by the folk, who then became greatly advantaged.

Having finished the *yagya* at Kachala Ghat, Maharaj Shri proceeded on to Shukara Kshetra [at Soron, some miles north of Etawah, between Mathura and Bareilly, a place famous as the birthplace of the poet Tulsi Das, composer of epic poem 'Ram Charit Manas']. The *purohit* (priest) of the *tirth* (sacred place) there, together with the devout populace, all turned out to form a grand procession to welcome their *dharma acharya* (religious teacher). At the end there had been a gathering wherein the public and the respective organisations had the opportunity to meet and greet him.

Some particular individuals, having come from Kasaganja (in Etah district, about 20kms southwest of Soron) requested that Maharaj Shri set out for Kasaganj. Having seen the abundant restlessness of the devotees Shri Charan proceeded to Kasaganj. Here also a grand procession turned out and his welcome was by means of *aarati pujana* (Aarati worship) at various places. *Here you stayed in a tent in a garden.* The *darshan* seekers stayed from dawn until 11-12 at night as did those caught up in the heat of curiosity.

Several times important individuals came from Agra and at their request Maharaj Shri proceeded from Kasaganja to Agra. *At this place your abode was Bhadawar House (the residence of the Maharaja of Bhadawar) and for some days you stayed at Hari Parvat. You kept going with a continual programme of darshan, dikshaa (initiation), upadesha (lecturing) etc.*

Because of entreaties from scholars and folk of Moradabad (a town to the north of Agra), you proceeded from Agra to Moradabad. A huge procession turned out to welcome you. At different places the folk welcomed their religious preceptor by means of *pujana aarati* (Aarati worship). The immense crowd of *darshan* seekers increased. All were becoming satisfied in getting the *darshan* of Shri Shankaracharya's, a really charming way to hear his *upadesha* (counsel). In this manner, by degrees, the promulgation of *dharma* was done.

At the beginning of the hot season Maharaj Shri again travelled to Jyotish Peeth. The mountain people there were in difficult circumstances at this time and for some days past. For a long time there had been no rain in the mountains and the people were very distressed. All the crops in the fields were becoming completely parched and there wasn't even a hint of any possibility of that it would rain. But the day that Maharaj Shri entered the building of the *peeth* a cloud was seen on the tops of the mountain. By the second day the whole sky had became covered, and then it rained too. For four days it rained continuously. All of the mountain people became very pleased and from all their mouths these words came, 'This rain has been from the blessing of Maharaj Shri'.

From far and wide people rushed for *darshan* of Maharaj Shri. Whilst taking *darshan*, thoughtful and honest devotees said; 'Maharaj, we hear that since your arrival it has been raining. This is clear too, that before your coming there had been no rains for three months. All the population were stirred up lamenting. With it raining we are all delighted and this all the effect of your coming to this place.'

Maharaj Shri did the *chaaturmaasya vrata* of this season of 1949 at this very place and from his *dharma upadesha* (lessons in religious matters) the mountain people were happily guided in the direction of Vedic *dharma. Having finished the chaaturmaasya-vrata you again departed to travel for the promulgation of dharma. He roamed to places such as Prayag (Allahabad), Kashi (Varanasi), Calcutta, Haridwar, Dehra Dun, Mussoorie etc – and from place to place he flew the victory flag of sanatana dharma.* There was a spiritual awakening in all places. In the population there was unprecedented enthusiasm, and the great sowing of the seeds of the belief of in-love-ness with the deliverance of God.

['Guru Deva and Language

When the preceding Shankaracharya [Swami Brahmanand Saraswati] went to Lucknow, people told him that the town possessed an Urdu culture and spoke Urdu language. He replied that it would not matter. He would do his duty irrespective of the extent of the benefit people derived from his visit.' - Reference from p 46, *'Orange Book',* by Shankaracharya H H Swami Shantanand Saraswati,, The Study of Normal Psychology, 1981]

In 1950 Maharaj Shri's was dwelling in Lucknow. At that time Raja of Dilipur, Shri Pashupati Pratap Singh was there as a *darshan* seeker of Shri Charan. One day he made a request of Maharaj Shri, 'This is an idea, that there is an *ashram* built in Prayag (Allahabad). I have a mansion of my own which is situated in Alopi Bag. I wish to make a gift of it to the *gaddi* of

Jyotirmath.'

Maharaj Shri refused this request of his. *The reason was, that your guidance was this; that he did not accept any offering left at pujaa (worship).* Wherever he went, an information notice was displayed in front of his *shivira* (camp), stating that:-

इस शिविर में को भेंट पूजा – द्रव्य आदि नहीं चढ़ेगा ।

"isa shivira men koii bhenta, puujaa - dravya aadi nahiin chadhegaa"

NO MATERIAL OFFERING, OBJECT etc. IS TO BE OFFERED IN *PUJA* AT THIS *SHIVIRA*.

But at the repeated insistence of the Raja Sahib, Maharaj Shri said, 'If you give a *"bayanaamaa"* (a buyer's contract) in our name, then we will accept.'

At this he became willing.

After this Maharaj Shri summoned the secretary of the Raja of Dilippur and asked the price of the mansion. The secretary said, 'Last year this mansion was for sale. At that time Raja Sahib was demanding a price of one hundred thousand *rupees* for it, but only a buyer at sixty-five thousand applied. Because of this the mansion was not sold.'

After this Maharaj Shri considered, that, 'If sixty-five thousand will come from that *"khadaana"* (mine), then from that can also come one hundred thousand. Therefore, why not give the price of one hundred thousand?'

One day Maharaj Shri summoned the Raja of Dilippur and gave to him one hundred thousand *rupees* as the price of the mansion and *rupees* for the expenditure of registry etc and said that, 'In Allahabad we give our name to a *byanaamaa* (contract) of the mansion.'

The *raja* requested a man from Maharaj Shri and Maharaj Shri granted him his private attendant to accompany him. The contract was drawn up and the Maharaj Shri became the named buyer of the mansion.

After the *bayanaamaa* had been completed, there was a rumour in Allahabad, that asked, 'Where did Maharaj Shri's hundred thousand *rupees* come from?'

But he did not accept any *dravya* (matter, wealth) and there was no income coming from somewhere. Previously then, the registrar said, 'The *rupees* were given in front of me.'

They asked of him, 'How were the notes?'

He did say, 'The ordinary fixed manner, such exactly it was.'

The people were very amazed.

Two months later when Maharaj Shri himself came to Allahabad, the people asked of Maharaj, 'Maharaj Shri does not accept anything from anyone and yet Maharaj Shri gathered together and gave one hundred thousand *rupees*? By this the people are very astonished. Where did that one hundred thousand *rupees* come from?'

Maharaj Shri said that, 'The coming of these *rupees* is not in the hands of any man.'

When many questioned, then Maharaj Shri said, 'At the time of the Maharabharata, when Draupadi's cloth became longer, then thousands of yards it grew. Where did the cloth come from? Another thing is this that, the *sari* that Draupadi was wearing, that very cloth came. It was not just some red, some green, some yellow. When Bhagwan gives then he gives all, and gives the genuine real thing. If the work could be done at the time of the Mahabharata, that now also can be. The essence of Bhagwan always exists, in Him no end comes.'

At the time that this mansion was sold, its condition was

ramshackle. Maharaj Shri had made, completely renovated and renewed a special place of Jyotirmath, in Prayag (Allahabad). He had it made as one huge ashram, which today is distinguished by the name "Brahmanivaas" – 'Abode of Brahma'. In that, above and below are dozens and dozens of rooms, which can be a dwelling place for large numbers of *sadhak*, *brahmachari*, *sannyasi* etc.

[Regarding the allusions to miracle working contained in this chapter, it is worth noting this comment from an authoratitive account of the Shankaracharya tradition:-

'The Shankaracharyas are not public wonder-workers and are not sought out for the manifestation of yogic powers. The only exception to this was the previous *guru* of Jyotirmatha [Swami Brahmananda Saraswati] who displayed wonders, such as lighting ritual fires and producing *prasada* offerings, which disquieted the priests of the Badrinath temple.' - Extract from page 133, *'A Tradition of Teachers: Shankara and the Jagadgurus Today'*, William Cenkner, Motilal Banarsidaa, 1983.]

९

नवाँ अध्याय

महान् आध्यात्मिक नेतृत्व

प्रयाग में लगभग एक महीना निवास करने के बाद महाराज जी काशी होते हुए कलकत्ता पधारे। इस समय भारतीय दर्शन-परिषद् की रजत-जयंती कलकत्ता में मनाई जा रही थी। विश्व के अनेक दानिक एकत्र हुये थे। महाराज श्री को उस जयंती-समारोह में अध्यक्ष-पद पर आसीन कराया गया। सभापति के पद से आपका उपदेश हुआ। विश्व के उच्चकोटि के दार्शनिकों ने जब महाराज श्री का उपदेश सुना, तो मुग्ध हो गये। कुछ दार्शनिकों की जिज्ञासा हुई कि महाराज श्री से एकान्त में मिला जाय।

दूसरे दिन भारत के सर्वमान्य दार्शनिक-शिरोमणि डा। सर्वपल्ली राधाकृष्णन् को आगे करके अमेरिका के प्रसिद्ध दार्शनिक डा। काँगर और डा। शिल्प रात्रि में लगभग १० बजे श्री शंकराचार्य-शिविर में आये। महाराज श्री ऊपर की छत पर विराजे थे। एकान्त था। कोई प्रकाश नहीं था। बाहर चाँदनी छिटकी थी। गुरु के सानिध्य में उनका एक सेवक अध्यात्मराज्य की अनन्तानन्दानुभूति में निमग्न था। द्वारपाल ने आकर कहा "डा। राधाकृष्णन् जी के साथ इंग्लैंड व अमेरिका के दो दार्शनिक दर्शनार्थ आये हैं।" आगन्तुकों की सूचना देकर द्वारपाल खड़ा था। लगभग एक मिनट बाद महाराज श्री ने कहा, "यह कौन समय है मिलने का? कोई समय तो दिया नहीं गया था।" समीपस्थ सेवक को ऐसा लगा कि महाराज श्री कहते हैं, "कह दो नहीं मिलेंगे," क्योंकि ऐसे समय में प्रायः ऐसा ही

होता था । सेवक ने प्रार्थना की, ''यदि महाराज श्रीं उचित समझें, तो दो-चार मिनट दे दें । दिन में इन लोगों को अवकाश न मिलता होगा ।'' महाराज श्री ने कहा । ''अच्छा तो लिवा लाओ ।''

आगे डा। राधाकृष्णन् उनके पीछे डा। काँगर और उनके बगल में डा। शिल्प थे । सब लोग एक के बाद एक प्रणाम करके सामने एक कालीन पर बैठ गये । परिचय समाप्त होने पर डा। राधाकृष्णन् ने महाराज श्री से कहा, ''डा। काँगर वेदान्त के सम्बन्ध में कुछ सुनना चाहते हैं । तत्वदर्शन के लिये वे महाराज श्री की सहायता चाहते हैं ।'' महाराज श्री ने कहा –

''वेदान्त प्रतिपाद्य तत्व तो स्वतः सिद्ध पदार्थ है । वह स्वयं प्रकाश है । उसको प्रकाशित करने के लिये अन्य किसी प्रकाश की अवश्यकता नहीं ।'' डा। काँगर ने जिज्ञासा प्रकट की ''वेदशास्त्र में जो तत्वप्राप्ति के साधन हैं, वे व्यर्थ तो नहीं कहे जा सकते ।'' महाराज श्री ने कहा, ''साधन जो हैं वे ब्रह्म को प्रकाशित करने के लिये नहीं हैं । उनका तात्पर्य केवल अविद्या की निवृत्ति में है । साधन अविद्या का नाश करते हैं । ब्रह्म का प्रकाश नहीं । जो स्वतः प्रकाश है । उसको देखने के लिये किसी अन्य प्रकाश की आवश्यकता नहीं । जैसे सूर्य स्वतः प्रकाशमान है, उसको देखने के लिये किसी अन्य प्रकाश की आवश्यकता नहीं है । सूर्योदय के पहिले अरुण का उदय होता है, किन्तु अरुणोदय केवल रात्रि के अंधकार को हटाता है । वह सूर्य को प्रकाशित नहीं करता । सूर्य तो स्वयं प्रकाश रूप है । जितने साधन है वे सब अविद्य को ही निवृत्त करते हैं । आत्मा का प्रकाश नहीं करते । आत्मा तो स्वतः प्रकाश रूप और सबका साक्षि है ।''

सारगर्भित उपदेश सुनकर डा॰ राधाकृष्णन् गद्गद हो कर सहसा बोल पड़े – कितनी सरलता से कितने गूढ़ प्रश्न को महाराज ने हल कर दिया। इसके बाद श्रीचरण को कष्ट देने के लिये क्षमा याचना करते हुये, शिष्टाचारपूर्ण भाव से सब लोग विदा हुये।

कलकत्ता में लगभग एक महीना विश्राम करके महाराज श्री पटना आ गये। श्री शंकराचार्य-शिविर, अरोड़ा बिल्डिंग में बिहार के राज्यपाल श्री अणे महोदय ने ता॰ २३ मार्च को आकर पूज्यपाद श्री शंकराचार्य जी महाराज का षोडशोपचार पूजन किया और लगभग ४५ मिनट तक शान्तचित्त से उपदेशामृत का पान किया।

दूसरे दिन बिहार के मंत्रिगण महाराज श्री के दर्शनार्थ शिविर में आये। महाराज श्री ने लगभग एक घण्टा तक उनसे बातें कों और धर्म तथा नीति सम्बन्धी महत्वपूर्ण विषयों पर उपदेश दिया और कहा, "परमात्मा व्यापक है और अन्तर्यामी है। सभी के भले बुरे कर्मों को वह जानता है। अल्पज्ञ मनुष्यों की दृष्टि तो बचाई जा सकती है, परन्तु अन्तर्यामी परमात्मा से छिपाकर कोई कार्य नहीं किया जा सकता।"

२६ मार्च, १९५१ ई॰ को पटना से हवाई जहाज द्वारा प्रस्थान कर लक्कऊ के अमौसी अड्डे पर उतरे। यहाँ पर लखनऊ व उन्नाव एवं कानपुर के लोगों ने भव्य स्वागत किया। यहाँ से कार द्वारा महाराज श्री कानपुर पधारे। जन-समुद्र उमड़ पड़ा। सड़कों पर अपार भीड़ और ऊपर मकानों से महिलाओं द्वारा पुष्पवृष्टि ने अपूर्व दृश्य उपस्थित कर दिया। फूलबाग से विराट् शोभायात्रा निकाली गई। सम्पूर्ण मार्ग झंडियों और तोरणों से भव्य रूप में सजाया गया। वाल्मीकि, याज्ञवल्क्य, पाराशर, चाणक्य, शाण्डिल्य आदि महर्षियों

के नाम वाले फाटक द्वारा सजाये गये। उनसे होकर जाती हुई शोभायात्रा का दृश्य कानपुर के इतिहास में एक नवीन पृष्ठ हो गया। मार्ग में पग-पग पर पूजन किया गया। आरती उतारी गई। भक्तों की टोली की टोली ने पुष्प-मालायें लिये स्वागत अभिनन्दन किया। बीसों भक्तों भक्त बड़े बड़े कटोरों में केसरिया चंदन लिये हुये मार्ग में सबको चन्दन लगा रहे थे। पादुकाओं पर पुष्प मालाओं का ढेर इतना ऊँचा हो जाता था कि कई बार पुष्प हटाये गये। इस प्रकार महाराज श्री की शोभायात्रा जयपुरिया हाउस के विस्तृत मैदान में ही सभा के रूप में परिणत हो गई।

कानपुर की जनता की ओर से श्रद्धांजलि समर्पित होने के बाद महाराज श्री ने अपने उद्बोधन में कहा, "वैसे हमारे लिये स्वागताभिनन्दन की कोई आवश्यकता नहीं। किन्तु भारतीय संस्कृति के अनुसार गुरु का स्वागत एवं शिष्टाचार भी हो तो ठीक है, उसे हम स्वीकार करते हैं। किन्तु इससे आगे हमारा स्वागत यह है कि आप हमें अपना कुछ समय दें। क्योंकि जैसा देवता होता है, वैसा ही उसका पूजन होता है। जैसा मेहमान हो, वैसा स्वागत होना चाहिये। हम हिमालय से उतरे हैं, तो हमारा स्वागत भी हिमालय जैसी कोई बड़ी चीज से होना चाहिये। समय ही संसार में सबसे बड़ी मूल्यवान् वस्तु है, उसी से हमारा स्वागत करो। जो वस्तु आपको अत्यन्त प्रिय हो वही अर्पण करो। हमने देखा है कि सबसे प्रिय वस्तु मनुष्य को दुर्गुण होता है। उसे छोड़ने के लिये मनुष्य तैयार नहीं होता। धन खर्च करता है, अपमान सहता है, शरीर क्षीण होता है तो भी उसकी पर वाह नहीं करता। इसलिये हमें अपना परम प्रिय दुर्गुण अर्पण करो। वही हमारी सेवा पूजा है। यही भेंट हम लेते हैं। कानपुर में थैलियाँ भेंट करने की प्रथा है। पर हम

कंकड़-पत्थर रुपया-पैसा की थैली से संतुष्ट होने वाले नहीं। हमें तो जनता के दुर्गुणों की थैलियाँ चाहिये।"

इस प्रकार प्रतिदिन शिविर के विस्तृत सुरम्य उद्यान में ८ से १२ हजार जनता के समक्ष सायंकालीन उपदेश होते रहे। महाराज श्री का निवास कानपुर में डेढ़ मास रहा। प्रतिदिन जनता बढ़ती ही गई। दर्शनार्थियों का ताँता लगा ही रहता। इस अवधि के अनन्तर श्री महाराज का कार्यक्रम प्रयाग जाने का बना। यह समाचार सुनकर धार्मिक जनता अधिक संख्या में एकत्रित हुई और सायंकालीन भाषण के पश्चात् लगभग ५० हजार जनता एक स्वर से प्रार्थना करने लगी "अभी महाराज श्री कुछ समय और ठहरें और अग्रिम चातुर्मास्य-व्रत कानपुर में ही हो।"

किन्तु पूर्व निश्चयानुसार १३ मई, १९५१ को महाराज श्री कार द्वारा कानपुर से प्रयाग पधारे। प्रयाग की जनता प्रातःकाल ८ बजे से ही प्रतीक्षा में खड़ी थी। नगर से पाँच मील आगे कई प्रतिष्ठित नागरिक अपनी-अपनी मोटर में स्वागत करने के लिये पहिले से ही उपस्थित थे। ब्रह्मनिवास आश्रम, प्रयाग में कार से उतरते ही षोडशोपचार पूजन हुआ और जनता में अत्यंत हर्ष उल्लास की बाढ़ आ गई।

ब्रह्मनिवास आश्रम में नित्य प्रातःकाल ८॥ से १० बजे तक दर्शनार्थियों एवं दीक्षार्थियों की भीड़ लगी रहती। कभी-कभी दीक्षा में अत्यधिक भीड़ होने के कारण ९ व ९॥ बजे जाता। सायंकाल ८॥ बजे सामूहिक दर्शन व उपदेश होते। अग्रिम चातुर्मस्य-व्रत के लिये सभी प्रांतों से प्रार्थनायें आने लगीं। कलकत्ता, पटना, लखनऊ, नागपुर, बम्बई, से विशेष अनुरोध हुआ। अन्त में महाराज श्री ने चातुर्मास्य -व्रत प्रयाग में ही करना निश्चय किया। धार्मिक संस्थाओं

एवं धार्मिक जनों में उत्साह की अपूर्व लहर फैल गई। अपने-अपने ढंग से सभी लोग गुरुपूर्णिमा महोत्सव को वृहत्तर और सुन्दरतम बनाने के लिए प्रयत्नशील हो उठे। गुरुपूर्णिमा-महोत्सव अत्यन्त हर्ष एवं उत्साह के साथ मनाया गया। चातुर्मास्य-व्रत काल में दर्शन, पूजन, दीक्षा, उपदेश आदि का क्रम पूर्ववत् चलता रहा। गुरुवार और रविवार को सामूहिक उपदेश आश्रम के विस्तृत प्रांगण में होते थे। भीड़ इतनी अधिक होती थी कि सम्पूर्ण प्रांगण श्रोताओं से भर जाता था। उपदेश के समय आश्रम में एक विशिष्ट धार्मिक मेला लग जाता था। कभी-कभी श्रोताओं के अत्यधिक एकत्र हो जाने पर महाराज श्री का सिंहासन आश्रम के फाटक के ऊपर वाली छत पर लगाना पड़ता था, जिससे जनता सुचारु रूप से महाराज श्री का दर्शन और उनके उपदेशामृत का पान कर सके।

लखनऊ, जबलपुर, सूरत तथा बम्बई पधारने लिये श्री चरण के पास प्रार्थनायें आने लगीं। अधिक प्रार्थनाओं का आना देख कर प्रयाग के विद्वानों ने प्रार्थना की कि वर्ष में एक बार माघ मास में सब तीर्थ तीर्थराज प्रयाग में आकर निवास करते हैं। इस समय यदि महाराज श्री प्रयाग छोड़ कर अन्यत्र जायँगे, तो सभी तीर्थों की अवहेलना होगी और तीर्थराज का अपमान होगा। इस दृष्टि से इस वर्ष के माघ में अवश्य ही आप अपने दर्शन एवं उपदेश से तीर्थराज की शोभा बढ़ावें। प्रार्थना स्वीकार कर ली गई। कार्यक्रम पूर्ववत चलता रहा। किन्तु माघ मेले में आये हुये कल्पवासियों की प्रार्थना पर माघ भर प्रति रविवार व गुरुवार को स्थान पर नित्य उपदेश होता रहा।

२३ फरवरी, १९५२ ई० को श्री शंकराचार्य-सेवक-संघ द्वारा शिवरात्रि महोत्सव बड़े धूमधाम से मनाया गया। कार्यक्रम मध्याह्न

से प्रारम्भ होकर ८ बजे रात्रि तक चलता रहा। सायंकाल सामूहिक दर्शन उपदेश के समय शिवरात्रि के अवसर पर महाराज श्री का सामूहिक पूजन हुआ। आश्रम का प्रांगण दर्शनाथिंयों से भर गय और सभी ने सामूहिक पूजन में व्यक्तिगत रूप से अपनी-अपनी थाली में आरती की। यह आरती अपने-अपने स्थान से ही सामूहिक रूप में की गई इसका दृश्य अत्यन्त मनोरम और अपूर्व था।

Chapter 9
Great Spiritual Leadership

After staying in Prayag (Allahabad) about a month, Maharaj Shri went to Kashi (Varanasi) before then going on to Calcutta. At this time the Silver Jubilee of the Bharatiya Darshan-Parishad (Assembly of the Society of Indian Philosophy) was to be celebrated in Calcutta. Many were collected together daily and Maharaj Shri was sitting as president at that grand anniversary. *So, from the seat of president your instruction had been.* The highpoint of all was when they heard the *upadesha* (teaching) of Maharaj Shri, then they became enamoured and some philosophers were asking Maharaj Shri whether they could meet with him alone.

[It is said that at this event in December 1950 Guru Dev posed the question;-

'What is the difference between *Jiva* and *Brahman*?

The difference is the same as the difference between rice and paddy. Remove the skin of the paddy and it is rice. Similarly, remove the covering of *Maya,* and the *Jiva* will become *Brahman.*']

The next day, at about ten o'clock at night, the famous American philosopher Dr. Conger, Dr. Schilpp, and an eminent philosopher respected by all in India, Dr Sarvapalli Radhakrishnan, all arrived at Shri Shankaracharya's camp. Maharaj Shri was seated on the upper floor. He was alone. There was no light. Outside was a speck of moonlight. Near the *guru* sat an attendant engrossed in the royal state of endless bliss. The gatekeeper came and said, 'Dr Radhakrishnan has come with two *darshan* seekers, philosphers from England and America.' Having given notification of the visitors the gatekeeper waited.

After about a minute, Maharaj Shri said, 'What time is this to meet? No time was given.' Maharaj Shri spoke to the nearby attendant, 'Say we will not meet because at this time it is generally thus.'

The attendant requested him, 'If Maharaj Shri understood properly, then he will give two, four minutes. These people will not get any opportunity to meet in the day.'

Maharaj Shri said, '*Achchaa* (Okay) then cause them to be brought.'

Soon came Dr. Radhakrishnan, and behind him Dr. Conger, and at his side Dr. Schilpp.

Sir Sarvepalli Radhakrishnan
President of India 1962-1967

One after the other, these people did pranaam (salutation) and went to sit on the carpet in front of you. Having become acquainted, Dr. Radhakrishnan asked of Maharaj Shri, 'Dr. Conger wishes to hear something in connection with *Vedanta*. He desires the assistance of Maharaj Shri for *darshan* of the truth.'

Maharaj Shri said, 'The truth of the subject of *Vedanta* then, is that the meaning is spontaneously obtained. This is the light of the self. No other light is necessary in order to discover it.'

'Those *sadhana* (means) to gain the truth which are given in the *Veda Shastra*, they cannot be called useless?'

Maharaj Shri said, 'Those *sadhana* (means), they are not for making Brahman apparent. Their significance is only for the disappearance of *avidyaa* (ignorance, illusion). The *saadhana* fades the *avidyaa*, it does not bring the light of Brahman, that light is spontaneous. No other light is necessary in order to see that. It is not necessary to have any other light in order to see that which is spontaneously radiant. Before the sunrise the dawn rises, but daybreak is only to drive away the darkness of the night. It is not to make the sun evident. The sun then is lighted by itself. However much *saadhana* is done, that much the *avidyaa* is got rid of. The *aatmaa* (soul) is not lighted. The *aatmaa* then is spontaneously the form of light and the witness of all.'

Having heard this *upadesha* (lesson) so full of pith, Dr. Radhakrishnan became very happy and suddenly said, 'With how much simplicity did Maharaj solve this difficult problem?' After this he implored Shri Charan to excuse them for giving inconvenience and all the people departed with a feeling that this was the proper behaviour.

[In the Hindi book *'Amrit Kana'* – a collecton of quotations of Guru Dev, there is also mention of a speech on 22nd December 1950, by a speaker called 'Dr. Paal', almost certainly Professor Paul Arthur Schilpp (1897 - 1993), an associate of former President of India Dr Sarvepalli Radhakrishnan,:-

'To-day we are here to do homage to his Holiness, Shri Jagatguru Shankaracharya Ananta Sri Vibhusita Swami Brahmananda Saraswati of Jyotirmath, Badarikasram - the Superman, the seer, the sage, who is one of the few rare individuals amongst the billions of the citizens of the world, whom we would unhesitatingly choose if and when we would be called upon to describe the spiritual and cultural capital of our nation, if and when the world would feel the need of evoking the part our nation can play in it, who is beyond any controversy, one of the rare few who have contributed and can still contribute something to universal peaceful progress, who have risen by their talent and genius above their fellow countrymen, above their fellowmen of the world and have thus gained a place for themselves at the head of humanity, at the extreme spearhead of civilization.

Standing here at a time when everywhere in the world everybody feels not a little bewildered at an immense increase in the sense of human power, we can hardly exaggerate the necessity of teachers like his Holiness the Jagatguru.

You will pardon me if I venture; at this assemblage of eminent philosophers, to refer to an aspect of our Hindu Philosophy which seems for the time being, to be too much belittled by the power-intoxicated world.

Our Vedic philosophers.... ....

The civilized world today is indeed in an age of spiritual chaos, intellectual doubt and political decadence. Civilized man today no doubt has acquired immense scientific and mechanical resources, but seems hopelessly to lack the wisdom to apply them to the best advantage. This is why we witness a growing sense of frustration seizing every mind almost everywhere. The whole world seems to be suffering from an epidemic of hysteria................

We do not know which way the truth lies. Perhaps even here it will be true to say that every truth, however true in itself, yet taken apart from others, becomes only a snare. In reality, perhaps, each is one thread of a complex weft, and no thread can be taken apart from the weft. But this much seems to be certain that there is this paralysing fear and alarm almost everywhere in the world-everywhere even the most powerful minds have not succeeded in escaping it altogether. Everywhere humanity is beginning to feel that we are being betrayed by what is false within, - we are almost giving way to find ourselves spiritually paralysed.

This indeed is a deadly malady. The patient here must first of all be brought to see that he is sick and to want to get well and to do of himself what is needed to get well. Perhaps something is away both with the heart and the brain.

The world needs philosopher-teachers like His Holiness Shri Jagatguru Shankaracharya who can reveal the world of values and can make us realize that, that is the real world. The world badly needs guidance to a creed of values and ideals. The world needs a teacher who can dispel our fears and can remove all sense of frustration or least in so far as it is only an internal malady.

We need a teacher who has succeeded in gaining for himself freedom to be alone, who does not require any power, who can cure both heart and Brain. We are in an age in which the meeting of the traditionally alien cultures of the Orient and the Occident has become inevitable. We need a teacher with sufficient gift of intellectual imagination and divine inspiration who can help the smooth working of this meeting, the working out of this meeting in such a way that the values of each civilization complement and re-inforce rather than combat and destroy those of the other. We cannot avoid the sight of conflicting economic, political, religious, artistic and other ideological doctrines and the consequent fear and feeling of helplessness, We need a teacher who can teach us how to get out of the crisis in valuation in this realm of conflict, who can teach us how to avert the danger of spiritual paralysis facing us.

His Holiness Sri Jagatguru Shankaracharya, having gained the freedom to be alone, did also fully realize the means of escaping from loneliness. In these days of doubts and difficulties if we can at all safely turn our eyes for guidance to any one it should be to this superman the overpowering influence of whose genius appears indeed in the light of divine inspiration, the superman who has succeeded in ridding himself of any ambition for power.

Saintly guidance from a seer like Sri Jagatguru alone can ensure an abiding peace.']

For about a month Maharaj Shri relaxed in Calcutta then moved to Patna. On March 23rd 1951, Shri Aney, His Eminence the Governor of Bihar, came to Shri Shankaracharya's camp in the Arora Building. He did the *shodashopachara* (*puja* with the sixteen methods of worship), doing worship of Pujyapaad (worthy of worship) Shri Shankaracharya Ji Maharaj, and with calm thought he drank the nectar of *upadesha* (counsel) for about forty-five minutes.

The next day the ministers of Bihar came to Maharaj Shri's camp to get *darshan*. For about an hour Maharaj Shri talked with them about *dharma* and about politics, giving an *upadesha* on things that are really important, saying, 'Paramaatma (Supreme Soul) is multi-faceted, and pervading the inner parts of the universe. He knows the good and bad actions of all. One can escape the vison of human beings of limited knowledge, but there can be no hiding from the Almighty Supreme Self.'

On 26th March 1951 he set out from Patna by means of an aeroplane, setting down at Amausi Airport, the stopping place for Lucknow. There the people of Lucknow, Unnao and Kanpur gave him a grand welcome. From there Maharaj Shri proceeded to Kanpur by car. A sea of people surged. On the roads were immense crowds and from on tops of houses the women showered flowers, affording an unprecedented scene. From Phoolbag a very splendid procession turned out. The entire route was arrayed in such a beautiful way with flags and arched gateways. Doors and gates were adorned with the names of *maharshis* (great saints), such as Valmiki, Yagyavalkya, Parashara, Chanakya, Shandilya etc.

You went with them in a beautiful procession, adding a new page to the history of Kanpur. On your footsteps in the road, pujana (worship) was done and aarati (worship with lighted lamp) was offered up. Crowds of devotees welcomed and greeted you with garlands of flowers. Dozens of devout devotees went about with great bowls of saffron-coloured sandalwood (paste), applying sandalwood paste to all on the street. So high was the pile of garlands of flowers put on the wooden sandals of the *guru*, that many times they had to be removed. In this way Maharaj Shri's procession transformed into an assembly in the expansive open field of Jayapuriya House.

After the populace of Kanpur had delivered their offerings of faith, Maharaj Shri told to them in his *upadesha* (teaching); 'Such welcome and praise for us is not necessary. But, according to *bhaaratiya sanskriti* (Indian culture) etiquette exists concerning the welcome of the *guru* and so it is fit. To that we agree. But henceforth, our *svaagata* (welcome) is this, that you give us some of your time. Because, according to the deity, such is the worship. Similarly when the guest comes you should give welcome accordingly. We are come down from the Himalayas, then our reception also is similarly like the Himalayas, you should give some big thing. In *samsara* (worldly existence) time is the most precious thing, therefore do our *svaagata* (welcome) with that. Deliver that thing that is extremely precious to you. We see that of all the things beloved by man, are the *durguna* (defects, flaws, blemishs, faults). Man is not ready to let go of them. Wealth he expends, disgrace he bears, the body it becomes feeble, but he is not concerned. Therefore, offer your best loved flaws to us. This is our service and worship. These are the gifts we receive.

In Kanpur it is a custom to make gifts of *thaili* (small bags). But we are not someone who is contented with a *thaili* (small bag) of stones and jewels, *rupees* and *paisa* (*paisa* are small coins). You should give to me bags of the *durguna* (flaws) of mankind.'

In this manner, in the beautiful expansive garden of the *shivira* (camp), daily in the evening time he was *upadasha* (lecturing) in front of eight to twelve thousand people. Maharaj Shri stayed in

Kanpur for one and a half months and every day the crowds became bigger joining the row of *darshan* seekers. After this period Maharaj Shri made a programme to go to Prayag (Allahabad). Hearing this news, a great number of devout people collected in one place, and after the evening speech, with one voice about fifty thousand people joined to request:- 'Now Maharaj Shri will please stay more time and first be in Kanpur for *chaaturmaasya-vrata* (fast of the four months of rainy season).' But as per prior arrangement he left Kanpur for Prayag (Allahabad) by car on 13th May 1951. [Allahabad is about 195kms SE of Kanpur]

In the early morning at eight o'clock the people of Prayag were standing in a state of expectation. *Several respected townspeople were ready ahead of time waiting with their motor cars five miles outside the city to welcome you.* When he alighted from the car in Prayag (Allahabad) at Brahmanivas Ashram he was worshipped with *shodashopachaara* (*puja* with sixteen methods of worship), and there became an increase of much joy and light in the people there.

From eight-thirty until ten o'clock at Brahmanivas ashram there were constantly crowds of *darshan* seekers and those seeking *dikshaa* (initiation). Sometimes there were excessive crowds for *dikshaa* caused by those going from nine o'clock to nine-thirty. In the evening time from eight-thirty there was community *darshan* and *upadesha* (lecture). For the *chaaturmasya-vrata* (rainy season four-month fast) prior requests came from all directions. There had been special requests from Calcutta, Patna, Lucknow, Nagpur and Bombay. In the end Maharaj Shri decided to do *chaaturmaasya-vrata* in Prayag (Allahabad). A wave of unprecedented enthusiasm spread in the religious organisations and religious community. In their own ways all the people rose to make an effort to create a great and beautiful festival of Guru Purnima [celebrated at the full moon in the month of *ashadha*, on Wednesday, 18th July 1951]. The great festival of Guru Purnima evoked much joy and enthusiasm.

At the time of *chaaturmasya-vrata* (rainy season fast) *darshan*, *pujana, dikshaa, upadesha* proceeded as per the usual routine up until now. On Thursdays and Sundays the community *upadesha* was convened in the expansive courtyard of the *ashram*. The crowds were so great that the courtyard was full of listeners. At the time of *upadesha* (discourse) the *ashram* was a time of special religious assembly. Sometimes when there were too many listeners gathered together in the one place, Maharaj Shri's Sinhaasana (Lion throne) was raised above the gate and placed on a terrace. By doing this the folk could get a good view of Maharaj Shri's, obtaining his *darshan* and drinking his *upadeshaamrita* (immortal nectar counsel).

Requests came to Shri Charan for him to grace Lucknow, Jabalpur, Surat and Bombay with his presence. Having seen the requests coming, the scholars of Allahabad requested him that once a year, of all pilgrimage places, that each year he stay at Tirthraaj Prayag ('King of Pilgrimage Places, Allahabad'), in the month of *maagha* (11th month of Hindu year, falling in February 1952). If at this time he ignores Prayag and goes elsewhere, then this will disrespect all places of pilgrimage and dishonour Tirthraaj.

[Tirthraaj Prayag = 'Raaj (king) of places of pilgrimage, Prayag' - the phrase is found in *Guru Gita* in verse 17 - *'tiirtharaajah prayaagashcha gurumuurtyai namo namah..'*]

With this view, certainly in the month of Maagh this year, you enhanced the magnificence of Tirthraaj with your darshan and upadesha. Having accepted the request he proceeded with his programme as before. But at the persuasion of those *kalpavaasa* (those conducting traditional rituals on the banks of the Ganga during the month of Maagh), on Sundays and Thursdays there were regular *upadesha* throughout Maagh.

On Friday 23rd February 1952 the Shankaracharya Sevak Sangha (the Shankaracharya Disciples Organisation) invoked the great festival of Shivaratri with great grandeur. The programme began at began at noon and went on until eight o'clock at night. On this occasion in the evening time there was community *darshan, upadesha* and communal worship of Maharaj Shri. The courtyard of the ashram was full of *darshan* seekers and all those who participated in the communal worship had their own *aarati* tray. This *aarati* was in a communal form with each in his own place [offering camphor flame], the scene was very attractive and unprecedented.

*

[The following quotations are attributed to Guru Dev, said to have been included in publicity material in 1952:-

'One should know as to how to live in the world and he will be happy. Your body and wealth is useful in the world and your mind is useful on the path to God. Do not apply too much mind in the world than necessary otherwise it would be a waste and a loss to both material and spiritual aspects of life. Just like putting more than necessary gum to paste the envelope. The gum will be wasted and the envelope will be spoiled.

'Either live and leave yourself at the entire mercy of God or act according to the dictates of the *Shastras*. The kitten will not move from its place unless the mother cat removes it, even though the male cat may kill it. In this case the mother cat takes care and hides it from the male cat. The young one of a monkey on comprehending danger at once runs to the mother and she takes it to the place of safety! If it runs to some other side than the mother then it would be a risk of its life. Similarly if people act according to their mind and not according to the *Shastras* then they will be mislead and again fall in the circle of birth and rebirth.'

१०

दसवाँ अध्याय

अन्तिम धर्म-प्रचार-यात्रा

६ मार्च, १९५२ ई० को महाराज श्री की यात्रा का मुहूर्त्त प्रयाग से लखनऊ पधारने का निश्चित हो गया। यह समाचार प्रयागवासियों के मध्य बिजली की तरह फैल गया। १२ बजे मध्याह्न में यात्रा प्रारम्भ होने को थी। किन्तु प्रातःकाल से ही जनता आतुर हो होकर आश्रम में दर्शन के लिये एकत्र होने लगी। शहर में चारों ओर से भक्तों का ताँता लग गया और थोड़ी ही देर में आश्रम भर गया। यात्रा के समय जब महाराज श्री अपने कमरे से बाहर निकले तो भक्तों को यह विछोह सहन नहीं हुआ। क्या स्त्री, क्या पुरुष सभी रो पड़े। इस यात्रा के समय भक्त लोग विशेष अधीर हो उठे – कौन जानता था कि यह आपकी अन्तिम यात्रा है। महाराज श्री ने एक दृष्टि से सभी को तृप्त करते हुए कार में बैठने के पूर्व अपने सेवकों को आदेश दिया, "शीघ्र चलो हमारे बैठते ही कार चल पड़नी चाहिये" इतना कहकर वे कार में बैठ गये। आश्रम में ऊपर नीचे भीतर बाहर सड़क पर इतनी अधिक भीड़ थी कि मोटर को आश्रम से बाहर निकलने में बड़ी कठिनाई पड़ी। आँखों में आँसू भरे हुए भक्तों की भावनाओं से द्रवित हुए श्री भगवान् का कोमल हृदय सिहर उठा। व्यथित हृदय भक्तों के गगन भेदी जयकारों के बीच आश्रम से भगवान् की यात्रा प्रारम्भ हुई। मार्ग में स्थान-स्थान पर सड़क पर जनता श्री चरण के दर्शन की प्रतीक्षा करती हुई खड़ी मिली। कहीं-कहीं सहस्रों नर-नारी फूल-माला, शंख-घंटा-घड़ियाल, आरती और पूजन की सामग्री लिये

उपास्थित मिले ।

लखनऊ से लगभग ७ मील दूर नागरिक जन अपनी अपनी मोटरकारें, जीपें और लारियाँ लेकर सैकड़ों की संख्या में श्री भगवान् के स्वागत में ४ बजे से ही प्रतीक्षा कर रहे थे । लगभग ५॥ बजे श्री भगवान् की कार वहाँ पहुँची । आरती पूजन आदि के अनन्तर जीपों में वैदिक मंडलियाँ वेद पाठ करती हुई भगवान् की कार के आगे चलीं । पीछे सभी भक्त जन अपनी-अपनी कारों में चले । इस प्रकार नागरिकों ने श्री चरण का अभूतपूर्व स्वागत किया ।

लखनऊ में नित्य दिन में ११ से १२ बजे तक दर्शन सायंकाल ६ से ८ बजे तक कीर्तन, प्रवचन व उपदेश होते रहे । भगवान् शंकराचार्य के पदार्पण से लखनऊ में अपूर्व धार्मिक जागृति हो गई । श्री शंकराचार्य-सप्ताह मनाने का निश्चय किया गया । श्री चरणों के प्रति नागरिकों की जो अगाध श्रद्धा थी, उसे वर्णन कर सकना किसी के लिये सम्भव नहीं । श्री चरणों के प्रति कृतज्ञता के भाव प्रदर्शित करने तथा इस समारोह के बहाने श्री चरण के दिव्य अमृतमय सदुपदेशों से नगर निवासियों को अधिकाधिक लाभान्वित करने के लिये इस समारोह का आयोजन किया गया । श्री शंकराचार्य सप्ताह समारोह शनिवार, २२ मार्च १९५२ से प्रारम्भ हुआ । श्री शंकराचार्य शिविर में श्री शंकराचार्य सेवक मंडल लखनऊ द्वारा श्री चरण-पादुका का सामूहिक पूजन हुआ पूजन के अन्त में जब आरती का समय आया तो उपस्थित विशाल जन-समूह में जो जहाँ था वहीं उसने अपनी अपनी आरती जलाई । सहस्रों हाथ आरती की थालियाँ लिये हुये ऊपर उठ आये । मैदान भर में सहस्रों दीपशिखाएँ छोटेछोटे चक्करों में घूमने लगीं । जो जहाँ थे, वही खड़े हुये । सबने श्री चरणों की आरती उतरी । सैकड़ों घण्टे-घड़ियाल एक साथ बज रहे थे ।

ज्योतिर्मय दृश्य और शंख घंटों की तुमुलध्वनि से अन्तःकारण गद्गद और प्रफुल्लित हो उठा। वायुमंडल सत्व प्रधान हो गया। सामूहिक प्रार्थना हुई। गुरुचरणों के प्रति भक्ति की एक हिलोर उठी और एक छोर से दूसरे छोर तक सबके सब उसमें वह उठे। भक्ति से मुग्ध प्रशान्त दिव्य वातावरण में भगवान श्री का उपदेश हुआ।

लखनऊ के इतिहास में यह प्रथम अवसर था जबकि नगर में किसी के नाम से सप्ताह मनाया गया हो। इस नगर के नाम (लक्ष्मणपुर) के साथ त्रेतायुग की स्मृति है और लाखों वर्ष पूर्व का इतिहास इसके पीछे है। विलासिता प्रेमी मुगल नवाबों के उत्कर्ष एवं पराभव की कहानी कहनेवाली अट्टालिकायें आज भी खड़ी हैं। ऐसे भौतिकता प्रधान नगर में धर्माचार्य के प्रति यह श्रद्धा धर्माचार्य के तप एवं उनकी महत्ता का द्योतक है।

प्रथम दिवस के कार्यक्रम में प्रातःकाल साढ़े चार बजे से हो भक्तगण अपने-अपने मुहल्लों में प्रभातफेरियों के लिये निकल पड़े। भगवान् के शिविर में भी भक्तगण अपनी-अपनी मोटरों में लाउडस्पीकर लगाये हुये अपने को तीन दलों में बाँट कर नगर के समस्त प्रधान मार्गों में प्रभातफेरी के लिये चल पड़े। साढ़े चार से साढ़े सात बजे तक भगवान् शंकरा-चार्य तथा सनातन धर्म के जयघोषों से नगर गुंजायमान रहा। नागरिकों ने घरों से बाहर निकल-निकल कर प्रभात फेरियों के जयकारों में अपनी जयकारें मिलाकर उनका स्वागत किया। सभी ने भगवान शंकराचार्य के अतुलित प्रभाव का अनुभव किया।

सायंकाल भगवान् ने विधान सभा मार्ग से सभामण्डप के लिये प्रस्थान किया। बीसों मोटरें, जीपें, कारें पीले-पीले झंडे फहराती हुई

शंकराचार्य तथा सनातन धर्म के जयघोष तथा वेद पाठ करती हुई आगे चलीं। भक्तों ने मार्ग में पचासों फाटक बनवाये और जगह-जगह आ रती पूजन काप्रबन्ध किया। भगवान् की मोटर को घेरे हुये सहस्रों जन दौड़ाते हुये चल रहे थे। सैकड़ों साइकिलें दौड़ा रहे थे। हर एक समय हर एक मनुष्य एक्सीडेन्ट के मुँह में था। किन्तु भगवान् की दया से किसी से किसी प्रकार की दुर्घटना नहीं हुई।

श्री चरणों के प्रति जनता का भक्तिभाव देखकर हृदय गद्गद हो उठा। बड़े-बड़े सुप्रतिष्ठित स्थूलकाय विद्वानों को शंख फूँकते भगवान् की मोटर के बगल में दौड़ते देखा गया। जिस मार्ग को पैंतालीस मिनट में पार करने का अनुमान था, उस मार्ग को पार करने में दो घण्टे पैंतालीस मिनट लग गये। साढ़े दस बजे रात जुलूस सभा-मण्डप में पहुँचा। स्वर्ण शिविका द्वारा भगवान् मंच पर पधारे। सिंहासन पर समासीन करा कर नगर की ओर से श्री चरणों की पादुकाओं का पूजन किया गया। अभिनन्दन पत्र समर्पित किये गये। निश्चित कार्यक्रम के उपरान्त भगवान् का अमृतमय उपदेश हुआ सप्ताह में प्रतिदिन प्रातःकाल ४॥ बजे से ७॥ बजे तक प्रभातफेरी, ९ से १२ बजे तक पंचदेवों-भगवान् शंकर, विष्णु, देवी, सूर्य एवं गणेश-की आराधना ६॥ से ७ बजे तक सभामंडप में भजन, कीर्तन, ७ से ९ तक सन्तों के उपदेश और अन्त में ९ बजे से भगवान् शंकराचार्य का अमृतोपदेश होता रहा। अन्तिम दिवस धन्य-धन्य जयकारों के गगनभेदी उद्घोषों के बीच उल्लासपूर्वक वातावरण में चिरस्मरणीय सप्ताह समाप्त हुआ। जिन सौभाग्यशाली सहृदय नेत्रों ने इसका आनन्द लिया, वे जीवन भर भूल नहीं सकेंगे। एक लाख से अधिक जनसमूह के मध्य ऐसा अद्वितीय उत्सव हुआ कि इसके सम्बन्ध में चर्चा करते हुये लोगों के प्रेमाश्रु छलक पड़ते,

कण्ठ गद्गद हो जाता, वाणी धन्य-धन्य के अतिरिक्त अधिक कहने में अवरुद्ध हो जाती। इस प्रकार ३१ मार्च, १९५२ ई० को यह अभूतपूर्व श्री शंकराचार्य-सप्ताह-महोत्सव समाप्त हुआ,

इसके बाद महाराज श्री लखनऊ में लगभग एक महीना रहे। आपका निवासस्थान, शंकर-निवास (१९ विधान सभा मार्ग), उस समय वास्तव में शंकर-निवास हो गया। प्रातःकाल ९ बजे से लगभग २ बजे तक दर्शन व दीक्षा के लिये मेला लगा रहता। आश्रम के संन्यासी तथा व्रचारियों से भी अपनी-अपनी शंकाओं का समाधान करने के लिये लोग उनके कमरों में भीड़ लगाये रहते। कितने ही भक्तगण प्रातःकाल से ही आश्रम के बगीचे में और कमरों में जिसको जहाँ सुबिधा दिखती बैठ कर जपध्यान करने के लक्ष्य से आ जाते और मध्याह्न में श्री चरण दर्शन के उपरान्त ही वापस जाते।

सायंकाल ५ बजे से ही भक्तों का आना आरम्भ हो जाता। आश्रम के विस्तृत मैदान में ऊँचे तख्त पर भगवान् शंकरचार्य का सिंहासन लगता बगल के तख्तों पर संन्यासी, महात्माओं के आसन लगते, सामने विद्वानों और ब्रह्मचारियों के आसन रहते और व्यवस्थित रूप से महिलाओं तथा पुरुषों के लिये बैठने का प्रबन्ध रहता। भगवान् का मंच फूल मालाओं से सजाया जाता। पर्व-तिथियों पर विशेष रूप से सजावट होती। इस प्रकार सभा का दृश्य अत्यन्त चित्ताकर्षक होता।

सायंकाल ६ बजे से भगवन्नाम संकीर्तन से उपदेश सभा का कार्यक्रम प्रारम्भ होता। ६॥ बजे से संन्यासी महात्माओं के प्रवचन होते और ७ बजे श्री चरण पधारते। अपने कमरे से महाराज श्री

चलकर ही आते और दोनों ओर से भक्तगण 'जय हो जय हो' की गम्भीर ध्वनि के साथ पुष्प वृष्टि करते। वैदिक पंडित स्वस्तिवाचन करते हुये आगे-आगे चलते। उसी समय मंच पर स्वस्तिवाचन का पाठ किया किया जाता। उपस्थित जन समूह खड़ा होकर जयकारों से आकाश गुंजायमान कर देता। श्री चरण सिंहासन पर विराजते और सभा पुलकित हो उठती। महाराज श्री का उपदेश लगभग सवा सात से आठ बजे तक नित्य होता था।

उपदेश के पश्चात् भगवान् अपने कमरे में आ जाते और सभामंच पर भगवान् चन्द्रमौलीश्वर की सामूहिक आरती होती। उधर बाहर आरती होती इधर विशाल जनसमूह श्री चरण के पीछे-पीछे आकर हाल में निकट से दर्शन करने के लिये एकत्र हो जाता। लगभग एक घण्टा भगवान् को यहाँ दर्शन देने के लिये हाल में बैठना पड़ता। वहाँ से उथकर महाराज श्री छत पर चले जाते। यहाँ भी एकान्त में उपासना आदि समझने वालों की संख्या इतनी अधिक हो जाती कि १२ बजे अर्द्धरात्रि तक भी सब लोगों को समय न मिल पाता और १२ बज जाने पर सब केवल दर्शन प्रणाम करके लौट जाते। इस प्रकार प्रातःकाल से १२ बजे अर्द्ध रात्रि तक आश्रम में मेला-सा लगा रहता।

इस विधि से लखनऊ में श्री महाराजजी ने डेढ़ मास तक निवास किया। तत्पश्चात् २१ अप्रैल, १९५२ ई० को सायंकाल देहरा एक्सप्रेस से देहरादून के लिये प्रस्थान किया। स्टेशन पर श्री चरण के दर्शन के लिये अपार जनता एकत्र हुई। लखनऊ स्टेशन का लगभग २ फर्लांग लम्बा प्लेटफोर्म स्त्री-पुरुषों से खचाखच भर गया। नीचे रेल की लाइनों पर भी लोग हजारों की संख्या में श्री महाराज के दर्शन की एक झाँकी पाने की उत्सुकता में आशान्वित खड़े थे। लोगों के

हृदय में श्रद्धा भक्ति थी। प्रेमाश्रुओं की उमंग से नेत्र झलझला रहे थे। हर जगह भीड़ की अधिकता थी। हर व्यक्ति धक्कों से दबा जा रहा था। पर हर मुख से रह-रह कर निकल पड़ता था, 'भगवान् शंकराचार्य की जय हो।'

पूर्व निश्चित कार्यक्रम के अनुसार श्री भगवान् एक सुसज्जित बंद कार द्वारा ६ बज कर ४५ मिनट पर स्टेशन पहुँचे प्लेटफार्म के बाहर ही श्री चरण को इस बंद मोटर से उतार कर एक सुसज्जित खुली मोटर पर आसीन किया गया जिससे स्टेशन पर श्री चरण के दर्शनार्थ आई हुई जनता को ठीक से दर्शन हो सके। यह कार प्लेटफार्म के अन्दर लाकर उस जगह खड़ी की गई जहाँ एक ओर महिलाएँ और दूसरी ओर पुरुष अपनी-अपनी आरतियाँ लिये खड़े थे।

वैदिक विद्वानों ने स्वस्तिवाचन पाठ प्रारम्भ किया और सबों ने अपनी-अपनी आरतियाँ जलाई। प्लेटफार्म भर में बीसों हजार आरतियाँ एक साथ जगमगा उठीं। हजारों शंख-घंटा-घड़ियाल की मंगल ध्वनि सहसा होने लगी। सैकड़ों हाथों में झंडे-झंडियाँ लहरा रहे थे। उस समय लखनऊ का चारबाग स्टेशन भव्य मन्दिर बन गया। भगवान् शंकराचार्य के जय घोषों से वातावरण गूँज उठा और भक्तों का हृदय गद्गद हो गया। नास्तिकों का मस्तक झुका और नागरिकों ने धर्म सम्राट को विदाई में अनन्त आरती जलाकर इस तथ्य का प्रदर्शन किया कि जो धर्म ज्योति आपने जलाई है वह अनन्त एवं अखण्ड है और शाश्वत काल तक जगमगाती रहेगी।

५० हजार से अधिक नर नारियों ने भक्ति-गद्गद हृदय और अश्रुपूरित नेत्रों से जगद्गुरु शंकराचार्य को अभूतपूर्व विदाई दी।

भीड़ इतनी अधिक थी कि प्लेटफार्म पर तिल रखने की जगह न रहने की बात चरितार्थ हो गई। जिस डिब्बे से महाराज श्री देहरादून जाने वाले थे, वह फूल-मालाओं से बहुत ही सुन्दर ढंग से सजाया गया था। यद्यपि महाराज श्री के कार और रेल के डिब्बे में कुल ५ या ६ गज का ही फासला था पर भीड़ के कारण वहाँ तक पहुँचाने में १५–२० मिनट लग गये। जिस समय फूल-मालाओं से सजा हुआ डिब्बा महाराज जी को लेकर आगे बढ़ा, 'भगवान् शंकराचार्य की जय हों', के गगनभेदी स्वर से आकाश गूँज उठा। लखनऊ की जनता ने जिस भक्ति और श्रद्धा से महाराज श्री को विदाई दी, वह लखनऊ के इतिहास में चिरस्मरणीय रहेगी।

२२ अप्रैल, १९५२ को प्रातःकाल ९ बजे आप देहरादून पहुंचे। स्टेशन पर नागरिकों द्वारा भव्य स्वागत के पश्चात् आपको कसभंडा-हाउस, जो शहर से बाहर एक बड़े बगीचे के बीच स्थित है, ठहरया गया। भीड़ भाड़ से आये हुये महाराज श्री को यह शान्त-स्थान अनुकूल पड़ा। ऋषीकेश के काली-कमली-क्षेत्र के मंत्री, पं० श्रीदत्त शास्त्री द्वारा विशेष आग्रह किये जाने पर महाराज श्री, २५ अप्रैल को संध्या समय देहरादून से ऋषीकेश, रामनगर आये। मार्ग में जनता ने गाजे-बाजे के साथ श्रीचरण का भव्य स्वागत किया और वहाँ आत्म विज्ञान-भवन में "श्री शंकराचार्य निवास" में ठहरे। सत्संग भवन में दो दिन उपदेश हुआ और निश्चयानुसार २८ अप्रैल को कार द्वारा मंसूरी पधारे। मार्ग में मंसूरी की सीमा प्रारम्भ होते ही जहाँ-जहाँ नियमानुसार मोटर रुकती आई जनता स्वागत के लिये एकत्र मिली और सभी स्थानों पर सब ने बड़ी श्रद्धा-भक्ति और उत्साह के साथ श्री चरण की आरती उतारी। टोल गेट एवं क्रीकेट गेट पर विशेषरूप से आरती पूजन का समारोह हुआ। लायब्रेरी

(पुस्तकालय) के सामने हजारों की संख्या में नागरिकों ने घण्टा-घड़ियालों की तुमुल ध्वनि करते हुये "श्री शंकराचार्य" एवं सनातन धर्म के गगन भेदी जयकारों से भगवान् का स्वागत किया । कई राज्य परिवारों ने श्री चरण का पूजन किया, आरती उतारी और अपनी-अपनी श्रद्धा-भक्ति का परिचय दिया ।

पर्वतीय धार्मिक जनता की प्रार्थनाओं पर महाराज श्री ने इस वर्ष अपना चातुर्मास्य-व्रत भी यहीं किया । यह महायज्ञ "प्रताप भवन" में हुआ, जो नगर के केन्द्र, मुहल्ला कुल्हड़ी में ऊँचाई पर स्थित है । यहाँ के नैसर्गिक दृश्य अत्यन्त मनोरम हैं । ७ जुलाई, १९५२ ई० को गुरुपूर्णिमामहोत्सव बड़े ही समारोह के साथ सम्पन्न हुआ । श्रीचरण के पूजनार्थ प्रातःकाल ९ से १२ बजे तक श्री चरण पादुका का पूजन अनेक भक्तों और श्रद्धालुओं ने किया । सायंकाल ५ से ९ बजे रात्रि तक सार्वजनिक सभा का कार्यक्रम बड़े ही आनन्दपूर्वक सम्पन्न हुआ । लखनऊ, कलकत्ता, कानपुर, इटावा, प्रयाग, जबलपुर, काशी, देहरादून, बम्बई, दिल्ली, आदि प्रायः सभी बड़े-बड़े नगरों से आये हुये भक्तों ने अपने-अपने नगर की श्रद्धां-जलियाँ अर्पित कीं और अनेक धार्मिक सामाजिक संस्थाओं की श्रद्धांजलियों के तार और पत्र पढ़कर सुनाये गये । अन्त में भगवान् का शुभाशीर्वादात्मक उपदेश हुआ ।

चातुर्मास्य-व्रत के समय नित्य सायंकाल दर्शन होता था और सप्ताह में दो बार, गुरुवार और रविवार को सामूहिक उपदेश होते रहे । इस अवसर पर मंसूरी नगर निवासियों ने २३ सितम्बर १९५२ ई० को परम हर्ष व उत्साह के साथ "श्री शंकराचार्य दिवस" महोत्सव मनाया । मंसूरी जैसे विलासी शहर में जहाँ लोग भोग-विलास करने के लिये ही आते हैं धर्म का जयघोष हुआ । अपूर्व

धार्मिक जागृति हुई। भगवान् शंकराचार्य की शोभायात्रा किताबघर से निकाली गई जुलूस गांधी चौक, लंढौर बाजार तथा सनातन धर्म मन्दिर होता हुआ हिमालय क्लब में समाप्त हुआ। जुलूस का आकार बहुत विशाल था। सड़कों पर इतनी भीड़ हो गई कि सुगमता से चलना कठिन हो गया। घरों की छतों पर भीड़ जुलूस देखने के लिये एकत्र थी। विभिन्न स्थलों पर भगवान् का पूजन व आरती की गई। जुलूस २ बजे दिन से चलकर ६॥ बजे हिमालय क्लब में समाप्त हुआ। वहीं एक सार्वजनिक सभा हुई, जिसमें अभिनन्दन-पत्र और श्रद्धाञ्जलियाँ समर्पित की गई। महोत्सव के अवसर पर नगर की सजावट हुई और नगर ही नहीं आस-पास की धार्मिक जनता का मंसूरी में सागर-सा उमड़ आया। लोगों की इतनी अपार भीड़ इतना वृहत् जुलूस मंसूरी नगर के इतिहास में एक अभूतपूर्व घटना थी। मंसूरी जैसे शहर में श्रीचरणों के प्रति इतनी श्रद्धा एवं आस्तिकता महाराज श्री के व्यक्तित्व की महानता की विचित्र परिचय कराती थी।

८ अक्टूबर १९५२ ई। को लगभग २ बजे महाराज श्री का प्रताप भवन मंसूरी से कार द्वारा प्रस्थान हुआ। सहस्रों नर-नारी भगवान् की कार के आगे पीछे चल रहे थे वास्तव में मंसूरी की जनता का यह प्रत्यक्ष चित्रण था। आप - देहरादून पधारे और वहाँ आपने तीन दिन निवास किया। ११ ता। को ३॥ बजे सायंकाल सहारनपुर के लिये मोटर से यात्रा हुई। ५ बजे आप सहारनपुर पहुंच गये। सतयुग आश्रम से आपकी शोभायात्रा निकाली गई। जुलूस घंटाघर नेहरू मार्केट सब्जीमण्डी वामनजी रोड चौक फौवारा सराफा पुराना बाजार आदि प्रमुख स्थानों में होता हुआ रामलीला भवन में समाप्त हुआ। सभी के मुख से यही कहते सुना गया, "आज तक कभी ऐसा भव्य

जुलूस नहीं देखा ।''

रामलीला भवन महाराज श्री का निवास स्थान एक भव्य मन्दिर बन गया । प्रातःकाल से ही भक्तजन हाथों में फूल-मालाएँ लिये कितने ही पूजन की सामग्री लिये भगवान् के दर्शन पूजन की अभिलाषा से आ जाते । नित्य पचासों दीक्षायें होतीं । शहर में यह आम चर्चा हो गई कि इतने उच्चकोटि के गुरु का इतने सुलभरूप में प्राप्त होना कठिन है । इसी भाव से भावित होकर दीक्षा के लिये जनसमूह आतुर हो उठा ।

२२ अक्टूबर १९५२ ई० को महाराज श्री प्रातः ८ बजे मोटर कार द्वारा प्रस्थान करके अम्बाला पधारे । धर्माचार्य के अम्बाला पदार्पण पर उनके स्वागतोपलक्ष में विराट और भव्य शोभायात्रा निकाली गई । नागरिकों का उत्साह देखते ही बनता था । नगर की सभी धार्मिक सामाजिक संस्थाओं ने भाग लिया । ८॥ बजे सायंकाल में अभिनन्दन सभा का कार्यक्रम हुआ, जिसमें सनातन धर्म सभा, राष्ट्रीय-सेवक-संघ, ब्राह्मण सभा, हिन्दू महासभा की ओर से अभिनन्दन-पत्र समर्पित किये गये ।

१३ नवम्बर को प्रातःकाल ५ बजे भगवान् ने मोटर द्वारा अम्बाला से देहली के लिये प्रस्थान किया । १२ नवम्बर १९५२ ई० को ही अम्बाला निवासियों को यह ज्ञात हो गया था कि कल प्रातःकाल महाराज श्री उन्हें छोड़कर देहली जा रहे हैं । अतः ४ बजे से ही अम्बाला निवासी नर-नारी महाराज श्री के अंतिम दर्शन के लिये शिविर में एकत्रित होने लगे । ५ बजते-बजते अपार जनसमूह इकट्ठा हो गया । परिणामस्वरूप अम्बाला पार करने में मोटर को दो घण्टे से अधिक समय लग गया । लोग प्रेम से विह्वल हो रहे थे ।

उनकी अश्रुपूर्ण आँखें उनके हृदय की आंतरिक वेदना का प्रदर्शन कर रही थीं। अम्बाला से चल कर देहली से १० मील पहिले, महाराज श्री ने दिन भर विश्राम किया और संध्या समय वहाँ से चलकर ७ बजे भारत की राजधानी दिल्ली पधारे। स्वागत हेतु नगर की धर्मप्राण जनता गांधी ग्राउंड में सागर की भांति अपार रूप धारण किये थी। सहस्रों नर-नारियों और नगर की प्रमुख धार्मिक-संस्थाओं ने महाराज श्री का तुमुल हर्ष ध्वनि एवं जय-जयकारों के साथ स्वागत किया और ११ गोलों से महाराज श्री की वन्दना की।

दिल्ली स्टेशन के समीप, क्वींस गार्डन में श्री शंकराचार्य शिविर निर्माण किया गया और वहीं महाराज श्री ने निवास किया। नगरनिवासियों, नगर की प्रमुख धार्मिक संस्थाओं एवं पंडित मण्डली की ओर से स्वागतसभा हुई और भगवान् के चरण कमलों में श्रद्धांजलियाँ एवं अभिनन्दन पत्र अर्पित किये गये। स्वागताध्यक्ष ने अपने स्वागत भाषण में कहा, "महाराज श्री उत्तर भारत की धर्मपीठ के धर्म-सिंहासन पर समासीन होकर हमारा पथ प्रदर्शन करने के लिये भगवान् आदि शंकराचार्य के पवित्र उद्देश्य को सार्थक करने के लिये देश के कोने-कोने में जनता से निकट सम्पर्क स्थापित कर हमें इहलोक और परलोक का राजमार्ग बताने के लिये भ्रमण कर रहे हैं। आपकी सर्वांगीण आदर्श-व्यवस्था देखकर सभी को ज्योतिर्मठ पर गौरव होने लगा है। आप किसी रूप में रुपये पैसे स्वीकार नहीं करते और अपने दैवी बल से ही इस प्रकार धर्म-प्रचार यात्राएँ कर रहे हैं। यह इतने बड़े स्वाभिमान और गौरव का विषय है कि उसका उल्लेख शब्दों में नहीं किया जा सकता। आपकी यह नीति हमें आपके स्वरूप में व्यास, वसिष्ठ और भारद्वाज आदि प्राचीन महर्षियों का दर्शन कराती है। आपका स्वर्णछत्र धर्मछत्र है, जिसकी

मंगलमयी शीतल छाया में आकर सभी लोग सुख शान्ति का अनुभव करते हैं। आपका स्वर्ण-सिंहासन धर्म सिंहासन है, जो धर्म और अधर्म के निर्णय का अन्तिम स्थान है। आपके सम्मुख रहने वाले दो स्वर्ण-दण्डु धर्म और नीति के प्रतीक हैं। दाहिनी ओर का धर्म-दण्ड है और बाँई ओर का नीतिदण्ड है। आपके सम्मुख चलनेवाली दो ज्योति (मशालें) वेद और शास्त्र के प्रतीक हैं। दाहिनी ओर की ज्योति, अपौरुषेय वेद का प्रतीक है और बाँई ओर की ज्योति शास्त्र का प्रतीक है। ये दो ज्योतियाँ इस बात को स्पष्ट करती हैं कि आप वेद और शास्त्र के प्रकाश से लोक का अज्ञानान्धकार मिटाने के लिये यहाँ पधारे हैं। भगवान् शंकराचार्य का देहली में शुभागमन हमारे नगर के इतिहास में स्वर्णिम घटना है।"

हजारों की संख्या में प्रतिदिन श्रद्धालु नागरिक जन भगवान् के दर्शन करते और प्रातःकाल का दर्शन बंद हो जाने पर भी सायंकाल तक शिविर में भीड़ बनी ही रहती। नागरिकों के लिये श्री शंकराचार्य शिविर मेला-स्थल हो गया। सायंकाल ६॥ बजे से गांधी-ग्राउंद में उपदेश सभा का कार्यक्रम प्रारम्भ हो जाता। लगभग ७॥ बजे "हर हर महादेव शाम्भो काशी विश्वनाथ गंगे" की मधुर संकीर्तन ध्वनि के बीच श्री भगवान् शंकराचार्य की शिविका पंडाल में प्रवेश करती। शिविका से उतरकर महाराज श्री सिंहासन पर विराजते और छत्र, चमर, दण्ड आदि युक्त पार्षदों सहित झांकी को देखकर अपार जनसमूह का हृदय गद्गद हो उठता। लगभग ८ बजे नित्य भगवान् का उपदेश प्रारम्भ होता था। देहली के धार्मिक सत्संग में अपार भीड़ का होना प्रत्येक मनुष्य को संतुष्ट होकर जाना और नित्य श्रोताओं की संख्या बढ़ती जाना राजधानी के इतिहास की प्रथम घटना थी।

दिल्ली में अत्यधिक भीड़ होने के कारण महाराज श्री का विचार कुछ दिनों के लिये पूर्ण एकान्त सेवन करने का हो गया। २८ नवम्बर, १९५२ ई० को श्री भगवान् क्वीन्स गार्डन से उठकर ७ कैनिंग लेन, नई दिल्ली पधारे। यहाँ सायंकालीन सभाओं का कार्यक्रम स्थगित कर दिया, किन्तु नित्य सार्वजनिक दर्शन प्रातः १० से १२ बजे तक चलता रहा।

४ दिसम्बर को १२ बजे दिन में राष्ट्रपति डा। राजेन्द्र प्रसाद महाराज श्री दर्शन के लिये शिविर में आये। दर्शन किया श्रद्धांजलि समर्पण की और चरणोदक लिया। श्री भगवान् शंकराचार्य ने राष्ट्रपति से बातें करते हुये कहा, "पहिले नरेन्द्र लोग तपस्वियों और महर्षियों से अपने शासन कार्यों में परामर्श लिया करते थे। योग और तपस्या के कारण उनकी बुद्धि विमल होती थी। उन्हें लोभ और लोक वासना नहीं रहती थी और न उन्हें यही डर रहता कि राजा इस बात से अप्रसन्न हो जायगा। वे जो परामर्श देते थे वह राजा और प्रजा दोनों के लिये हितकर होते थे। जब से महर्षियों का सम्पर्क राजाओं ने छोड़ा तभी से रसातल को चले गये।" यह कहते हुये आगे कहा, "आपका नौकर आपको क्या सलाह दे सकता है? वह तो आप का ही नेत्र देखेगा। इसलिये प्रमुख सम्मति का काम महर्षियों से लेना चाहिये, जो भविष्य पर भी विचार कर सकते हैं। आप लोगों को यह भ्रम नहीं रहना चाहिये कि धर्मनीति राजनीति की विरोधिनी है। हमलोग जनता को सदाचारी बनने का उपदेश देते हैं। जनता जितनी सदाचारी होगी उतना ही शासनकार्य भी सुचारु रूप से चलेगा।" राष्ट्रपति महोदय बड़ी गम्भीरता से श्री शंकराचार्य महाराज की बातें सुनते रहे। महाराज श्री ने उपासना सम्बन्धी गम्भीर तथ्यों पर संक्षेप में प्रकाश डालते हुये कहा "वद्यार्थी अपना

पाठ्यक्रम स्वयं नहीं बना सकता। इसके लिए शिक्षाविद् की आवश्यकता पड़ती है। इसी प्रकार वास्तविक सुख-शान्ति का मार्ग समझने के लिये अनुभवी गुरु की आवश्यकता होती है।" इसी प्रसंग में अपने गुरुदेव के कुछ अनुभव सुनाते हुये श्री चरण ने संक्षेप में अपनी जीवनी पर भी कुछ प्रकाश डाला। बताया कि जब गुरु जी उत्तर काशी में मिले, तब सब से पहिले हमने यही कहा, "पहले हमें ऐसी विद्या दीजिये कि किसी के आगे हाथ न फैलाना पड़े बाद में हम परमार्थ समझेंगे। यह उन्हीं की कृपा का फल है कि प्रारम्भ से अभी तक हमने कभी किसी के सामने हाथ नहीं पसारा।"

डेढ़ घण्टे के बार्तालाप में शंकराचार्य महाराज ने राष्ट्रपति जो को व्यक्तिगत और सामाजिक जीवन के उत्थान के प्रधान तत्व तथा शासक और शासित के हित के मौलिक सिद्धान्तो का इस सुगमता से संक्षेप में दिग्दर्शन कराया कि राजेन्द्र बाबू मंत्रमुग्ध होकर सब सुनते रहे। राष्ट्रपति जी के कार्यक्रम के अनुसार महाराज श्री से बातचीत करते हुये निर्धारित समय से २५ मिनट अधिक हो गये, किन्तु जब महाराज श्री ने स्वतः उनके जाने की आज्ञा दी, तभी गये।

महाराज श्री का निवास इस समय कैनिंग लेन, नई दिल्ली में हो रहा था। एकान्त एवं विश्राम की दृष्टि से ही आप गांधी ग्राउंड से यहाँ चले आये थे। किन्तु थोड़े ही दिन लोगों का आना जाना कम रहा। धीरे-धीरे आगन्तुकों की संख्या बढ़ती ही गई। तब महाराज श्री ने फिर निर्णय किया कि चुपचाप स्थानान्तरण कर दिया जाय। इस लक्ष्य से, १९ दिसम्बर १९५२ ई० को, आप आगरा चले आये। यहाँ महाराज श्री का निवास सिविल लाइन्स में डा० भट्टू, प्रिंसिपल मेडिकल कालेज, की कोठी में हुआ।

यहाँ प्रायः शान्तिपूर्वक विश्राम रहा। केवल दर्शन प्रणाम ही सामूहिक रूप से चलता रहा। २२ जनवरी। १९५३ को आचार्यचरण आगरा से प्रस्थान करके २३ जनवरी को मध्याह्न में काशी पधारे और ब्रह्म निवास आश्रम सिद्धगिरि बाग में आपने निवास किया। आपका काशी पदार्पण भी प्रधानताः विश्राम की दृष्टि से ही हुआ था। इसलिये इस सम्बन्ध में जनता कि सुचना नहीं दी गई थी फिर भी एक दूसरे से सुनकर काफी संख्या में दर्शनार्थ लोग आने लगे। जब देखा कि दर्शनार्थियों की भीड़ उत्तरोत्तर बढ़ती ही जाती तो यहाँ भी सार्वजनिक दर्शन का समय १० से १२ बजे दिन में नियत कर दिया। बाहर से आये हुये दर्शनार्थी-भक्तों सायंकाल भी दर्शन दिया करते थे।

इस प्रकार कुछ तक दिनों काशी में निवास करके रविवार ४ मई, १९५३ ई० की रात को भक्तों को दर्शन देकर ८॥ बजे वेदध्वनि के बीच काशी से कलकत्ता के लिये प्रस्थान किया। भक्तों की दौड़-धूप एवं भीड़-भीड़ से बचने के लिये यात्रा का समाचार गुप्त ही रखा गया। ब्रह्मनिवास अश्रम से बाहर निकलकर आप सुसज्जित पिक-अप पर समासीन हुये। गगन भेदी जयकारों के बीच महाराज श्री की गाड़ी मुगलसराय से लिये चल पड़ी। उसके पीछे भक्तों की गाड़ियाँ और लारियाँ भी चल दीं। यहाँ देहली मेल में एयर कंदीशन डिब्बा महाराज श्री के लिये सुरक्षित था। सूचना न होते हुये भी प्लेटफार्म पर बहुत भीड़ एकत्र हो गई। गाड़ी पर आसीन हो जाने पर भक्त मंडली एक-एक करके डिब्बे में जा जाकर महाराज श्री के दर्शन किये और १०॥ बजे रात्रि में गगनभेदी जयकारों के बीच महाराज श्री का मेल रवाना हुआ। यात्रा सानन्द सम्पन्न हुई और कलकत्ता में ५६ वालीगंज, सरकुलर रोड पर निवास हुआ।

Chapter 10

The Final Dharma-Promulgation Tour

On 6th March 1952 Maharaj Shri resolved to leave Prayag (Allahabad) to find time to travel to Lucknow [238 kms NW of Allahabad]. This news spread like lightening amongst the inhabitants of Prayag (Allahabad). The journey was to begin at twelve o'clock noon but from daybreak the restless folk gathered together in the *ashram* for *darshan*. From the four directions of the city rows of devotees came and in a little time the *ashram* was full. When the time came to travel and Maharaj Shri appeared outside his room, then the devotees could not endure the separation.

Which woman cried? Which man cried? They all cried! At the

time of this his departure the devotees became epecially unsteady. *So, who could have known this was to be your last tour?* But by one sight of Maharaj Shri everyone became satisfied. Before becoming seated in the car he gave this instruction to his attendants, 'Quickly go, we should move as soon as we are sitting in the *"car"*!' Having said as much he sat in the car.

There were such crowds, above, below and within the ashram, and outside on the road the motor car had great difficulty leaving the *ashram*. The eyes filled with tears and as the emotions of the devotees were caused to flow, the tender heart of Shri Bhagwan trembled. Bhagwan's travel commenced amidst the cheers of the distressed devotees, which pierced the heavens, At places along the way the people stood on the road waiting to get *darshan* of Shri Charan. Here and there he was met by thousands of men and women, ready with garland of flowers, conch shell, bell, gong, implements of *aarati* and *pujana* (worship)

From four o'clock in the afternoon, about seven miles distant from Lucknow, several hundred citizens from there were waiting in a number of their own motor cars, jeeps and lorries to welcome Shri Bhagwan. Shri Bhagwan's car reached there at about five-thirty. After *aarati*, *pujana* etc, the Vedic associations recited in the jeeps ahead of Bhagwan's car with all the devotees following behind in their cars. In this manner the citizens gave a wonderful welcome to Shri Charan.

In Lucknow, regularly in the day from eleven to twelve there was *darshan* and from six-to-eight there was *kirtana*, *pravachana* (discourse, sermon) and *upadesha* (lecture). By the very prescence of Bhagwan Shankaracharya in Lucknow there was an unprecedented spiritual awakening there. Shri Shankaracharya Saptah (the week of Shri Shankaracharya) was certain to please. Every citizen had solid faith in Shri Charanon ('Blessed feet'), it is not possible to portray that.

Shri Charanon's brilliant counsel full of immortal nectar, caused the residents of the city to be very grateful towards Shri Charan. The magnificent Shri Shankaracharya Week began from

Saturday 22nd March 1952 and in the Shri Shankaracharya camp, by means of the Shri Shankaracharya Mandala Lucknow, there was a communal *pujana* (worship) of the sandals of Shri Charanon (Blessed Feet). At the end of *pujana*, when the time came for *aarati* (ceremony with lighted camphor lamps), then those present in that huge communal group did their own *aarati* burning wherever they were. Thousands of hands raised their *aarati* trays. In the whole field there were thousands of tiny, tiny flames circling and revolving. Everyone stood still. From all the *aarati* of Shri Charanon arose the sound of hundreds of bells and gongs ringing together as one. The scene abounded with light and with the noisy sounds of conch shells and bells. The inner self arising to be very happy and blossoming. The atmosphere became predominantly *satva* (pure). There had been communal prayer.

A wave of devotion arose towards the feet of the guru and from one end to the other everybody arose in you. In the simple calm heavenly atmosphere of *bhakti* (devotion) there was the *upadesha* (lesson) of Bhagwan Shri.

In the history of Lucknow this was the first occasion when the city invoked a 'week of' any name. The name of the city (Lakshmanpur) is remembered from the Treta Yuga and the history goes back hundreds of thousands of years before. Today there still stand the upper rooms of buildings that tell tales of excess and defeat of the amorous lovers, the Mughal Nawabs (Mohammedan governors). In the city which is chiefly materialistic, this faith towards the Dharmacharya (the religious preceptor), this penance to the Dharmacharya and shows the greatness of the Dharmacharya.

From half past four in the early morning on the first day of the programme the spiritual community went around their own neighbourhoods doing a dawn *prabhata pheri* ('morning walk'). Also the community of devotees in the camp of Bhagwan went off in the early morning in three groups on all the principal roads to all parts of the city, with loudspeakers attached to their motor cars. From half past four until half past seven the city was buzzing with cheering for Bhagwan Shankaracharya and Sanatana Dharma.

From the houses the residents appeared outside cheering, welcoming those who were going around doing the *prabhata pheri* ('morning walk', rallying), cheering again and again. Out and away all experienced the influence of Bhagwan Shankaracharya.

In the evening Bhagwan departed for the Sabha Mandap (the committee's pavillion) by way of Vidhan Sabha Marg (Legislative Assembly Road). Dozens of motor vehicles, jeeps, cars flying yellow flags went ahead, cheering Shankaracharya and Sanatana Dharma, and reading *Veda*. Devotees had made archways in the road and arranged *aarati* worship in different places. Thousands of people ran to encircle the motor car of Bhagwan. Several hundred cyclists came rushing. All the time everyone was expecting an accident but by Bhagwan's kindness there was no tragedy of any kind.

Having seen these feelings of devotion from the people towards Shri Charanon, his heart became very happy. Great big distinguished scholars were seen running beside Bhagwan's motor car blowing conches. That route was guessed at taking no longer than about forty-five minutes, but actualy in taking that route it took two hours and forty-five minutes. At half-past ten at night the cavalcade of cars came to the Sabha Mandap, the committee's pavilion. Bhagwan arrived on the platform on a gold palanquin. Seated securely on the Sinhasana (lion throne), *pujana* (worship) was done to Shri Charanon's sandals by the citizen's. Then there was a welcome address delivered after which came the settled programme of Bhagwan's *upadesha* (lecture) abounding in immortal nectar.

Every day during the week, from four-thirty until seven-thirty was the *prabhata pheri* ('morning walk', rallying), and from nine o'clock until twelve o'clock worship of Bhagwan's five deities, Shankara (Shiva), Vishnu, Devi (goddess), Surya (Sun) and Ganesh. From six-thirty to seven in the Sabha Mandap (the pavilion of the committee) were *bhajana* (hymns) and *kirtana* (singing praise of God). From seven to nine the *upadesha* of the *santon* (the pious or religious persons), and at the end, from nine o'clock being the *amritopadesha* (nectar lecture) of Bhagwan Shankaracharya.

*

At the end of these blessed days the memorable week was finished, the sound of *jaya karen* (cheers) hailing victory arose in the middle of the splendid atmosphere to pierce the sky. They who were lucky enough to perceive this *ananda* (bliss), they cannot forget this for their entire life. To be in the middle of this gathering of more than a hundred-thousand people was such a great occasion beyond comparison. In this connection, talking about past events people still spill tears of love, in telling of the abundant blessings, the throat becomes obstructed, the voice becomes silenced. This wonderful Shri Shankaracharya Saptah Mahotsava (the Great Festival of the Week of Shri Shankaracharya) ended on 31st March 1952, after which Maharaj Shri stayed in Lucknow for about a month longer.

Your dwelling place was at Shankar Nivas, 19 Vidhan Sabha Marg, Lucknow, and in truth at that time it did become "Shankar Nivas" (The Abode of Siva). In the daytime from nine o'clock until two, crowds stayed there for *darshan* (lecture) and for *diksha* (initiation). The folk crowded into the rooms for the *sannyasi* of the *ashram* and the *brahmacharis* too, to remove their doubts. Actually, from early morning there were many devotees in the garden of the spiritual community and in the rooms. Wherever they were thay could be seen sitting, having come with the aim of doing *japa* (mantra repetition) and *dhyana* (meditation). And at noon went for *darshan* of Shri Charan before returning again [to meditate].

From five o'clock in the evening devotees would start to arrive. In the expansive field, up on a platform near the Sinhaasana (lion throne) of Bhagwan Shankaracharya, the *samnyasis* and *mahatmas* would sit, in front of which sat the scholars and the *brahmacharis*, and in the established fashion seating was arranged for the ladies and the men. The dais of Bhagwan was arrayed with garlands of flowers. On *parva-tithiyon* ('half-lunar and lunar' -

pious days) it became decorated with a special appearance. In this manner the sight of the Sabha (gathering) was very alluring.

From six o'clock in the evening the *upadesha* (lecture) programme of the Sabha began with *sankirtan* (repeating the name of the deity) of the name of the Lord. From six-thirty were the sermons of the *sannyasi mahatmas* and then Shri Charan arrived at seven o'clock. Maharaj Shri walked from his own room, and from both sides came the profound sound of *"jaya ho jaya ho"* - 'Victory be. Victory be.' Showering of flowers on him, Vedic Pandits (Brahman scholars) walked ahead chanting benedictory mantras. On stage at that time were read the benedictory mantras. The heavens hummed with the assembly of individuals standing giving *jaya kar* (cheers hailing victory).

Shri Charan took his seat upon the Sinhasana (Lion Throne) and the assembly arose rejoicing. The *upadesha* of Maharaj Shri was given regularly from about a quarter past seven until eight o'clock.

[Over an hour of sound recordings of Guru Dev survive, and even a few minutes of movie footage (which appears to have been recorded at this venue during March / April 1952). The following is a translation of parts of a lecture by Guru Dev captured on a wire-recording: -

और मनन वह मन क्या है । मन गया परमात्मा को ढूंढने के लिए और वहीं चलो समाप्त हो गया पकड़ा गया और पकड़ा जायेगा अवश्य जैसे लवण के पुतली लवण का चित्र बना कर के समुद्र में छोड़ दिया जाएं कि जाओ - तुम इसका समुद्र - की पैमाइश करो इसका थाह लो कितना गहरा समुद्र है । तो पुतली चली तो जायेगी वोह नम नमक की जो प्रतिमा है । वह चली जायेगी पर लौट कर चली आ सकती ही है । वोह लौट न जाने नहीं कोई सच कठिनई नहींवोह लौट कर जाने न कोई कठिनई है । जहां समुद्र में गई गल गई लौट कर कौन कहे कि कितना गहरा समुद्र है । इसलिए मुमुक्षु

जब परमात्मा का अनुभव करता है।तो फिर लौट कर तब कह ही
नहीं सकत है ।

कैसा परमात्मा है?

कैसा आत्म है?

गूढ़ तरु वह उस में लीन ही हो जायेगा । कहना सुनना तभी तक
है । बोलना बताना तभी तक है । जब तक परमात्मा को देखा नहीं ।

'And that thought…. What is mind?

Mind went in search of Paramatma (Supersoul, God) and it
finished going there, and was caught - and certainly it will be
caught.

Like a doll made of salt, having made an image of salt, and drop it
into the ocean, it will go.

<Go, measure how deep this ocean is, how deep is the ocean?>

Then the doll will proceed.

Then the salt statue gets wet.

There is no difficulty to go but there is difficulty to come
back.There is difficulty returning, in returning from wherever he
has gone. Wherever it entered the ocean, it is drowned.

Who can then speak of <How deep is the ocean?>

Therefore, desiring mumukshu (salvation), when Paramatma is
experienced, who then will come back when the seeker
experiences what Paramatma is, or what atma (individual soul) is?

The "guudh taru" ('the tree that is concealed' – i.e. the root). He will become absorbed in That.

For this reason, to speak and to listen takes us only so far,
to talk and to explain, only so far, whilst one has not seen
Paramatma.

दो प्रकार के मन हैं - एक शुद्ध एक् अशुद्ध। जो अशुद्ध मन है
उस करके तो अप्राप्य है। और जो शुद्ध मन है उस करके
अनुद्रष्तव्य है।

'There are two kinds of mind. One is *shuddha* (clear), and the
other one is *ashuddha* (impure). If the mind is impure, doing that
work (of attending to Paramatma) is impossible. If the mind is
pure that work is to be seen.

दो प्रकार के मन हैं - एक शुद्ध एक् अशुद्ध। जो अशुद्ध मन है
उस करके तो अप्राप्य है। और जो शुद्ध मन है उस करके
अनुद्रष्तव्य है। दोनों श्रुतियों का अर्थ तो गया - दो प्रकार के मन
होने के नाते एक मन तो संसारी है उसमें तो परमात्मा दूर - अति
दूर है।

एक मन शुद्ध है जहां शम - काम संकल्प नहीं है को मन शुद्ध
है। शुद्ध मन अनुद्रष्तव्य है। शुद्ध मन से ही अनुभव होता है। तो
हमारा कर्तव्य क्या होता है कि हम जिससे परमात्मा को जानेंगे

उसको बनाओ। परमात्मा तो बनी - बनाई चीज है। उसे हम बना नहीं सकते हैं। किन्तु जिससे हम जानेंगे वो साधन हमे बनाना चाहिए। अब आहार शुद्धि पर जोर दिया अब जो इसको नहीं समझते इसके महात्म को परन्तु -

आहार शुद्धौ सत्त्व शुद्धिः सत्त्व शुद्धौ ध्रुव स्मृतिः

लिखा है आहार शुद्धि से सत्व - अंतःकरण की शुद्धि है। अंतःकरण की चार वृत्तियां हैं - मन बुद्धि चित्त अहंकार। अंतः करण एक चीज है उसके चार वृत्ति हैं चार भेद हैं चार पाद हैं। वो कौन हैं - मन बुद्धि चित्त अहंकार। मन और बुद्धि चित्त और अहंकार। ये चार - एक का भी नाम से सो - तब भी अंतःकरण का बोध होता है।

बुद्धि कहो तब भी अंतःकरण आ गया केवल मन कहो तब भी अंतःकरण आशय अहंकार कहो तब भी अंतःकरण आशय और यह सब है - मन बुदि चित्त और - - - - सो इसलिए ये हो चार वृत्तिय हैं यही संसार में आत्म को भरमाया करती हैं।

'One mind is pure, wherever there is control over the lust-driven senses, that mind is pure. The pure mind is to be observed. Only with a pure mind is perception possible. In that case what is to be done?

We should get an understanding of Paramatma.

Paramatma has made, is making, something wonderful, That. We cannot make anything. But from that, we should understand to perform that *sadhana*. Now pure food gives strength, now who does not understand this? However, to one who is a *mahatma*:-

"आहारशुद्धौ सत्त्वशुद्धिः सत्त्वशुद्धौ ध्रुव स्मृतिः"

"aahaarashuddhau sattvashuddhih; sattvashuddhau, dhruva smritih"
'From correct food, correct activity, all activities become purified, memory becomes firm'.

It is written that from purity of food is purity of *antah karana* (inner existence). *antahkarana* has four conditions which are; *mana* (mind), *buddhi* (intellect), *chitta* (consciousness), & *ahankaara* (egotism). *antah karana* is one thing, there are four states, there are four differences, there are four parts. There are what? *mana, buddhi, chitta, ahamkaara* - *mana* and *buddhi*, *chitta* and *ahamkara*. These four by one name also that then is the sense of *antahkarana*.

Say *"buddhi"* then also *antakarana* has come, only say *"mana"* then also the intention is *antahkarana*, say *"ahankaara"* then also the intent is *antahkarana* and this is all - *mana, buddhi, chitta & ahankaara*. Thus therefore there are four states, in this very place the *sansaara* (mundane existence) fills the *aatma* (self) with *maayaa* (illusion).

जन मन को फुर्सत मिले संसारी जंजालों से तब परमात्मा की तरफ चले। जब संसारी विषयों से मन को अवकाश आप देते नहीं हो बस कपाट बन्द करो। जैसे जो चोर घर में घुस गये हैं वो तो घुसें पर बाहर वाले

न आने पावें इसी वास्ते कपाट लगाओ। अर्थात इन्द्रियां जो हैं – जो वासना – जो विषय – वासना हृदय में आगई है वो तो चोर घर में घुस गया और बाहर की विषय – वासना जो अभी तक नहीं है वो दुसरे चोर हैं। तो पहिला कर्तव्य क्या होता है कि कपात लगा दो। बस कपाट लगा दो बाहर के चोर न आने पावें और भीतर को गिरफ्तार करने की कोशिश वाला करो। पहिला कर्तव्य है समझ लो

कि भीतर चोर घुस गय तो क्या करना चाहिए कपात पहले लगाना
चाहिए। जो वासना - जो बाहर की वासना यें अभी न हीं आई हैं।
वो तो आने न पायें अर्थात जो चोर नहीं घुसे हैं वो घुसने न पायें
और जो घुसा है उसको पकड़ कर गिरफ्तार करो। अर्थात जो वासना
भीतर है उसको तो भगवान की प्राप्ती के लिए सदाचारी बनकर के
उस वासना को हताओ। और उस वासना को सबको नष्ट करो।
और बाहर की वासना आने न पावे। क्यों कि वासना ही मुख्य
अनर्थ - कारी है। जैसी - जैसी वासना आपकी बढ़ेबी सांसारिक
वैसी ही - उलझन बदेगी और उतना उसी - उसी प्रकार से आपू
संसार से दूर - बहुत मातायें वृद्धा हो गई मरने को चली फिर भी वो
कहती हैं कि हम पौत्र का विवाह देख लेते तो अच्छा था। पेप्ले
लौघेद् - बतलाइये पुत्र काविवाह तो देखी चुकीं पौत्रो को देख लेती
और पौव के सन्तान भी देख लेती तो और किस - किस के हो
जाते। कितनी बड़ी दिवासना। मालूम पड़ता है कि इन्हे फिर लौट
के इसी घर में आना है। कितनी बड़ी झुल है। ये नहीं सोचते कि
पुत्र का विवाह हो जाय पौत्र का हो जाय।

'If the individual mind meets with the chance of worldly
difficulties, then go towards Paramatma.

When there is the chance for the mind to dwell on worldly matters
you do not yield. It is enough just to close the shutter.
In the manner a thief enters in the house, so that he cannot enter
from outside, so he cannot take steps to come, a door is attached.

Those who through their imagination perceive anything with the
senses or imagines in the heart, that thief comes entering in the
house. And beyond the senses and imagination, that which is
present is it not a thief. So what is first necessary is that a screen is

affixed. If enough screen is attached then no thief can take steps to come inside and attempt to sieze anything within.

First it is necessary to understand what to do if the thief is entering inside. What should you do?

Firstly you should close the screen. He to whom imagination does not come, to him no thief enters. He who would enter does not step. He who would enter, he is seized and captured. If that is the impression inside, then it this is made correctly for obtaining Bhagwan. Remove that imagination and destroy all that desire, all that desire, and from outside the desire does not come stepping in.

Why is desire the primary misfortune? It is similar in that as your worldly desires grow, so also you grow entangled, and from so many different kinds you desire of *samsara*. Many mothers become old women - who go to die again, as also we say that, 'to see our grandson's marriage would be good'.
(The audience laugh)

You should say (ask yourself), 'Son's marriage then you will see completely, get to see the grandson, and taken to see grandsons perpetually and where will you be going?

How much of a great desire which cannot be fulfilled?
It appears that again you will be coming to this house?

How great is a body?

Then don't consider that son's marriage and become a grandson (by being reborn as your own grandson!).

इसी से हमारे यहां जगत को मिथ्या कहते हैं । जगत मिथ्या है और परमात्मा में ही जगत अध्यक्त है कल्पित है कल्पित चीज की सहज सत्ता नहीं होती । ये बात जो हम कह रहे हैं - वेदान्त के सिद्धान्त का अनुवाद कर रहे हैं ।

'Really this our universe is said to be illusory. The world is an illusion, and really in Paramatma the world is prepared, it is false, the nature of an illusion is that it has no power. These words that we are saying – we are doing an interpretation of the theory of *Vedanta*.

पांच प्रकार के कर्म माने गाये हैं । चार तो हि निहित है । एक अविहित है । पांच प्रकार के कर्म हैं ।

नित्य कर्म नैमित्तिक प्रायश्चित्त काम्य कर्म निषिद्ध नित्य कर्म नैमित्तिक कर्म प्रायश्चित्त कर्म काम्य कर्म

ये पांच प्रकार के कर्म करने के लिए शास्त्र परन्तु निषिद्ध कर्म करने के लिए शास्त्र कभी भी आदेश नहीं । नित्य कर्म अविहित है । और चार प्रकार – के कर्म विहित हैं ।

नित्य कर्म क्या है – संध्या वन्दन आदि । संध्या है । द्विजातीय जातक आदि के लिए संध्या है गायत्री का जप है । पर जो लोग गायत्री जप के अधिकारी नहीं माने जाते वेद – शास्त्रानुसार उनके लिए भगवद् नाम स्मरण ही नित्य कर्म है । उन्हे खाली नहीं रहना है बल्कि ये ही कोई भगवान का नाम जपना चाहिए । नित्य कर्म प्रातः कालः उठो पृथ्वी को नमस्कार करो

कालः सत्तं समस्तमेव ।

नित्य ही प्रातःकाल उठ कर के पृथ्वी को वन्दन करो । तब पृथ्वी पर चरण धरो । उसको नमस्कार कर के । यह हमारे यहां भारत की जो है सभ्यता है । दिन भर पृथ्वी पर रहना है आपको मल मूत्र आदि करना है । सारा प्रपंच आपको पृथ्वी के ऊपर करना है । इस वास्ते पृथ्वी को नमस्कार पहले । पृथ्वी के पश्चात यदि माता – पिता

जीवित हैं तो माता की चरण – स्पर्श करो पिता का चरण स्पर्श करो –

'आत्रु देवो भव पित्रु देवो भव

माता – पिता का वन्दन करो । इसके पश्चात् आचार्य देवो भव् । शुरु यदि हैं तो उनका चरण स्पर्श करो । नहीं हैं तो उनके शिष्य नमस्कार करो । शिष्य भी नहीं है तो मानसिक प्रणाम करो जिसके अभी तक गुरु नही है तो भगवान तो गुरुर्ब्रह्मा गुरुर्विष्णु गुरुर्देवो महेश्वरः गुरुः साक्षात् प्रब्रह्म तस्मै श्री गुरवे नमः

ये सब सबका शुरु का शुरु परमात्मा ब्रह्म ही है उनको प्रणाम करो । ये हमारे यहां का नित्य कर्म है । ये माता का वन्दन करना पिता का वन्दन करना । क्या होगा माता – पिता पुत्र के वन्दन करने से बहुत बड़े मोरे – फूले नहीं हो जाते । पुत्र जा के माता का चरण स्पर्श करे तो माता जो है बहुत लम्बी – चौड़ी नहीं हो जाती है । वो प्रसन्न हो जाती है । आशीर्वाद देवी है । तब उसके आशीर्वाद से पुत्र जो है तब आगे बढ़ता है अपने कार्यों में । जीव को आशीर्वाद लेना चाहिए । पहले माता का आशीर्वाद लो उसके पश्चात पिता का आशीर्वाद । फिर आचार्य का आशीर्वाद लो । ये आशीर्वादों से आप लोगों की वृद्धि होगी । इसलिए अब इस पर कोई उदाहरण देना है आशीर्वाद ही से हम कैसे माने कि हमको उदाहरण क्या है कि केवल आशीर्वाद ही से हमारा कल्याण हो जायगा । तो हम उदाहरण देते हैं कि जैसे कमठ कूर्मि और मत्स्य ।

'Five kinds of *karma* are; *nitya karma, naimittika, praayashchitta, kaamya karma, nishiddha - nitya karma* (daily duty), *naimittika karma* (special occasional duty*), praayashchitta karma* (expiate)*, kaamya karma* (ritual).

These five kinds of *karma* do for the purposes of *Shastra,* but *nishiddha karma* is never instructed in the *Shastra - nishiddha karma* is that which is forbidden. And four kinds of *karma* are performed.

What is *nitya karma?*

Evening, *vandana* (worship) etc. Evening is for the purpose of the twice-born, new-born babe etc, repetition of Gayatri. But those people who are not authorised of the Gayatri *japa,* according to the *Veda Shastra,* for them *nitya karma* is the remembering of God's name. There they should not be unoccupied, but these really should be doing *japa* of Bhagwan's name.

nitya karma, get up early in the morning, bow to the ground;

"कालह् सत्तं समस्तमेव"

"kaalah sattam samastameva"
'Morning is most excellent of all'.

Really, regularly rise at dawn, and adore, do obeisance to the earth. Afterwards, place the foot on the earth. Do her adoration. Here, this is our Bharat (India), this is politeness.

All day remain on the earth. You do excretion - urine etc. All the worldly affairs you are doing on the earth.
This is for the sake of the earth, bow first. The earth, afterwards if mother father are alive; then touch mother's foot, touch father's foot.

"मात्रु देवो भव पित्रु देवो भव"

"maatru devo bhava, pitru devo bhava"

Do adoration of mother and father. Afterwards, this;

"आचार्य देवो भव"

"aachaarya devo bhava"

If they (the *aachaarya* - teacher) are there, then touch foot. If not then do salutation to their disciple. If there is also no disciple, then do mental *pranaam*. If no *guru* just now then to Bhagwan;

"गुरुर्र ब्रह्मा, गुरुर्विष्णु, गुरुर्देवो महेश्वरः गुरुः साक्षात् प्रब्रह्म तस्मै श्री गुरुवे नमः"

*"gururra brahma, gururvishnu, gururdevo maheshvarah guruh
saakshaat prabrahma tasmai shrii guruve namah"*

These all, beginning of beginning of all. Paramatma really is Brahma, to them do *pranaam*.

These here are our *'nitya karma'*. These; mother's obeisance to do, father's obeisance to do. What will come from not doing mother father son's obeisance? The fruits do not grow abundantly, the fruits will not come. If son does not go to touch the foot of mother, then mother is not going to be very great. Her becoming delighted is the *ashirvaadi* (benediction) of the goddess. Then with the blessing the son then grows in his own tasks. In life you should accept this blessing. Firstly mother's blessing then afterwards father's blessing.

Again, take the *aachaarya's* blessing. By these blessings you people will have progress. Therefore, now we give you an example of the meaning of *ashirvaadi* (benediction), of the example of how the welfare comes from the *ashirvaadi*, then we give an example in which the tortoise, turtle and fish .... (There are three types of protection and service.)

1) *uttam* (Highest) *kurmvat* (quality of tortoise)
2) *madhyam* (Middle) *matsyavat* (quality of fishes)
3) *nikrista* (Lower) *panchirvat* (quality of birds)

The *kurma* (turtle) protects its eggs by concentrating on them from a distant place, without keeping them near. The *matsya* (fish) protects its eggs by focusing eyes on the eggs without going near the eggs. The *panchi* (bird) protects its eggs by covering them, always sitting on the eggs.

In the manner of the tortoise, the great spiritual *guru* helps, protects and guides his sincere disciple by concentration and observation of the behaviour of his disciples. By the blessing of the *guru* the life of disciple become purposeful and develops faster at spiritual progress.

The disciple should not copy the behaviour of *guru* and his duty is that he should follow the orders and instructions as given by the *guru*. By the blessing of the *guru* the life of the disciple shines in the world. Therefore each and every disciple should worship his *guru*.

There is some distance and separation among mother, father and *guru* but there is no distance or separation with Paramatma. Therefore, every moment is the power of the Supreme to be realised and remembered by everyone. The great spiritual *guru* can change the life of his disciple by keeping the hand on the head of the disciple and make him like his own life.

The knowledgeable and realised *guru* feels that this world is like keeping the *amla* (sour plums) in the hand but realising that Paramatma is inside.

The great *guru* keeps himself separate from his own body. If someone says that you are my Brother, Father, Mother then this is also one of the ways of separation. But Paramatma never keeps separate from *atman*, By the control of the mind and the senses and deep concentration, is the true *yoga*. When mind is totally concentrated then he merges with Brahma.

viyoga - separated from God; is the root cause of all suffering and being engaged in union with God is the path of highest blissfulness. It can be realised by *sadhana*, the practice of *yoga*. The techniques of *yoga* are for self-realisation and the *guru* is the guideline.']

*

After *upadesha* Bhagwan would go to his own room and on the dais of the Sabha was a collective *aarati* of Bhagwan Chandramoulishwara (the Lord with the moon on his matted hair - Shiva). *Aarati* (camphor flame worship) occurred outside. Here afterwards a vast gathering came together near Shri Charan for *darshan*. For about an hour Bhagwan sat in this state for giving *darshan*. From there Maharaj Shri arose to walk on the terrace. Here in seclusion he could worship etc with a number of followers. *So many more came that also up to twelve o'clock in the night you could not get the time to meet all of the people.* At twelve o'clock he returned only for *darshan pranaam*. In this way, in the ashram it stayed like a *mela* (festival) from the early morning until twelve o'clock in the middle of the night.

In this manner Maharaj Ji stayed in Lucknow for up to one and a half months. After that, on 21st April 1952, he was to depart by the Dehra Express for Deharadun. At the station an immense crowd collected together for the *darshan* of Shri Charan. The platform at Lucknow Station, approximately two furlongs long, became completely full with men and women. Also, on the railway line below, thousands of people were standing possessed of the desire to get a look of the *darshan* of Shri Maharaaj. There was reverence and devotion in the hearts of the people. The eyes were made to shine by the abundance of tears of love. The crowd kept increasing in that place. Everyone was going to be squashed by the pushing. But from every mouth appeared, "Bhagwan Shankaracharya *ki jaya ho.*" - 'Victory be to Bhagwan Shankaracharya'.

In accordance with the decided programme, Shri Bhagwan reached the station by a well-decorated closed car at six forty-five. Actually, beyond the platform Shri Charan descended from the closed motor car and sat in a well-decorated open motor car, from which the *darshan*-seeking people could have a good *darshan* of Shri Charan at the station. Having brought this car onto the station platform, at that standing place, in one direction were ladies, and in the other direction were men, standing for their own *aarati* (ceremonies of camphor burning).

Vedic scholars began chanting *mantras* and all lit their *aaratis* (camphor flames worship). In the whole platform tens of thousands of *aaratis* shone together as one. At once the auspicious sound of thousands of conch shells, bells and gongs rang out. Flags were waving in several hundred hands. At that time Charbagh Station was made into a beautiful *mandir* (temple). The atmosphere buzzed with the sound of "Bhagwan Shankaracharya *ke jaya*" – 'Victory of Bhagwan Shankaracharya', and devotees hearts became very happy. Atheists bowed their heads, and the citizens burned an interminable *aarati* (ceremony of camphor flames) to 'Dharma Samrat' (the Emperor of Dharma). This demonstrates the truth that 'The one who has had his own light lit, that is eternal and perfect, and remains shining until time eternal'.

With very happy devoted hearts and with tearful eyes more than fifty-thousand men and women gave a wonderful send-off to Jagadguru Shankaracharya (World-*guru* Shankaracharya). One could successfully say that the crowd was so great there that there was not a spot left on the platform.

The compartment in which Maharaj Shri was travelling in to Dehradun was arrayed in a beautiful way with garlands of flowers. Although the distance between the car and the railway compartment was only five or six yards, because of the crowd it took fifteen to twenty minutes to reach there. At that time flower-garlands were taken to array Maharaj Ji's compartment, and the sky resonated, piercing the heavens with the sounds of "Bhagwan Shankaracharya *ki jaya ho*" - 'Victory be to Bhagwan Shankaracharya'. With faith and reverence the folk of Lucknow gave such a send-off to Maharaj Shri, that memorably remains in the history of Lucknow.

You reached Dehradun early in the morning at nine o'clock on 22nd April 1952 [Dehradun is some 555 kilometres NW of Lucknow]. *At the station there, there was a grand welcome from the citizens and afterwards you stayed outside the city at Kashmanda House, located in the middle of an extensive garden.* Having come from the crowds, for Maharaj Shri this was a comfortable peaceful place.

At the specific persistence of Pandit Shridatta Shastri, administrator of the Kali Kamli Kshetra of Rishikesh, Maharaj Shri then went to Ramnagar, Rishikesh on the evening of 25th April 1952. [Rishikesh is about 43kms SE of Dehradun, a route that goes through dense jungle.] In the road the people gave a grand welcome to Shri Charan, with a band of musicians. There at Atma Vigyan Bhavan he stayed in "Shri Shankaracharya Nivas" ('Dwelling place of Shri Shankaracharya').

[Atma Vigyan Bhavan is situated south of Rishikesh, established as Baba Kamliwala Panchayat Kshetra, founded by Baba Vishuddhananda aka. Baba Kali Kamli Wale.]

In the Satsang Bhavan you stayed doing upadesha for two days, then according to plan, on 28th April you set out for Mussoorie by car. [Mussoorie is 77kms NW of Rishikesh, via Dehradun.]

On the outskirts of Mussoorie, wherever the car was meant to stop, a crowd of welcoming people would meet together and at all such places all would offer *aarati* (camphor flame worship) to Shri Charan with great respect, veneration and enthusiasm.

At the Toll Gate and at Cricket Gate there were magnificent special *aaratis* worshipped. In front of the library thousands of citizens noisily sounded bells and gongs. Bhagwan was welcomed with "Shri Shankaracharya" and "Sanatana Dharma", the cheering making a hole in the heavens. Several royal families made worship of Shri Charan, offering *aarati* and presenting their own faith and devotion.

At the request of the religious hill people, Maharaj Shri also made this year's *chaturmasya-vrata* (rainy season fast) right here. This *mahayagya* (great sacrifice) was at Pratap Bhavan in the centre of town, situated on the top in Muhalla Kulari (in the Mall).

Here there is a very pleasing natural view.

On 7th July 1952 the great festival of Guru Purnima was accomplished, being the treasured worship of Shri Charan. From nine until twelve several devotees and the faithful did worship of the sandals of Shri Charan. From five in the evening until nine o'clock at night was a programme of public gathering which was accomplished with great pleasure. Devotees came from Lucknow, Calcutta, Kanpur, Etawa, Prayag (Allahabad), Jabalpur, Kashi (Varanasi), Dehradun, Bombay, Delhi, etc probably from all the main cities [of North India]. Devotees presented the offerings of faith of their own city and telegrams of several religious community organisations, and letters were listened to. At the end was Bhagwan's auspicious blessing, of *upadesha* (discourse).

[A book containing quotations of Guru Dev was being compiled, by Brahmachari Mahesh, later to be known as Maharishi Mahesh Yogi. He wrote the introduction to this book on 7th July 1952 whilst staying at Pratap Bhavan, Musoorie. The quotations were published as *'Amrit-Kana'* ('Drops of Immortal Nectar') – translated and reproduced in companion volume to this book, entitled, 'Guru Dev as Presented by Maharishi Mahesh Yogi'.]

At the time of *chaturmasya-vrata* (the rainy season 'four-month fast') there were regular evening *darshans* with community *upadesha* (discourse), twice a week on Thursdays and Sundays. At this time the residents of Mussoorie, with utmost joy and enthusiasm, agreed that there should be a great festival on 23rd September 1952 celebrating Shri Shankaracharya Day - the cheering of *dharma* in Mussoorie, that easy-going town where people come for pleasure and merriment! This was a religious awakening.

The procession of Bhagwan Shankaracharya's turned out to start from the Kitab Ghar (Book House), it went on to Gandhi Chauk (the Square), Landaur Bazaar and Sanatan Dharma Mandir (Temple), to finish at the Himalaya Club.

The procession was very large, so that it became so crowded that it became difficult to walk in the streets. Crowds of people collected together on the rooftops to see the procession. At various places worship and *aarati* of Bhagwan was performed.

[There are five known photographs taken of Guru Dev in Mussoorie, all apparently taken on Tuesday 23rd September 1952. The images show Guru Dev seated in the lion throne set upon a open-chassis vehicle. The disciples surrounding Guru Dev in this photograph are not too easy to identify, but the moustached face of the handsome man to the left of the photo, standing in the background, appears to be that of Dandi Swami Narayanand

Saraswati. The attendant standing to the far left of the photo closely resembles Swami Swaroopanand Saraswati. To the right of the picture the attendant could well be a young Swami Shantanand Saraswati, whilst unmistakeably at the front is Brahmachari Mahesh (aka. Maharishi Mahesh Yogi), with his arm outstretched. To the lower left of photo one can just make out the shape of the steering wheel of this unusual vehicle.]

The procession started at two o'clock and finished at six-thirty in the Himalaya Club.

[Apparently several of the photographs were taken at the suggestion of a businessman who visited a local studio. Later, in 1968, Delhi Photo Company rediscovered the images of Guru Dev taken at Mussoorie. Fateh Chand Pasricha and Bhagwati Prasad Shankar had established Delhi Photo Company in 1937 before opening a studio at Mussoorie in 1938. Delhi Photo Company is still run as a family business, and is currently in the hands of Ajay Shankar (grandson of founder Bhagwati Prasad Shankar). Hand-tinted photographs of Guru Dev and high-resolution black-and-white prints of Guru Dev are available from:- Delhi Photo Company, 78, Janpath, New Delhi – 110001, India.]

At that place of Mussoorie there was a public assembly wherein letters of congratulation and offerings of faith were delivered. At the time of the great festival the town had been decorated but it was not really about the city, the religious people had come flooding in to Mussoorie like an ocean. Such a large procession, such an immense crowd of people, unique in the history of the town of Mussoorie. In the city of Mussoorie so much reverence and *astikata* (belief in the existence of God) was done towards Shri Charanon, it was a wonderful introduction to the great personality of Maharaj Shri.

*

On 8th October at about two o'clock Maharaj Shri journeyed out of Pratap Bhavan, Mussoorie by car. Thousands of men and women walked in front and behind the car. In truth this was a portrayal of the people of Mussoorie. *You arrived at Deharadun and stayed there for three days.*

On the 11th October at three-thirty dusk you travelled by motor car for Saharanpur. At five o'clock you arrived at Saharanpur. [75kms SW of Deharadun] Your procession turned out from Satyuga Ashram and went to Ghanta Ghar (the Clock Tower), Nehru Market, Sabji Mandi, Vaman Ji Road, Chowk Phauwara (Fountain Square)*, Saraph Purana Bazaar, etc.* Having been to the principal places it finished at Ramaleela Bhavan. This is what everyone had to say, 'Until today we had never seen such a beautiful procession'.

Ramleela Bhavan was the place Maharaj Shri stayed, one beautiful *mandir* (temple) had been made there. Really, from the early morning, how many devotee people were coming with garlands of flowers in their hands and paraphernalia of *pujana* (worship), desiring *pujana* of Bhagwan? Regularly, hundreds of initiations occurred. This became a matter of public discussion, so much so that at the Zenith it became difficult to gain access of the *guru*. This produced a feeling so that there arose a mob seeking *diksha* (initiation).

*

[It was planned that Guru Dev would again visit Delhi, and it seems that Brahmachari Mahesh went ahead to Delhi to pave the way for Guru Dev's arrival. Apparently, a press conference was convened by Shri Shankaracharya Reception Committee, Delhi and on the 15th October 1952 at 5 p.m., in the Young Man's Tennis Club Queen's Gardens, Brahmachari Mahesh announced that:-

'His Holiness Shri Jagatguru Shankaracharya Swami Brahmanand Saraswati Maharaj will be visiting your city about the 12th of November 1952 and stay here for about a month for *dharmopadesh (dharma upadesha)*.']

On 22nd October 1952, at eight o'clock in the early morning, Maharaj Shri departed by car to go to Ambala. [82kms NW, in Punjab, just south of Chandigarh] At the act of the *dharmacharya* (religious preceptor) going to the place, to denote their welcome, they turned out an enormous and beautiful procession. He was really made to see the enthusiasm of the citizens. All the religious community organisations took to their feet. At eight-thirty in the evening was the assembly's welcome, wherein welcome addresses were delivered from the Sanatana Dharma Sabha, Rashtriya Sevak Sangha, Brahman Sabha and the Hindu Mahasabha.

On 13th November, early in the morning at five o'clock, he was to depart from Ambala for Delhi but on 12th November the citizens of Ambala became acquainted with this, that Maharaj Shri was leaving them and going to Delhi. [Delhi is 192kms south of Ambala] Therefore, from four o'clock the inhabitants of Ambala, the men and women, collected together in the *shivira* (camp) for a last *darshan* of Maharaj Shri. At five o'clock it had become an immense mob. The consequence of this was that it took a period of more than two hours for the motor car to get to the other side of Ambala. The people were agitated with love. Their eyes were tearful, they were displaying the inner pain of their hearts. From Ambala he went to within ten miles of Delhi.

Maharaj Shri relaxed the whole day and in the evening time at seven o'clock he left there, setting out for the capital, Delhi. In order to welcome him, the religious folk there appeared like an immense sea in the Gandhi Ground. Thousands of men and women and the leaders of religious institutions gave Maharaj Shri a welcome with noisy sounds of rejoicing and applause, and saluted Maharaj Shri with eleven rounds' of gunfire.

Near Delhi Station, in Queen's Garden the Shri Shankaracharya *shivira* (camp) was organised, and there Maharaaj Shri stayed. The reception committee was from residents of the city, respected religious institutions of the city and the association of *pandits*. They delivered offerings of faith to the lotus feet of Bhagwan and a welcome address.

The president of the welcome committee spoke his own welcome speech:- 'Maharaj Shri, having become seated on the Dharma Sinhasana (the Lion Throne of Dharma) of North India, for the purpose of showing us the way of Bhagwan Adi Shankaracharya's pure goal, is roaming about close to the people in the various corners of the land, to inform us of the Raj Marg (the Royal Way), of this world and the other world. Having seen your comprehensive ideal method all are proud of Jyotirmath. You do not accept in any form, *rupees* or *paisa*, and your Dharma Promotion Tours are from your divine power. So great is the self-respect and pride of the matter, thereof no mention can be made in words. This is your guidance to us.

*

[A Sanskrit Poet of Benares, an *"ashu kavi"* (spontaneous poet), Pt. Veni Madava Sastri *'Shashtrartha Maharathi'* decided to create a series of verses in praise of Guru Dev, of which these five verses survive.:-

प्रार्थना

praarthanaa
Prayer

वन्देऽहं यतिराजराजरमणं योगीन्द्रचक्रायुधं
चातुर्वर्ग्यफलप्रदं सुविहितं मोक्षच्छटाच्छादितम् ।
योगानन्दतरंगतानतननं त्रैलोक्यनाथं शिवं
ब्रह्मानन्दसरस्वतीं गुरुवरं ज्योतिर्मठाधीश्वरम् ॥

vande aham yatiraajaraajaramanam yogiindrachakraayudham,
chaaturvargyaphalapradam suvihitam
mokshachchhataachchhaaditam.
yogaanandataramgataanatananam trailokyanaatham shivam,
brahmaanandasarasvatiim guruvaram
jyotirmathaadhiishvaram..1..

I praise Brahmananda Saraswati, the most excellent among the
gurus, the supreme lord of Jyotirmath who loves the king of the
kings of ascetics, who has the *chakra* of the chief of the *yogis* as
his weapon, who gives the fruits of the four classes, who is well
known, who is covered with the lustre of liberation, who spreads
the sounds of the waves of bliss arising from *yoga* (the union of
the individual soul with the cosmic soul), who is the lord of the
three worlds, who is gracious and kind.

साक्षाद्ब्रह्मपदार्विन्दयुगलं पैशल्यकल्लोलकम्
नैष्कर्म्याद्यखिलेश्वरं कृतिमतामानन्ददधारान्वितम् ।
ध्यानज्योतिरखण्डरखण्डवरणैरद्वैतमानन्त्यकम्
ज्योतिष्पीठमहेश्वरं गुरुवरं प्रत्यक्षदेवं भजे ॥२ ॥

saakshaadbrahmapadaarvindayugalam paishalyakallolakam,
naishhkarmyaadyakhileshvaram
kritimataamaanandadhaaraanvitam.
dhyaanajyotirakhandakhndavaranairadvaitamaanantyakam,

jyotishhpiithamaheshvaram guruvaram pratyakshadevam bhaje..2..

I worship the great lord of Jyotishpeeth, the most excellent among the *gurus*, who is God present before the eyes, who with his two lotus feet appears to be Lord Brahma in person, who is a wave of tenderness, who is the universal lord, inactive in the beginning, who among the learned ones is endowed with streams of bliss, who in his meditation by going beyond the parts to the wholeness, to the light, is non-dual and infinite.

सर्वानन्दकरं महाप्रभुवरं साक्षाच्छिवं सात्विकं
लोकनामुपकारकं निगमतो मार्गप्रभोद्दीपकम् ।
शान्तं दान्तमपीह सर्वजगतां तापत्रयोन्मूलनं
वन्दे तं गुरुदेवदेवसदनं ज्योतिर्मठाधीश्वरम् ॥३ ॥

sarvaanandakaram mahaaprabhuvaram saakshaachchhivam saatvikam,
lokanaamupakaarakam nigamato maargaprabhoddiipakam.
shaantam daantamapiiha sarvajagataam taapatrayonmuulanam,
vande tam gurudevadevasadanam jyotirmathaadhiishvaram..3..

I praise him, the Gurudeva who is the dwelling place of the *devas*, the supreme lord of Jyotirmath, who creates bliss for all people, who is the most excellent among the great Lords, who is Shiva in bodily form, who is endowed with the quality of *sattva*, who helps all people, who has the light to awaken the path described by the scriptures, who is peaceful and restrained and who destroys the three afflictions of all people.

शास्त्रे साधुकथासुधा सुललिता कैवल्यनैर्गुण्यिका
सर्वानन्दकरी सुरत्रसनालावण्यलीलाम्बुधिः ।
राराजीति विशिष्टभावगहना यस्य प्रसादाद्भुवि
ब्रह्मानन्दसरस्वतीं गुरुवरं प्रत्यक्षदेवं भजे ॥४ ॥

shaastre saadhukathaasudhaa sulalitaa kaivalyanairgunyikaa,

sarvaanandakarii suratnarasanaalaavanyaliilaambudhih.
raaraajiiti vishishhtabhaavagahanaa yasya prasaadaadbhuvi,
brahmaanandasarasvatiim guruvaram pratyakshadevam
bhaje..4..

I worship Brahmananda Saraswati, the most excellent among the
gurus, who is God present before the eyes, by whose grace the
ocean of the *leela* with the best salty taste, which is the nectar of
the stories of the saints found in the scriptures, very charming,
transcendental, beyond the three *gunas*, an excellent state
unfathomable creating bliss for all beings --- shines brilliantly in
the world.

यद्द्वारे निखिला निलिम्पपरिषत्सिद्धिं विधत्तेऽनिशं
श्रीमच्छ्रीलसितं जगद्गुरुपदं नत्वात्मतृप्तिं गताः ।

लोकाज्ञानपयोदपाटनधुरं श्रीशंकरं शर्मदं
ब्रह्मानन्दसरस्वतीं गुरुवरं ध्यायामि ज्योतिर्मयं ॥५॥

yaddvaare nikhilaa nilimpaparishhatsiddhim vidhatte anisham,
shriimachchhriilasitam jagadgurupadam natvaatmatriptim
gataah.
lokaagyaanapayodapaatanadhuram shriishankaram sharmadam,
brahmaanandasarasvatiim guruvaram dhyaayaami
jyotirmayam..5..

At whose door the whole galaxy of gods pray for perfection day
and night.
Adorned by immeasurable glory, preceptor of the whole world,
having bowed down at His feet, we gain fulfilment.
Skilled in dispelling the cloud of ignorance of the people, the
gentle emancipator,
Brahmananda Saraswati, the supreme teacher, full of brilliance, on
Him we meditate.]

*

In your appearance it is like receiving the *darshan* of the maharishis of old, Vyasa, Vasishtha and Bharadvaja etc. Your gold umbrella is the umbrella of *dharma*, who once having come in the shadow of the one who abounds in auspiciousness, all people experience the pleasure and peace. Your gold throne is the Lion-Throne of *dharma*, which is the final place of resolving *dharma* and *adharma*. In front of you are two attendants with the gold *danda* (mace-like poles), symbolising *dharma* (righteousness) and *niiti* (good behaviour). On the right is the *dharma-danda* and the *niiti-danda* to the left. In front of you go two attendants with lighted torches, symbols of *Veda* and *Shastra*. The right side is a symbol of the divine *Veda* and the left side is a symbol of the light of the *Shastra*. The two flames clearly say that you have arrived to destroy darkness and ignorance of the world with the light of the *Veda* and *Shastra*. Bhagwan Shankaracharya's auspicious arrival in Delhi is a golden occasion in the history of the city.'

Upadesha in Delhi.

Every day thousands of faithful citizens had *darshan* of Bhagwan and when the early morning darshan became stopped they too stayed making crowds in the camp until the evening. For the citizens Shri Shankaracharya Shivira became a *mela-sthala* (a place of festival). From six-thirty in the evening the programme of *upadesha* (instruction) assembly began. Bhagwan Shankaracharya's palanquin entered into the *pandal* (marquee) of the camp at about seven-thirty, in the midst of the melodious *kirtan* sounds of "Hara Hara Mahadeva Shambho Kashi Vishvanath Gange" [a *bhajan* (hymn) to Lord Shiva].

Having descended from the *shivika* (palanquin), Maharaj Shri sat on the Sinhasana (lion throne). Having seen the scene - seeing the *chamara* (whisk), the *danda* etc. held by the attendants, the heart of the gathering arose to become very happy. Regular *upadesha* began at about eight o'clock. The religious people of Delhi appeared for *satsang* in immense crowds. Every man became satisfied, and the number of listeners increased, a principal occasion in the history of the capital.

Because of the excessive crowds in Delhi, Maharaj Shri decided to spend some days in service utterly alone. On 28th November 1952 Shri Bhagwan, having risen from Queen's Garden he arrived at 7 Canning Lane, New Delhi. Here the evening gatherings were suspended, but he was going for public *darshan* regularly from ten o'clock until twelve o'clock.

On 4th December at twelve o'clock in the day, President Dr Rajendra Prasad came in the *shivira* (camp) for *darshan* of Maharaj Shri. He did *darshan*, *shraddhanjali* (offering of faith) of surrender and for *"charanodaka"* (the holy water that washed the feet). Shri Bhagwan Shankaracharya conversed with the Rashtrapati (President) saying, 'Before, the kings would have discussions with *tapasviyon* (ascetics) and *maharshiyon* (great saints) for their advice on the tasks of government. Because of *yoga* and *tapasya* (austerity) their minds had become clear. There existed neither greed nor worldly desires, and they did not fear the king becoming displeased with what they said. Those who were given advice, that advice was beneficial for both *raja* (king) and *praja* (subject). But now things have gone to hell on account of *rajas* neglecting to keep the company of *maharishis*.'

Shankaracharya Swami Brahmanand Saraswati
and President of India Dr Rajendra Prasad, Delhi, 4th December
1952

Having related this he said afterwards, 'What advice can your servant give you? Only that which your eyes will [already] see. Therefore, first you should wish to accept advice from *maharshiyon* who can also imagine the future. You people should not remain confused about this, opposing religious guidance and statecraft. Us folk giving *upadesha* (instruction) make mankind righteous. However righteous mankind will be then that much the government also proceeds with a very beautiful appearance.'

His Eminence the President listened to the words of Shri Shankaracharya Maharaj with utmost seriousness. In a summary on the profundity connected with *upasana* (intercession) Maharaj Shri cast light saying, 'The student cannot make the syllabus for himself. For this an academician is indispensable. By this manner, to understand the way of real happiness and peace, the experienced *guru* becomes indispensible.' In this connection, in an extract of his own lifestory, listen as Shri Charan also throws light of some experience of his own Gurudeva. He told that when he met Guru Ji in Uttarkashi, 'At that time, before anything else we said, "Firstly, you ought to give me such knowledge that I do not have to outstretch the hand outwards. Afterwards we will understand *paramartha* (the greatest treasure, salvation)". This is the effect of Their kindness that from the beginning until the present we have never extended the hand in front of anyone!'

In one-and-a-half hours of conversation, Shankaracharya Maharaj explained to the President the chief elements of how to better the individual and the society, so that ultimately the ruler and the ruled would benefit. Rajendra Babu was charmed and enamoured with all that he heard, of the simple and succinct theories. According to the programme of Rashtrapati Ji's fixed period of conversation with Maharaj Shri there was an additional twenty-five minutes more. But when Maharaj Shri spontaneously gave him leave, only for for this reason did he go.

Maharaj Shri's quarters at this time remained in Canning Lane, New Delhi. *You had come here from Gandhi Ground with a view to being alone and relaxed.* But after a few days he rarely was. Slowly, slowly the number of visitors grew, so then Maharaj Shri again resolved to take to a different quiet place. *With this aim, on 19th December 1952 you proceeded to Agra.* [Delhi to Agra is approximately 200kms.] Here the dwelling of Maharaj Shri was in the Civil Lines, at the *kothi* (dwelling) of a Dr Bhatt, of Principal Medical College. Here it was generally quiet and relaxing. He only proceeded with a community appearance of *darshan pranaam.*

On 22nd January 1953 Acharya Charan departed from Agra, arriving in Varanasi at midday on 23rd January, and dwelt in Brahmanivas Ashram, Sidhagiri Bhag. [The distance from Agra to Varanasi is about 600kms.] *Your act of going to Varanasi was also with a view of excellent rest.* Therefore, in this connection, the masses were not informed. But again, having heard from one another the *darshan*-seekers came in numbers enough. When it was seen that the crowds of *darshan*-seekers grew greater and greater then the time of public *darshan* was restricted to between ten o'clock and twelve o'clock. When *darshan*-seeking devotees came from outside he gave *darshan* in the evening too.

In this way he stayed in Varanasi for some days. On the night of Sunday 4th May 1953, having given *darshan* to devotees, at eight-thirty he was to set out from the middle of Varanasi for Calcutta. News of the travelling was kept secret in order to escape from the heat of running devotees and crowds. *From Brahmanivas Ashram you appeared comfortably seated upon a well-decorated pick-up.* In the midst of cheers hailing victory making a hole in the sky, it happened that Maharaj Shri left for the train at Mughal Sarai [a railway junction 10kms from Varanasi]. Behind him came devotees in cars and also in lorries.

Here an air-conditioned compartment in the Delhi Mail was secured for Maharaj Shri. Without any notice a great crowd collected together on the platform. After becoming seated in the carriage, one-by-one the multitude of devotees went for *darshan* of Maharaj Shri, and at ten-thirty in the midst of cheers hailing victory, the Mail train of Maharaj Shri departed. [The distance from Varanasi to Calcutta is about 680kms]

The trip finished happily and he stayed in Calcutta at 56 Vali Ganj on Circular Road. [It seems that 56 Ballygunge on the Circular Road, Calcutta, was at one time the home of Sivaramakrishna Iyer, a former Accountant General who is said to have been very fond of entertaining people.]

११

ग्यारहवाँ अध्याय

महा-प्रयाग

इधर कुछ दिनों से महाराज श्री के स्वास्थ्य में शिथिलता आ गई थी। साधारण होमियोपैथिक औषधियाँ चल रहीं थीं। लाभ की गति मंद होने के कारण एल्योपैथी डाक्तरी उपचार आरम्भ किया गया। २० मई, १९५३ ई० को लगभग १ बजे डाक्टरों ने देखा और कहा "सब ठीक है। हृदय की गति ठीक है। नाड़ी बहुत अछी चल रही है।" डाक्टर के जाने के बाद महाराज श्री विश्राम करने लगे। लगभग १० मिनट बाद सहसा उन्होंने आँखें खोलीं और कहा "उठाओ।" उठकर बैठते ही शीघ्रता से अपने दोनों चरण सिकोड़ कर सुखासन की मुद्रा में बैठ गये और आँखें बंद कर लीं। इस प्रकार बैठे-बैठे एक बजकर १५ मिनट पर अपने पंचभौतिक शरीर को त्याग कर अपने स्वरूप में लीन हो गये। अध्यात्म का साकार विग्रह भूतल से उठ गया।

कलक्त्त नगर में यह समाचार तुरन्त ही बिजली की भाँति फैल गया। नागरिकजन महाराज श्री के अन्तिम दर्शनों के लिये समुद्र की भाँति उमड़ पड़े। जो जिस परिस्थिति में था, वह उसी परिस्थिति में अपने आप को भूलकर दौड़ पड़ा। टेलीफोन तार द्वारा देश के कोने-कोने में यह दुःखद समाचार तुरन्त पहुंच गया। दूर-दूर से वास्त्तविक समाचार और भावी कार्यक्रम जानने के लिये आश्रम में आने वाले तारों व ट्रंककालों का ताँता लग गया। यथासम्भव उत्तर में महाराज

श्री के पार्थिव शरीर को काशी ले जाने की सूचना दे दी गई। आल
इंडिया रेडियो से भी महाराज श्री के महाप्रयाण एवं अन्तिम संस्कार
के लिये उनके पार्थक शरीर को काशी ले जाने का समाचार प्रसारित
हुआ। सारे देश में शोक का वातावरण छा गया।

सभी प्रान्तों से धार्मिक-जन काशी चल पड़े-रेल से, मोटर से,
हवाई जहाज से, जिसे जो भी साधन उपलब्ध हुआ, उसी साधन
द्वारा काशी चल दिया – जो जिस अवस्था में था, बिना किसी तैयारी
के वह उसी अवस्था में चल पड़ा। लखनऊ प्रयाग, जबलपुर, इटावा,
कलकत्ता, पटना, बम्बई, नागपुर, इन्दौर, दिल्ही, आगरा आदि नगरों
के हजारों नर-नारी भगवान् के पार्थिक शरीर की अन्तिम झाँकी पाने
के लिये एवं अपनी-अपनी श्रद्धांजलि समर्पित करने लिये २० मई की
रात से ही श्री ब्रह्मनिवास आश्रम काशी पहुँचने लगे।

वहाँ कलकत्ता में निवास-स्थान पर दोपहर से ही दर्शनार्थियों की
भीड़ एकत्र होने लगी। संध्या होते-होते अपार जनसमूह इकट्ठा हो
गया। ९॥ बजे रात की गाड़ि से महाराज श्री का पार्थिव शरीर
काशी ले जाया जाने लगा। संध्या समय एक ट्रक पर महाराज श्री
को आसीन किया गया। बाजा, शंख, घंटा, घड़ियाल बजाता कीर्तन
एवं जयकार करता हुआ जुलूस निवास स्थान से रवाना हुआ। मार्ग
में इतनी अधिक भीड़ थी कि महाराज श्री की सवारी को स्टेशन
पहुंचने में तीन घण्टे से अधिक लग गये। हाबड़ा स्टेशन् पर जनता
को अन्तिम दर्शन देने के बाद, देहली एक्सप्रेस में महाराज श्री का
डिब्बा लगा दिया गया। डिब्बा पूर्णरूपेण सुसज्जित था। बीच में श्री
महाराज का पुण्याकृत दिव्य शरीर रखा गया और उसके चारों ओर
बर्फ रखी गई। पीछे भक्त मण्डली बैठ कर हरिकीर्तन करने लगी। ९-
५० बजे रात्रि में गाड़ी हावड़ा से रवाना हुई। मार्ग भर भक्तमण्डली

कीर्तन करती आई। दिन में लगभग ३ बजे गाड़ी मुगलसराँय पहुँची। मुगलसराँय से महाराज श्री के पार्थिव विग्रह को कार द्वारा काशी लाया गया और लगभग ४ बजे ब्रह्मनिवास आश्रम के प्राङ्गण में भक्तों के दर्शनार्थ सुशोभित किया गया। इस अन्तिम दर्शन से भक्तों के हृदय में, जो आघात पहुँचा, वह शब्दों द्वारा किसी भी प्रकार व्यक्त नहीं किया जा सकता। अपना-अपना हृदय थाम कर हो जैसे थे, स्तब्ध हो कर खड़े रह गये। तब फूल चढ़ाये और अन्तिम प्रणाम किये। फिर, जिस कमरे में महाराज जी दिन में विश्राम किया करते थे, उसी में ले जाकर स्नान कराया गया। पंडितमंडली द्वारा वेद पाठ के पश्चात् भगवान् का षोडशोपचार पूजन हुआ और तब अन्तिम यात्रा के लिये विशेष रूप से सुसज्जित विमान पर भगवान् को आसीन किया गया। विमान को एक सजे हुये ट्रक पर रखा गया और अन्तिम यात्रा आरम्भ हुई। आगे-आगे पुलिस बेंड, शनाई बजा रही थी तत्पश्चात् कीर्तन-मंडली, पंडित वृन्द, संन्यासीगण भजन कीर्तन कर रहे थे। विमान के आगे-पीछे भक्तगण का अपार जन-समूह चल रहा था। आश्रम से कमच्छा गुदौलिया इत्यादि स्थानों से होता हुआ जुलूस दशाश्वमेध घाट पर पहुँचा। यहाँ पर लाखों जनता सीढ़ियों और सैकड़ों बजरों, नावों पर पहिले से ही प्रतीक्षा में उपस्थित थी।

गंगा के तट पर विमान रखकर वैदिक विधान से भगवान् का अभिषेक हुआ फिर एक बड़े बजरे पर संन्यासीगण भक्तमण्डली एवं विद्वन्मंडली के बीच विमान रखा गया और वह बजरा केदारेश्वर महादेव की ओर चल पड़ा। बजरे के अग्ल-बगल भक्तों के पृथक्-पृथक् बजरे और नावें चल रही थां। केदारेश्वर महादेव के सामने केदारघाट पर पहुंच कर जल-प्रवाह की व्यवस्था की गई। यहाँ जल

प्रवाह के निमित्त विशेष रूप से निर्मित पत्थर का एक बड़ा संदूक दूसरी नाव पर लादा गया था। यहाँ पर महाराज श्री का विमान बजरे से उतार लिया गया और महाराज श्री का दिव्य विग्रह विमान से उतार कर उसमें रख दिया गया। साथ ही में महाराज श्री का कमंडलु और दण्ड भी रख कर संदूक में बंद कर दिया गया। तब नाव महाराज श्री के विग्रह को लिये हुये गंगा के मध्य की ओर चल पड़ी। अब अँधेरा हो गया था, अतः दूसरी नाव गैस बत्तियाँ लिये उसके साथ-साथ चल पड़ी। साथ ही भक्तों की नावें अगल-बगल चलने लगीं। मध्य में पहुंचकर नाव रुकी और यहाँ पर यह संदूक गंगा जी में उतार दिया गया। ब्रह्मचारी महेश जी संदूक को लिये हुये गंगा में कूद गये और संदूक के धरातल पर पहुंच जाने पर अन्तिम प्रणाम करके बाहर आये। जलप्रवाह होते समय उपस्थित जनसमूह अपने शोकातिरेक को रोक न सका; आंखें डबडबा आईं, कण्ठ अवरुद्ध हो गये और मुँह से शब्द न निकला और फूट-फूट कर रो पड़े।

महाराज श्री यह कहा करते थे कि जगत् में कभी किसी का कार्य पूरा नहीं हुआ। यही परम्परा आपने निभाई न जाने अपने तिरोधान का समय किस माप से इतना शीघ्र निश्चित कर लिया। पर अपने जीवन में, जो महान् आदर्श स्थापित कर गये, वे शताब्दियों तक जगत् का पथ प्रदर्शन करते रहेंगे।

Chapter 11

Great Confluence

Here at Calcutta, since some days, Maharaj Shri's good health was becoming lassitude. Ordinary Homeopathic medicines were continued but because he became feeble it appeared to be an advantage to begin using the remedy of an allopathic doctor [said to have been Shri Vidhan Chandra Roy].

At about one o'clock on 20th May 1953, the doctor saw him and said, '*"Sab thik hai"* (All is well)! The state of the heart is *"thik"* (fit). The pulse is moving, *bahut achchi* (very good).'

After the doctor went, Maharaj Shri relaxed and about ten minutes later he suddenly opened his eyes and said, '*"Uthao"* - 'You must lift (me)!'

Having arisen, he quickly drew both his feet to sit in the posture of *sukhasana* ('easy seat' - cross-legged) and closed the eyes. In this way he was sitting.

At one-fifteen, having abandoned his own body of the five-elements he became absorbed in his own Self. The Self arose from the form of the gross body, from the surface of the world.

*

This news instantly spread like lightning in the city of Calcutta. Like the surge of the sea citizens gathered for the final *darshan* of Maharaj Shri. Those who were in the surrounding area came running to you in that setting. By telephone line this trouble-giving news quickly reach in all corners of the country.

[In a recording of Brahmachari 'Swami' Satyanand made in about 1967 he speaks about hearing news of Guru Dev's death:-

'When in 1953 Guru Dev left this mortal frame and attained *nirvana,* I was at Benares, another place of pilgrimage for Hindus, and at that moment I was staying in the *ashram* of Guru Dev. Everybody knew that I am very attached to Guru Dev and devoted to Guru Dev, and then news came to Benares that Guru Dev has attained *nirvana*. I was sitting somewhere with a group of my friends and the news was relayed there. When my friends heard that Guru Dev was no more, they were very anxious about me and when they conveyed that news, they were rather alert to appraise whatever reaction is and what happened. I simply, when I heard that news I became very sad, very sorry and I just kept my head on the table before me. And all of them were very anxious what will become of me. But soon after, while I was very morose, sorrow, sad, entire world was empty for me and I did not understand what to do without Guru Dev, just a half a minute or two seconds after, a flash came and it appeared to me that Guru Dev was scolding me;

"What a fool you are! You have been with me for all these many months and years, and you heard my discourses too. Is it a moment of feeling sorry? Why should you be sorry today? And you think that I am gone, where am I gone? Till now whenever you wanted to meet me, you had to come to the place where I was, and today when I have attained *nirvana*, I am everywhere, I am omnipresent. Where have I gone? Very foolish for you to mourn on this occasion. I am with you, here, there, everywhere. Why should you be sorry?"

And the moment this flash came, my face became very brilliant, I became very cheerful. And when I raised my head, my friends who were standing there, very anxious and held in suspense, they were upset to see my brilliant and cheerful face. And then they said, "What has happened to you?" I said, "No, you can't understand, nothing has happened to me, I am alright, now let me go back to the *ashram* and make the necessary arrangements".']

From far and away a series of telegrams and trunk calls came to the ashram wanting to know the real information and the future programme. In answer, according to the circumstances, information was given about the taking of the material body of Maharaj Shri to Varanasi. Also via All India Radio news spread of the great departure of Maharaj Shri and the earthen body going to Varanasi for the final rituals. An atmosphere of shock spread through the entire country.

From all ends of India devout people travelled to Varanasi - by rail, by motor car or by aeroplane. By whatever means could be gained, by that means they travelled to Varanasi - and that was the situation, having to travel in that way without any preparation. From the cities of Lucknow, Allahabad, Jabalpur, Etawah, Calcutta, Patna, Bombay, Nagpur, Indore, Delhi, Agra etc thousands of men and women came to get a look at the material body of Bhagwan, and for delivering their *shraddhanjali* (offerings of faith), they arrived at Brahmanivas Ashram in Varanasi by the night of 20th May.

In Calcutta, at the dwelling-place there, a crowd of *darshan*-seekers had gathered by midday. By the evening an immense crowd had accumulated. In the evening time Maharaj Shri went, seated on a truck. A procession set out from the dwelling place, singing *kirtan*, playing instruments, conch shell, bell and gong. In the road there was such a large crowd that it took Maharaj Shri's carriage more than three hours to arrive at the station. At nine-fifty the earthly body of Maharaj Shri was to be taken to Varanasi by wagon. After giving a final *darshan* to the masses at Howrah Station, Maharaj Shri's wagon was attached to the Delhi Express. The wagon was wholly well-decorated. In the middle went the holy divine body of Maharaj Shri and ice was put on four sides. A circle of devotees stayed behind, doing *harikirtana* (singing praise of Hari, Vishnu). The train then departed from Howrah between nine and ten o'clock at night. Then the whole way the circle of devotees did *kirtana*.

Arrival at Mughal Sarai [the junction near Varanasi] was at about three o'clock in the day [of the afternoon of 21st May]. From Mughal Sarai the earthly body of Maharaj Shri was taken by car to Varanasi and at about four o'clock it was well-adorned and placed in the courtyard of Brahmanivas Ashram for devotee *darshan*-seekers. By this final *darshan* a blow was caused in the heart of devotees that cannot be conveyed by any kind of words. Standing having become stupefied, holding their hearts,. Then flowers were offered and they did the final *pranaam*.

Afterwards, in the room where Maharaj Shri would relax in the day, in there he was taken to be washed. After a circle of pandits read *Veda*, Bhagwan's *shodashopachara pujana* (*puja* with sixteen methods of worship) was done, and then for the special specific appearance for the *antima yatra* (the final journey), Bhagwan was seated on a well-decorated *vimana* (bier). The *vimana* was placed on a truck that had been decorated, and the final journey commenced. In front, the Police Band was playing *shenai* (Indian clarinet), after that a circle of *kirtan* (reciting), an assembly of *pandits*, the *sannyasi* community was singing *kirtana*. Behind the *vimana* moved an immense multitude of devotees. From the ashram, from Kamachcha, from Godoliya, from all sorts of places, the procession arrived at Dashashvamedha Ghat. Already waiting here on the steps and on several hundred boats were hundreds of thousands of people.

Having placed the *vimana* on the shore of the Ganga, Bhagwan's *abhisheka* was done according to Vedic ceremony. Then on a large *bajara* (barge-like boat) the *vimana* (bier) was placed in the midst of a circle of devotees of the *sannyasi* community and a circle of scholars, and that *bajara* moved in the direction of Kedareshwar Mahadev. Following the *bajara* were several other *bajara* and boatloads of devotees.

Having arrived at Kedar Ghat, in front of Kedareshwar Mahadev (temple), they settled the *jala pravaha* (the act of releasing something to the 'flow of the water'). Here, on account of the specific flow of water, a large box of fabricated stone was loaded on another boat. Maharaj Shri was taken from the *bajara* and Maharaj Shri's divine body was placed it in that box. Having also placed Maharaj Shri's *kamandalu* (water pot) and *danda* (staff) the box was closed. Then the boat with the body of Maharaj Shri moved in the direction of the middle of the Ganga. Now since it had become dark, another boat with gas-lamps moved alongside, together with boats of devotees following.

Having arrived in the middle of the river the boat stopped and the box was lowered into Ganga Ji. Then Brahmachari Mahesh Ji jumped into the Ganga, for the box. On the arrival of the box on the riverbed he came outside for doing the final *pranaam*. The time of the *jala pravaha* having arrived, the gathering could not stop their own abundant mourning; their eyes becoming filled with tears, throats becoming obstructed and no words were coming from the mouths, and disunited they fell to crying.

* * *

Maharaj Shri had said this, that;

'In the world, the work is never completed. Really, this is the *parampara* (succession), not going to be accomplished oneself. The time of one's disappearance. By what measure? So quickly the decision is taken.'

A few words from
Swami Swaroopanand Saraswati,
Shankaracharya of Dwarka
(interviewed by Robert Kropinski in Vrindaban, India, 1985.

'I was also his disciple, Brahmanand Saraswati's. He was my Guru. He would not accept any offerings from his disciples. Disciple should be such that he gives to his Guru everything. Then nothing belongs to the disciple, everything is Guru's. Guru should be such that he does not take anything from the disciple. He thinks only good of his disciple.

'The Lord, Shankaracharya Brahmananda Saraswati Ji Maharaj strictly adhered to the *varna* (caste) and *ashram* (four stages of life) systems. He believed in one's *varna* by birth. Whosoever came to him to become a disciple, he used to ask him which form of God he was in love with. Whichever form the new disciple had an interest in, that form he would explain to the new disciple, used to explain, either you should depend on your own inclination or else, he, after understanding your previous life and which form of

God you worshipped then, would instruct the initiate accordingly.

Without having an *ishtadevata* (a personal form of God), no one could have a *mantra* from him. The very meaning of *mantra* is *ishtadevata*. Therefore, along with every *mantra*, thinking or reflecting over the form of the *ishtadevata* is essential. Therefore, in all the modes of worship, one reflects over one's *ishtadevata* before chanting or meditating with one's *mantra*.

'The Lord, Adi Shankara was a great exponent of Vedic Sanatana Dharma. God, he taught, is grouped into six forms. He preached six types - five based on forms of God like Shiva, Shakti, Vishnu, etc. and one, *Nirakar*, without form. However, the worship of God without form being extremely difficult was reserved for renunciates. That is what Adi Shankaracharya had instructed.

Bhagwan Shree Shankara revived *Vedic Sanatan Dharma*. He said God has six forms. So accordingly, Maharaj Ji gave *upadesha* (initiation) to meditate upon those forms for the sake of our worship.

'This is a principle. A quotation from Goswami Tulsidas:-

"The *guru* who charges or takes money from his disciples in return for initiation, steals disciple's property and goes to damnable hell."

For that reason Gurudeva used to give *upadesha* (initiation) without any fees. He used to say "If I accept any gift from the disciple (or fees), then his sins are transmitted to me."

DROPS
OF
SERMON NECTAR

BY

SHRI GURU DEV

*

'So long passion for attaining God is not firm you shall fly hither and thither, without knowing, like a kite.'

*

'Be a worldly man through body and wealth and contemplate Him (Paramatma) in your heart. Thus you shall shine in the world and attain *summum bonum* as well.'

*

'The God is Almighty. If you attain power through worshipping the Almighty, in accordance with scriptures, there would be nothing impossible in the world.'

*

'He alone is the Adored One who does not let any evil take place. He alone can make one free from all evils, for He alone is Almighty.'

*

'He is perfect in the entire creation. He saves those from every evil who depend wholeheartedly upon Him.'

*

'Keep in mind the instance of Prahlad. Wherever Prahlad was taken to he was saved by his Adored One. Hence make yourself immune from every evil by making Him your Adored One.'

*

'Lord Vishnu, Shankar, Devi, Surya and Ganesh, each of these five deities, are equally capable of doing good to their devotees. One should make one of them one's favourite and should visualize him pervading throughout the creation.'

*

'He alone is the best devotee who sees his Adored One everywhere. For the devotee of Vishnu the Lord is omnipresent. He should see Lord Vishnu even in the images of Shankar, Devi, Ganesh and Surya etc. Likewise a devotee of Shankar, Devi etc. should visualize his Adored One omnipresent.'

*

'If a worshipper of Devi does not see her in the images of Vishnu and Shankar etc. this would imply that he is doubting the omnipresence of his Adored One. Such a devotee who sees his Adored One partially remains imperfect.'

*

'He who causes strife and envy among different schools and philosophies is but an outcome of not seeing his Adored One omnipresent.'

*

'Only through *karma* worship and enlightenment, as put in the *Vedas* -- His Canons -- can one have welfare in this and other world.'

*

'Deeds done with right, propriety, and God-given wisdom are powerful. Laws of *karma* are to be learned from the *Vedas* and religious preachers.'

*

'The world has to undergo disquietitude, maladministration, and natural calamities when deeds forbidden in scriptures take place and the subjects are afflicted.'

*

'By not observing duty toward one's self one is afflicted by the advent of such internal enemies as lust, anger, greed, arrogance and ignorance etc.'

*

'Pure *satwik* diet develops mind and controls the senses. He who has won his senses there is nothing impossible in the world.'

*

'Progress of a nation is possible only by righteous persons possessing God-given endowments.'

*

'The divine strength is to be accomplished to make a nation powerful. Subtle divine authority is the regulator of the concrete universe. Without its help neither can a nation become powerful nor peace and prosperity can be felt.'

*

'One should always keep one's glory shining and should elevate one's thought and make it generous in accordance with the scriptures. One should see one's Adored One omnipresent and perfect.

The devotee remains incomplete if he sees his Adored One in unentirety with sectarian view.'

*

'One should be happy when seeing reverence evoking feeling in gurus, compassion toward afflicted and rise of others and having mutual goodwill one should devote oneself whole-heartedly toward universal welfare by being sincere to one's self.'

*

'If you devote yourself contemplating, worshipping and singing in praise of your Adored One you ought to feel something or other and your desire ought to be more steady. If it is not so, be sure your devotion is not of right kind.'

*

'There are classes of devotion, too. As the syllabi of pupils in schools become subtle gradually, likewise the path of devotion unto the ultimate end becomes continuously subtler.'

*

'As the devotee makes progress in devotion need of subtler devices increases and a veteran guru alone can show the real path.
If fortunately one gets a noble guru well versed in the *Vedas* and having deep knowledge of *Brahman* and receives his cooperation till end, only one guru makes one's life meaningful. Otherwise so long the devotee does not attain God he should gradually go in the protection of great gurus. One must revere previous gurus, but if they are not helping in spiritual attainment wasting life by depending upon them out of hesitation is a grave error.'

*

'Perceiving omnipresence of the Adored One alone can eliminate the discord of all opposing feelings. This very thing is the firm basis of permanent formation. And this also is the means of permanent peace in this world and the other.'

*

'Pleasure and pain are results of one's own deeds. One should bear them calmly for they are one's own belongings. One has to welcome one's relatives even if he is wicked.'

*

'If sorrow comes take lesson from it and be cautious in future, so as not to perform any forbidden deed which may cause suffering.'

*

'There is a tenet of Ayurveda that sins of previous life appear in the shape of different afflictions, i.e. physical diseases. They are cured by medicine, chanting of some particular *mantra*, *havana* and worshipping Him. Hence when a disease is not cured by medicine other remedies, too, should be tried.'

*

'Learning the kind of worship from a deserving veteran guru one should devote one self to one's Adored One while performing the duties of one's caste and age.'

*

'Devotional song is sung in four voices namely *baikhari*, *madyama*, *pashyanti* and *para*. These days devotional songs are sung in *baikhari* voice with the help of playing *kartal* (small cymbals or wooden clappers) and *sistrum* (resonant percussive device).

Singers of such songs should not spend their whole life in singing in *baikhari* voice. They should try to produce the other three kinds of voices with the help of veteran gurus. The same applies to chanting of *mantras* too. Chanting of *mantras* has several stages. Contemplation too are of many kinds such as internal-external, concrete, subtle and ultra subtle. Hence devotee should keep searching great veteran gurus.'

*

'Noble gurus determine the kind of worship for the pupil keeping in view place, time, condition, strength, temperament and circumstance etc. and he enables him to proceed further on the path of devotion.'

*

'Human body is attained with great difficulties. Being born in human species is the only way out of the prison of birth and death. If one misses this opportunity out of negligence, lethargy and hesitation one is bound to undergo, forever, the plight of birth and death. Hence rise, awake, attain eternal peace and bliss by being in contact with the best of mankind.'

Glossary

aachaarya, acharya teacher
aadhyaatma, spiritual contemplation
aananda, joy, bliss
aastika, religious
aatmaa, soul
abhyaasa, practice
adharma, vice, sin
agni, fire
agyaana, ignorance
ahamkaara, egotism, arrogance, conceit, empty pride, vanity
ahimsaa, non-violence, inoffensiveness, benevolence
akshara, permanent
amrita, nectar
anishta, mishchief, evil
antahkarana, conscience, inner self
artha, wealth
arya, noble
ashaanti, unrest
ashram, hermitage
ashrama, stage of life
ashubha, unfortunate, inauspicious
asura, demon
atma, atman, Soul
avataar, incarnation
aviveka, absence of discrimination
bhaagya, destiny
Bhaarata, India
Bhagwan, Bhagwan, *bhagavaana,* Supreme Being, God
Bhagavat, God
bhagavattatva, essence of the divine
bhajan, hymn

bhakti, devotion
Bharat, *bhaarata* India
bhavaroga, birth-sickness
bhavasaagara, sea of experience
bhavateet, transcendental
bhoga, the experience of pleasure or a pain
bhuta-preta, ghosts
biij, seed
brahmana, brahmin, Hindu caste
Brahma, Absolute Divine Truth, Hindu god of creation
brahmachari, celibate student
brahmacharya, celibacy
Brahmanand, *brahmananda* Absolute bliss
brahma-nirguna brahma, without qualities),
brahmavidyaa, theology taught in the Upanishads
brahmin, learned or priestly caste
brhmanishtham, possessing knowledge of immortal self
chaitanya, consciousness
charan, ray of sun or moon
chela, disciple
chimtaa, the funeral pyre
chit, consciousness
chitaa, worry
chitta, faculty of reasoning
daana, charitable gift
daitya, demons
darshan, darshana Holy look, vision
deepak, light, lamp
Devaloka, the world of the gods, paradise
devataa, god
devataaon, gods/goddesses
dhaarmik, (virtuous, devout, religious, godly, upright, etc.)
dharma, righteous duty
dharmashaala, a dwelling house for pilgrims
dhoop, sticky incense, fragrant lamp
dhoti, sheet
dhyaana, dhyan, meditation
diksha, initiation

duhkha, pain, suffering
dushkarma, wicked action
Gangajal, the sacred waters of the River Ganga
Ganapati, Ganesha Hindu god with elephant trunk
Gandharvas, celestial musicians
Gandharva-Ved, Indian classical music
ganja, marijuana
gita, song
grihastha, householder
grhasthon, householders
guna, quality
gupha, cave
guru, teacher, master
gurudwara, Sikh temple
gyaanii, learned
gyan, gyaan, gnan, jyaan knowledge
hansa, swan
hare, lord
hawaii, pertaining to the air
Ishwar, Isvara, God
ishta, deity
jaati, caste
jagadguru, world teacher, universal teacher
jai, jay, jaya, jaaya hail, glory
japa, repetition of *mantra*
ji, term of respect
jiiva, the individual soul
jiivanmukti, liberated soul
jyotir, light
jyotishi, Indian astrology
kalpa, period of time
kalyaana, happiness, welfare, benediction, prosperity
kama, love
kamandalu, wooden pot
karma, law of action and reaction
karunaa, compassion
Kashi, Benares, Varanasi
kaupeen, loincloth

kiirtana, singing praise of God

kripa, grace

Krishna, dark, name of principal character of *Mahabharata* poem

kriyamaana, work now being done

kshatriya, caste of warriors, administrators

kshema, prosperity

kusang, kusanga, the company of evil men

ladduu, Sweetmeat made of *ghii* (ghee)

lingam, phallus

maayaa, maya, delusion of

maharaja, king

maharishi, maharshi, Great sage

maharishon, sages

mahatma, mahaatma, great soul

Mahesh, name of Hindu god Shiva

maitrii, friendship

mala, maalaa, rosary, necklace, garland

mala-mutra, excrement & urine

mandir, temple

manoraajyam, the realm of the mind

mantra, word or words of spiritual power

Manu Smriti or *Manu Samhita,* law book

maryaadaa, principled code of conduct

math, monastery

mauna, maun, silent

moksha, final liberation, beatitude, redemption, absolution, salvation, freedom

muditaa, cheerfulness, delight

mukti, liberation

naastika, nastika, unbeliever

nagar, town

niraakaara, without form

nirguna, without qualities

nitya, eternal

nityaananda, always happy

paapa, sinful

pandit, learned man

parabrahma, the Supreme Soul

Paramatma, *paramaatmaa,* Supreme Spirit, Supersoul, God
parmartha, the ultimate good, salvation
pishaachinii, she-devil
praana, breath
praanon, the five vital airs
praarabdha, already commenced *karma*
prana, breath
pranaama, salutation
pranava, name of OM *mantra*
prasad, blessing
pravritti, tendency, inclination or perseverance of mind
puuja, puja, pooja, ceremony, ritual
puujana worship
punya, meritous *karma*
purnima, poornima, full-moon night
purusha, male
purushartha, human wealth or purpose, work for fulfilment of life
puurna, poorna, perfect
raaga, attachment
raaj, raja, royal, king
rajasic, energetic, passionate
rajogunii, pleasure seeking, passion of love and pleasure
Rama, Raama, Raam, name of hero of *Ramayana* poem
raurava, a hell
rish,i sage, wise man
roga, disease
Rudra, name of Hindu god Shiva
saadhaka, one engaged in spiritual discipline
saadhana, spiritual practice or discipline
sachchidananda, Truth, Consciousness, Bliss
sadguru, genuine *guru*
sadagati, salvation, good conduct
sadhu, wandering holy man
sanchita, collected *karma*
samaadhi, stillness of the mind
sampradaaya, sect
samsaara, samsara, worldly existence, mortal world,
transmigration

samsaarii, worldly
samskaara, mental impressions
sannyas, vow of renunciation
sanyaasi, renunciate
Saraswati, name of Hindu goddess of learning, name of river
Sarvashaktimaan, Omnipotent, Almighty
satogunii, purity
satsanga, to take the company of the good or pious
sattvic, satvik, pure
satya, truth
shaanti, shaanti peace
Shastras, shaastra, Hindu Scriptures
Shankar, name of Hindu god Shiva
shikshaa, instruction
shishya, pupil
Shiva, name of Hindu god of destruction, lord of the *yogis*
Shivalinga, symbol of creative forces
Shivaratri, night(s) dedicated to worship of Hindu deities Shiva
and his consort Shakti
shloka, verse
shraddha, faith, veneration, reverence
shravana, devotion
shri, blessed
shrotiyan, well-versed in *Vedas*
shruti, information heard from the *Veda*
shubha, happy, auspicious
shuudra, one of the four castes, labourer
siddha, perfected being
siddhi, one who has acquired supernatural powers
smarana, remembrance
smriti, remembered, from the *Shastra.*
sthuula shariira, gross body
stotra, hymns of praise
suukshma shariira, subtle body
svarg, svarga, swarg, heaven
swami, renunciate
swaroop, svarupa, swarupa, divine form, real self, true self
tamasik, impure

tamogunii, impure, ignorant

tapasya, tapas, austerity

tilaka, tilak, mark of sandalwood paste applied to forehead, emblem of a sect

tri, three

tyaagi, unattached renunciates

upaasanaa, sitting near, devout meditation, worship, prayer

upadesha, upadesh, lecture, advice instruction, discourse, sermon

Upanishad, texts on *yoga,* to sit near

upekshaa, equanimity, indifference

vaanaprastha, forest dweller

vaidya, physician

vairagya, freedom from worldly desires

vaishya, trader

vanaprasthas, forest dwellers

varna, caste

Veda, ancient religious texts, *Rig Veda, Sama Veda, Yajur Veda, Atharva Veda*

veshyaa, whore

vigyaana, knowledge, wisdom, science, learning, philosophy, the soul

Vishnu, Hindu god of preservation

vishvambhara, (universal support)

viyoga, separation, disunion, detachment etc

vritti, flow of mental activity

vrittiyon, mental conditions, of friendship, compassion, delight & indifference

yaatra, yatra, journey, tour, pilgrimage

yagya, yajna, ritual, religious sacrifice

yakshini, demi-gods,

karna-pishachi, demons

yogadarshanam, Patanjali's Yoga Sutras

yogamaayaa, inner power

yoga-shaastra, yogadarshanam, of Patanjali, Yoga Sutras

yuga, period of time